1861

1861

THE LOST PEACE

JAY WINIK

GRAND
CENTRAL

NEW YORK BOSTON

Grand Central Publishing
Hachette Book Group
1290 Avenue of the Americas, New York, NY 10104
grandcentralpublishing.com
@grandcentralpub

First Edition: May 2025

Grand Central Publishing is a division of Hachette Book Group, Inc.
The Grand Central Publishing name and logo is a registered trademark of Hachette Book Group, Inc.

The publisher is not responsible for websites (or their content) that are not owned by the publisher.

Grand Central Publishing books may be purchased in bulk for business, educational, or promotional use. For information, please contact your local bookseller or the Hachette Book Group Special Markets Department at special.markets@hbgusa.com.

Library of Congress Cataloging-in-Publication Data

Names: Winik, Jay, 1957- author.
Title: 1861 : the lost peace / Jay Winik.
Description: First edition. | New York : Grand Central Publishing, 2025. | Includes bibliographical references and index.
Identifiers: LCCN 2024057222 | ISBN 9781538735121 (hardcover) | ISBN 9781538735114 (ebook)
Subjects: LCSH: Conference Convention (1861 : Washington, D.C.) | Lincoln, Abraham, 1809-1865. | Crittenden, John J. (John Jordan), 1787-1863. | United States—Politics and government—1857-1861. | United States—History—Civil War, 1861-1865—Causes.
Classification: LCC E440.5 .W76 2025 | DDC 320.97309/034—dc23/eng/20241219
LC record available at https://lccn.loc.gov/2024057222

ISBNs: 978-1-538-73512-1 (hardcover), 978-1-538-73511-4 (ebook)

Printed in the United States of America

LSC-C

Printing 1, 2025

For Evie Miller Winik, the amazing gem of my life.
For my cherished sons, and magnificent budding historians,
Evan S. and Nathaniel J. H. Winik.

Contents

Foreword

We think of Abraham Lincoln as a great humanitarian, statesman, and war leader. But when he arrived in Washington in February 1861 to be sworn in as America's sixteenth president, he was widely seen as a hick. In the vituperative and vicious press of the era, he was sometimes described as a "baboon" because of his gangly arms. He had never been an executive of anything or commanded troops in combat. He was at once clever, passionate, and dryly funny, but he was regarded as a poor impromptu speaker.

He did not see himself as the Great Emancipator. Nor did he believe the country was on the brink of a civil war. The South, he said, was merely bluffing at secession, though seven states had already seceded. Stopping in Cleveland on his way to Washington, he told the crowd, "There is really no crisis except an *artificial one*." Why, he asked, are Southerners so incensed? "Have they not all their rights now as they had ever had? Do not they have their fugitive slaves returned now as ever? Have they not the same Constitution that they have lived under for seventy-odd years?... What then is the matter with them? Why all this excitement? Why all these complaints?"

If Lincoln was unprepossessing—"small potatoes," a former cabinet member called him—he was not being unreasonable about the country's situation. Congress was not about to abolish slavery in the states where it was already legal. The question was whether slavery would be permitted in the western territories. But, so far, there were very few enslaved people in those territories, whose land for the most part was not well suited to an economy worked by slave labor. Most Americans, at any rate, wanted a compromise. Not a civil war.

What Lincoln could not quite grasp, even as the evidence mounted all around him, was that Americans were *angry*, especially at people unlike themselves. America in 1861 was not a mixing bowl. Indeed, as Jay Winik points out in his magisterial history of the outbreak of the Civil War, America was not really a nation, in the sense of one people with a shared background and values. The words "nation" and "national" appear nowhere in the Constitution. It was the United States, plural. People spoke of being "Carolinians" or "Tennesseans." Secession was in their history—beginning with the secession of the thirteen colonies from the British Crown in the American Revolution.

By the late 1850s, the poison of slavery had infected even the sacred places. Violence invaded the Capitol Building with its shiny new dome. In Congress, a haughty Massachusetts senator named Charles Sumner, an unapologetic Harvard-educated snob, mocked a senator from South Carolina. Using a gold-headed cane, the Southern senator's cousin almost beat Sumner to death, leaving Sumner stricken and bleeding beneath his desk on the Senate floor. Congressmen began coming to work armed with pistols and bowie knives.

The political parties were collapsing. The venerable Whig Party, with its great statesmen Henry Clay and Daniel Webster, had devolved into something called the Know-Nothings, who were anti-immigrant and anti-Catholic. Rancor ran everywhere. The Supreme Court had become extreme. In the *Dred Scott* case, the court ruled that Black people, even freed ones, could not be citizens, and that enslaved people were private property. Calumny and insult could flash around the country in a few seconds, thanks to a new technology called the telegraph.

The Union was unraveling. First to go was South Carolina, voting to secede on December 20, 1860. Then came Mississippi on January 9, followed quickly by Florida, Alabama, Georgia, Louisiana, and, on February 1, Texas. That month, as Lincoln made his way from his native Illinois to Washington, the threat of assassination was so great that he had to travel part of the way in a train separate from his wife and children. He had to secretly slip through the city of Baltimore in the dead of night lest he be waylaid by marauders known as "plug-uglies."

––––––––

Readers of Winik's number one national bestseller *April 1865* will recall it as a Homeric narrative, an epic drama with plot twists out of Dickens. In *1861: The Lost Peace*, Winik offers us all that and shows us more— that history can turn on contingency, on the vagaries of chance and personality, and that it is made by humans whose characters are often contradictory.

Major Robert Anderson of the US Army made an unlikely hero. He was shy and sensitive, a sometime poet, and prone to illness and depression. Decorated in the Mexican-American War, he said he hated war. Married to a Southern belle, he was sympathetic to the Southern cause and was himself an enslaver. Nonetheless, he felt duty bound. As the commander of federal troops in Charleston, South Carolina, acting mostly on his own initiative, he occupied Fort Sumter in Charleston Harbor, raised the Stars and Stripes, and announced that he and his men would die before they surrendered.

Suddenly, he became Horatius at the Bridge, his modest force of seventy men compared to the Spartan 300 at Thermopylae. Newspaper headlines shouted his name. A fuse had been lit.

––––––––

In Washington, President Lincoln, brand-new in his job, appeared overwhelmed, isolated, his authority undermined. "The man is not equal to the hour," said Charles Francis Adams Sr., one of the grandees of Lincoln's Republican Party. The president's secretary of state, William H. Seward, who fancied himself in every way Lincoln's superior except in title, was secretly negotiating with the Confederates, assuring them that Fort Sumter would be relinquished.

With the country on the brink of war, Seward tried to bully the president into dealing with the secessionists—with Seward himself as policymaker. But then came one of those moments when a man, through force of personality, changes history. Let author Winik tell the story:

> Rather than potentially escalate matters, the president chose not to rebuke him [Seward] in writing. John G. Nicolay and John M. Hay [Lincoln's secretaries] later noted that a less gracious president would have swiftly dismissed Seward. Aware of the difficulties that lay ahead, Lincoln instead wisely confronted Seward in private. He rejected his advice, sharply disagreeing that the administration had "no policy." On the question of who actually carries out policy, Lincoln was emphatic. "I must do it," he countered, because he was president. Finally, he eschewed any smothering of cabinet discussion. "I am entitled to have the advice," he said, "of all the cabinet." Backed into a corner, Seward suddenly appreciated Lincoln as a vigorous leader. As he learned, Lincoln could be pushed only so far. "Executive force and vigor are rare qualities," a shamed Seward wrote to his wife. "The president is the best of us." From then on, Seward became the president's most faithful cabinet secretary.

And so it began. Fort Sumter was besieged and fought back; war erupted. After four bloody years, the Union was restored; the enslaved people were freed. At the end, Lincoln was killed by an assassin who also grievously wounded William H. Seward.

It is impossible to know how our own tortured age will play out, whether democracy will survive and the anger that divides us will somehow abate. But it is fascinating and instructive to go back, in the skilled hands of Jay Winik, to a similarly chaotic time, before the fall, when the peace was lost.

Evan Thomas
Washington, February 2024

1861

Prelude

New Year's Day in the United States

On New Year's Day 1856, Washington, DC, burst to life. From the muzzles of massed cannons, thunder rolled across the city, and throughout the streets came the clamor of exhilarated conversation. That whole winter had seen the liveliest of social seasons. Every evening you could hear the tireless snorts of horses, the snap of whips, and the unceasing roar of liveries as carriages glided into line. Narrow cobblestone streets led to the lamplit windows of the sturdy redbrick homes of Georgetown and the old-fashioned estates of Kalorama. The aristocracy of the city moved effortlessly through a staggering round of concerts, banquets, balls, ballets, operas, private parties, and evening suppers. Seemingly everybody threw one and everybody went. There was music and supper and frivolity. Residents feasted on shad and strawberries, eggnog and hot punch.

Society ladies in flowing cream-colored dresses and billowing white gowns milled about in high-ceilinged drawing rooms, plucking glasses of champagne with their white-kid-gloved hands from passing servants and piling roasted duck on their plates. These women wore their largest necklaces and finest bracelets, rings, and earrings, some with massive stones. The more risqué among them wore low-cut evening dresses trimmed with antique lace or garlanded with roses, clematis, water lilies, violets, or scarlet honeysuckle. Not to be outdone, the men wore black broadcloth swallowtails with shiny buttons and sported mustaches, then the craze in Washington. Meanwhile, foreign officials, keeping tabs on the shifting

1

fortunes of the young republic, wore costumes neatly trimmed with their nations' colors or gold and silver lace. Throughout the afternoon and then into the evening, from one party to the next, ladies and gentlemen promenaded arm in arm, elegantly waltzed, or danced a chaconne in slow time or a quadrille in fast time.

And they ate. Across town, as candles burned brilliantly, heavy oak tables groaned with food prepared by distinguished chefs, the finest being the fashionable French caterer Charles Gautier, who prepared oysters and lobsters and terrapin, wild turkey and partridge and quail. At the same time, as they demolished their platefuls of food, the merrymakers could admire tables decorated with confectionery towers depicting not scenes of Americana but exotic themes, a fantastic array of castles, pyramids, and pagodas.

There was a rhythm to these affairs. At weekly "levees," days of excited conversation would invariably follow a nod, a smile, or a word sent by a powerful senator in an unusual direction. The women came prepared, always carrying calling cards, while the men looked forward to shaking the president's hand in the Blue Room—or exchanging a word with a cabinet official. And of course, ceaseless rustle begat more excited gossip, about who was up and who was down, the lifeblood of DC's power brokers.

It was all so elegant that one could scarcely notice that Washington was slumbering on the brink of an abyss. Or that the town was rife with hidden echoes of sedition and disarray, and that an undertone of conspiracy was coursing through the city.

Or that in due time the most significant decision in the life of the nation was about to be made, plunging the country into cataclysmic war.

Part I

1856

1

The Promise of America

For all the merriment, the capital, much like the rest of the country, remained a work in progress. After almost sixty years, it gave the impression of having only just been birthed. It had little of the luxury of Paris or the refinement of Vienna, little of the drama of Constantinople or the splendor of Saint Petersburg. There were few spectacular vistas, few intimate squares, and no gentle ocean breezes. If only for that reason, Washington was unique, and perplexing to the rest of the world. Among the great capitals on the world stage, it centered not around culture or commercial life, but politics and politics only.

From the outset, at the dawn of the century, its very design was ambitious, built more for a great power than the young republic that it still was.

To the west, the city stretched along the Potomac as well as the Eastern Branch, from the Anacostia River to Rock Creek, and then to the north along Boundary Street, later to be known as Florida Avenue. Designed by the great Pierre L'Enfant, Washington, with its diagonal streets and radiating circles, was to reflect the traditions of neoclassical monumentality. That was the conception at least. The reality told a different tale. Erected on a swamp and flanked by noxious flats in a stinking canal, the city emitted suffocating odors everywhere, which even wafted into the presidential quarters. The profusion of mosquitoes was terrible, and the stifling heat was even worse. Malaria was rampant. True, in one direction one might see finely suited gentlemen and elegant women slipping into their carriages, or clerks busily making their way to the Treasury Department.

But in another direction, one would glimpse unpaved roads and unsightly shacks, piles of broken brick and discarded stone, and backyard privies. Even more disconcerting to white visitors were the sweat-drenched enslaved people—on whose backs much of the capital was built—and their shanties clinging to the flanks of finer homes. At night, prostitutes copiously plied their trade, and gangs of rowdies disturbed citizens with their lawlessness.

As for the six main buildings of the government? Huge sums had been spent on the public buildings to finish them, but to no avail. There was the Capitol; the General Post Office and the marble Patent Office, diagonally across from each other on F Street; the Treasury Building on Fifteenth Street; the Executive Mansion (not yet known officially as the White House); and down by the Mall, the Smithsonian Institution. But they seemed unrelated to one another and, for the most part, remained incomplete.

Equally telling were the small brick structures housing the War Department and the State Department. The Army headquarters were awkwardly lodged in an old-fashioned house, as was the Navy Department. Workmen toiled, month after month, year after year, to finish the city. They struggled in the muck and the heat, during the daytime and at dusk. They chipped and carved away, chisels in hand, fashioning marble statues and stairs. And there was the skilled labor, the slave labor, and the imported labor.

After nearly ten years of backbreaking work, the gorgeous Library of Congress was still being worked on. The same could be said for the two new wings of the Congress, the Senate chamber and the ornate red-and-gold Hall of the House of Representatives, which everyone agreed would be magnificent once finished, with endless corridors, hideaways, and even gardens, not to mention rich, gleaming floors, great arched ceilings, and even shaded walks. For now, the glittering marble wings of the Capitol stretched bare and incomplete. The porticoes required one hundred Corinthian columns for completion, but only three were set in place, and the steps had yet to be erected. No wonder Henry Adams insisted, "The same rude colony was camped in the same forest, with the same unfinished Greek temples for workrooms and sloughs for roads."

One observer later wryly noted that in sixty years a "compact city" could be constructed, but "not Rome." He might have added: not Washington either. Because its few main buildings were spread far apart from one another, foreigners gibed that the capital was a city "of magnificent distances," and Anthony Trollope thought the city a disconcerting maze where one gets lost, as "in the deserts of the holy land." Or as Senator Charles Sumner once lamented, "What a difference between this place and Rome!" He repeatedly wished for "a walk in the streets of Rome, a stroll on the Pincian, a visit to the Vatican, a sight of St. Peter's—oh, for an hour, one brief hour, of any of these."

Even the breathtaking President's House failed to inspire outright awe. Just to the south of the mansion were sewage marshes and open drainage ditches upon which floated, one Washingtonian scoffed, "dead cats."

But for Americans, there was still much to admire inside and out of the fledgling White House. For one thing, it was the largest residence in America. For another, there were the large polished mirrors, the sparkling chandeliers, and the flowered carpets, not to mention the fruit trees and flower and kitchen gardens, as well as the greenhouses.

And of course, it basked not in wealth or glory, but in democracy.

Thus, on the other side of Pennsylvania Avenue, there stood the imposing bronze equestrian statue of the irascible founder of the Democratic Party, Andrew Jackson, the centerpiece of Lafayette Park. Meanwhile, by the northern portico stood a bronze statue of the author of the Declaration of Independence, Thomas Jefferson. Likenesses of George Washington were spread throughout the city.

There was a seasonal quality to the city, and for many, it was a winter resort. In April the air smelled of blooming flowers and jasmine, crab apples and roses. In July, the heat was oppressive. As the saying went, in the spring, Washington was a heaven; in the summer, it was a hell. But each autumn, after the unhealthy din of a humid Washington summer, the town came alive. Congress opened and the steady pulse of government was everywhere. The railway depot welcomed travelers streaming in from the North and the West. The wharves were equally busy with steamboats bearing Southerners arriving from Aquia Creek. As the legislators poured in, so did lobbyists, office seekers, claimants, delegations, inventors, and reporters. The city took on a life all its own: Senators brokered deals and breakfasted at the Fourteenth Street Willard Hotel on fried oysters and steak and onions. Congressmen wrote constituents, tended to patronage, and paid their dues.

So year after year, there was the constant bustle of guests arriving and guests departing. The small taverns were packed. Opera companies rolled into town, and so did minstrel shows and the theater. Elegant hotels and shabby boardinghouses alike were crowded, as were their halls and parlors, their dining rooms and bars. In a prologue to later problems, there were no empty beds left at the E Street infirmary. Meanwhile, shops decorated their windows, even as fish peddlers called out for customers with the steady refrain, "Get your *fresh* fish! Get your *fresh* fish!"

The jails were filled, and so was the lone poorhouse. Despite numerous churches, and the Young Men's Christian Association, visitors to Washington couldn't help but notice the deluge of gambling, the flood of saloon patrons and liquor venders, the influx of pickpockets and confidence men, the ubiquitous presence of vagrants shuffling about—and the prostitutes. The city, many believed, was tinged with "immorality." Nor was it helped by the fact that enslaved people were still bought and sold there, including in Lafayette Park.

So however exquisite the city was in conception, however vibrant it was when Congress started up, in every direction Washington seemed to evoke unfulfilled promise. Never did this seem to be more the case than in the fact that the Capitol's cast-iron dome, with the *Statue of Freedom* on top, was still unfinished, its gaping roof open to the sky and topped by scaffolding and a towering crane. Nor could it be forgotten that in the rotunda of the Capitol itself was a magnificent painting by John Trumbull of the draft of the Declaration of Independence being presented to the Congress. While a number of key details in the painting were actually wrong, what was not wrong was the unmistakable promise of the political faith of the young Americans as being free and independent, from one end of the continent to the other, from the North to the South.

And that promise seemed to be uniquely American. As Thomas Jefferson had intoned almost biblically in his first inaugural in 1801, speaking both as an aristocrat and as a Democrat, "We are all Republicans, we are all Federalists." Speaking to the future, he told the Congress sitting before him, "Some honest men fear that a Republican government cannot be strong. I believe this, on the contrary, to be the strongest government on earth." Pausing for effect, he added, "It is so. It will be so."

But in 1856, things were dramatically changing.

2

The Stain

For ten-year-old Silas Jackson and his fellow enslaved people, New Year's Eve that year would have a different meaning.

He was born at Ashby's Gap in Virginia; his father's name was Sling and his mother's was Sarah Louise. They were purchased by Tom Ashby, Silas's enslaver, from a trader of enslaved people in Richmond, Virginia. Silas admired his parents; his father was a man of "large stature" and his mother was "tall and stately." They originally came from the eastern shore of Maryland, but Silas knew few other details about them. He had six siblings: four brothers and two sisters; at least he knew their names. The only thing he remembered about his grandparents was that his grandfather managed to make his way to Philadelphia and eventually to save $350, which he used to purchase Silas's grandmother through the aid of a Quaker minister.

Headstrong and soft-spoken, Silas was a large boy for his age and had begun to work in earnest from the age of nine. "We all had hard taskwork to do—men, women, and boys," he told an interviewer much later in his life. The enslaved people raised tobacco and wheat, corn and other farm products. The work itself was unceasing, from early Monday morning to dusk on Friday. Work started at sunrise and continued all day to sundown, with no time to go to the cabin for dinner; the enslaved people instead carried their dinner with them, eating with their fingers. Day after day, week after week, the enslaved people were driven at "top speed" and "whipped at the snap of a finger" by one of the overseers: four hired white men.

Saturdays were a bit better; they were allowed to work for themselves, or to garden or cook or even do extra work. But they always had to be back by nine o'clock on Saturday night, when inspection was made; otherwise, they risked a beating. Meanwhile, Silas consoled himself with small triumphs, reveling in the fact that he could earn as much as 50¢ a day, enough to buy cakes, candies, or even clothes.

More often than not, when one of the enslaved people was sweating with the flu or sick with something else, they would be treated with a witches' brew of herbs, salves, and other remedies prepared by "someone who knew the medicinal value." For many, getting sick meant a death sentence. Not unsurprisingly, a number of enslaved people believed in ghost stories or voodooism (Silas did not). That said, for those who were considered "a valuable hand," when they took sick, Ashby would have one of the overseers go to Upperville for a doctor.

On Saturdays each enslaved person was provided ten pounds of cornmeal, a quart of "blackstrap," "six pounds of fatback," and three pounds of flour and vegetables. Every enslaved family, at least those that were intact, was provided small bits of acreage to raise their own chickens or vegetables, and if they did raise their own food, they received $10 extra at Christmas, "besides his presents." They were clothed modestly: In the summer, when the oppressively warm weather came, the women wore gingham clothes, the men overalls and muslin shirts, and straw hats to work in. In the cold weather, they wore woolen clothes, threadbare but all handsewn on the estate.

As Silas put it, describing his enslaver, Tom Ashby, "A meaner man was never born—brutal, wicked, and hard." Ashby ruled with an iron fist, and all the enslaved people lived in terror of him. He always carried a cowhide with him, and if he saw anything that did not "suit his taste," he would tie the enslaved person to a tree, man or woman, and then cowhide the victim relentlessly until the enslaved person would faint or incessantly whimper or spit up blood. Silas noted, "I've seen men beaten until they dropped in their tracks or knocked over by clubs, women stripped [naked] down to their waist and cowhided." Others had hot wax poured on them until they screamed or begged for mercy and passed out.

Mrs. Ashby was kind and loving to the enslaved people when her husband was not around. But when he was on the estate, it was an entirely different matter. One night Tom's father went to one of the slave cabins, where he overheard the enslaved people having a secret prayer meeting. He heard one enslaved person (Zeke) ask God to "change the heart of his master" and deliver him from slavery "so that he may enjoy freedom." This was a heresy of the highest order. Before the next day the man disappeared, and no one ever saw him again. But after that, down in the swamp when the moon was high, Silas could sometimes hear the grandfather who preyed on the cabin praying himself. Later Silas found out that just before Tom Ashby's father died, he confessed to the white Baptist minister that he had killed Zeke for "praying" and that in turn, "he was going to hell." Was there more on his conscience? A change of heart? Such as one grandmother who drowned herself in the river when she heard that "grand Pap was going away." In truth he was sold because he got "religious" and had fervently "prayed that God would set him and Grandma free."

Silas had never seen enslaved people directly "sold on the farm," but he had seen them taken away in chains before they "disappeared." He was also all too familiar with the feared stone building on the farm, where downstairs the overseer personally used one room, while he used the other room for some of the whippings. Often, at the least provocation, these whippings took place. Meanwhile, the women and girls sewed upstairs, wincing with each strap. They could hear the cries and the moaning of those being remorselessly beaten beneath them.

No one was taught to read or write; no one could read the Bible. As a result, Silas and his fellow enslaved people lived in a hermetically sealed world where information came largely from rumor and gossip and song. On Sundays, the enslaved people who wanted to worship—which was most of them—would gather in one of the large cabins, where they could take communion at "church." Sandy Jasper, Ashby's coachman and an enslaved person, was the preacher. Actually, he was allowed to go to the white Baptist church on Saturday with his family, and thus was better informed about what was taking place in the world because "he heard the white preacher."

It was whispered that other slave communities communicated with one another. For instance, there was the poignant story of one group of enslaved people who would gather on the banks of the Potomac and sing across the river to the enslaved people in Virginia, who in turn would "sing back."

Twice each year, after harvest and after New Year's, the enslaved people would have their protracted meeting or "their revival," after which they would then baptize one another in the creek. Sometimes in the winter, they would break the ice, singing "Going to the Water" or some other melodic hymn.

There were a number of enslaved people on the plantation who ran away, upon which the overseers let loose a frantic bevy of bloodhounds to find them. The incessant howls of the dogs were chilling. While some of the escapees were captured and sold to a Georgia trader, others were never caught. Often they would hide in the swamps or along the river, or squirrel themselves away on a train leaving Virginia, making their way to someplace "where they thought they would be safe." In turn, to intimidate the enslaved people, the overseers were connected with the patrollers.

During the afternoon, the enslaved people hummed familiar tunes as they worked. When the drudgery of the day was over, the enslaved people, worn out and drenched with sweat, retired to their cabins. Some played games, others cooked, and many, exhausted by the long days, simply collapsed.

Christmas was special; for once, there was a letup of the tireless cruelties. Ashby, the brutal enslaver, would call all the enslaved people together and give them presents and money, after which they then got to spend the day "as they liked." But on New Year's Day, eighty miles from where the social and political set were preparing to celebrate in Washington, DC, all the enslaved people "were scared." Why? That was the time for "selling, buying, and trading slaves."

In terror, Silas bided his time. He did not know "who was to go or who was to come." Would anyone ever come to the rescue of the enslaved people? He grimly watched, and he waited, completely ignorant of the titanic events unfolding in Washington.

Part II

THE
BEGINNING

3

The Senator

Unknown to Silas, in Washington, DC, there were those who wanted to come to the rescue, namely, the prominent liberal senator from Massachusetts, Charles Sumner. One of the great minds of the day on foreign policy, he would soon become the powerful chair of the Senate Foreign Relations Committee. On this spring afternoon, however, fate had something very different in store for him.

How does one describe Sumner? To his enemies he was humorless and intolerant and frequently annoyed those around him; to his friends, he was a high-minded man who hated slavery, who refused to compromise or temporize on its moral iniquities, and who spoke with great courage about racial injustice. And to all who knew him, he cut a large figure in political and social circles. He had blue-blooded manners and elevated tastes; he was a man of uncommon intelligence and refinement. An autodidact, he spoke French fluently, having mastered it in six months, as well as Italian, German, and Spanish. Not unsurprisingly, he also had an air of superiority about him, which often infuriated friend and foe alike. And he was vituperative, driving his adversaries to unmitigated fury with his insults.

Fastidious, he was a longtime bachelor with impeccable schooling; sophisticated, he was a graduate of the famed Boston Latin School. He also had BA and law degrees from Harvard. Meanwhile, at the Sorbonne in France, he had studied a range of subjects from geology to Greek history to criminal law. Lord Henry Brougham once declared that he had never met any man with the "natural legal intellect" of Sumner.

He was close to many of the great thinkers of the age: a good friend of Henry Wadsworth Longfellow's, of Horace Mann's, of Wendell Phillips's, and of the renowned jurist Joseph Story, who was his mentor at Harvard. He had even met the great French political scientist Alexis de Tocqueville, and he befriended the noted author Harriet Beecher Stowe. Sumner was a radical in an age when radicals were often despised; an early abolitionist, he fought equally tenaciously against segregation and for educational reform. And, too, he thought nothing of shocking eighteenth-century Boston with his opposition to misogynist laws, and like the young one-term backcountry congressman Abraham Lincoln, he was an ardent opponent of the Mexican-American War. Accused of utopianism, Sumner insisted his faith in reform was unshakable. "The utopias of one age," he once thundered, "became the realities of the next."

He almost never made it to the Senate. At just forty years old, he was elected by the slimmest of margins, a one-vote majority, and his abolitionist politics—so widely detested throughout much of the country—contrasted sharply with those of his illustrious predecessor, Daniel Webster, who was himself a proponent of the Compromise of 1850, the package of bills that diffused political confrontation between slave states and Free States on the status of territories acquired in the Mexican-American War. Once in the Senate, Sumner quickly became a sought-after orator. He spoke with great flourish, gesturing wildly with his hands and freely quoting from the Bible, that is, when he wasn't referencing the Greeks and hailing the Romans. Watching him, an awed Longfellow compared Sumner to "a cannoneer ramming down cartridges."

Enlightened and snobbish, Sumner never left anyone in doubt about what he truly believed. Slim, unusually tall—he was six foot four—he was a fussy dresser, invariably wearing tailored suits and checkered trousers. He had intense blue eyes, an aquiline nose, and a wavy mane of rich brown hair speckled with gray. And he had a rather sad smile. He was so conscious of his manners that he once admitted that "he never allowed himself, even in the privacy of his own chamber, to fall into a position which he would not take in his chair in the Senate."

For Sumner the politician, there was often a built-in tension he could never easily reconcile. Austere, able, experienced, and incorruptible, he had an abiding dislike of the compromises so common in politics. Privately, he could be warm and cordial; socially he could be quite pleasant, or charming, or as Kate Seward once said, even "sensitive." But on the floor of the Senate he frequently displayed an aloof and obstinate streak. Deep within him lurked a cold, insatiable vein. Once he made up his mind, he treated virtually any attempt to argue him out of it as an assault on his integrity. And he capitulated to no one.

So where others swayed with the political winds, this way or that, Sumner peered into the future with a keen sense of what was right and what was wrong. Never was this more apparent to the Senate and to the nation than when on May 19 and 20, 1856, he gave the most important speech of his already illustrious career: a withering two-day philippic titled "The Crime Against Kansas."

In preparation for the debate—violence and mayhem had erupted over the question of slavery in the Kansas Territory as it neared statehood—Sumner had been gathering his wrath. He confided to Salmon P. Chase, "I shall make the most thorough and complete speech of my life." He collected histories of North Carolina, South Carolina, and Georgia from the Library of Congress. He read *Don Quixote*. He prepared quotations from Cicero, Virgil, Dante, and Milton, as well as from British parliamentary debates. He referenced the fields of Marathon and Sparta when she ruled Greece; the English banner at Agincourt; and, for his final peroration, a passage from Demosthenes. The speech itself ran 112 pages once set in type by the congressional printer. And then he read the whole address to his friend, the distinguished New York senator William H. Seward, to practice before an audience. He was now ready.

On May 19, he spoke before a packed Senate gallery for three hours, and then again on May 20.

"My soul is wrung by this outrage," he bellowed. "And I shall pour it forth." In terms full of rebuke, Sumner spoke of a country steeped in rancor and saturated with chaos because of slavery. He denounced the Kansas-Nebraska Act, which allowed the people of the Kansas and Nebraska Territories to decide for themselves whether to allow slavery within their borders, and then he argued for the immediate admission of Kansas to the Union as a Free (i.e., non-slave) State. He went on to denounce slavery as a moral perversion and the "Slave Power"—the political arm of the enslavers—as just as bad. Their goal, he asserted, was to spread slavery everywhere, in the slave states as well as the Free States, and in Kansas itself. He said their motivation was the "rape of a virgin territory" with the complicity of federal officials, including even the president. Perhaps with more emotion than decorum, Sumner further declared, "Murderous robbers from Missouri, hirelings picked from the drunken spew and vomit of an uneasy civilization," were compelling Kansans to "the hateful embrace of slavery."

He continued: "It may be clearly traced to a depraved desire for a new slave state, hideous offspring of such a crime, in the hope of adding to the power of slavery in the national government."

Then Sumner made his speech personal, singling out two colleagues for attack—the authors of the Kansas-Nebraska Act. He heaped abuse upon Stephen A. Douglas, likening him to Don Quixote's illiterate but clever sidekick, Sancho Panza, and mocked Andrew P. Butler, a soft-spoken, cultured senator from South Carolina. Butler's home state, he said, with its "shameful imbecility from slavery," had sent to the Senate in his person a "Don Quixote who chose a mistress to whom he has made his vows, and...though polluted in the sight of the world, is chaste in his sight—I mean the harlot, slavery. For her his tongue is always profuse in words." Then, in the embodiment of bad taste, Sumner made fun of the elderly Butler's physical infirmity—he had a stroke-induced paralysis of muscles in his face, causing him to slur his speech.

Such language had rarely ever been heard within the Senate chamber itself, prompting Lewis Cass, the president of the Senate and formerly Andrew Jackson's secretary of war, to label it the "most un-American and unpatriotic" speech ever uttered there.

Sumner's speech produced a widespread uproar—in the Senate, as well as in the press, where even Republican praise was mitigated by concerns about Sumner's intemperate rhetoric.

No one challenged Sumner to a duel, but mainly because dueling was for social equals, which Southerners believed Sumner was distinctly not; to them, somebody as low as this Yankee "drunkard" deserved "a cowhide"—or a good caning. This was the view of the two-term congressman Preston Brooks, a cousin and neighbor of Andrew Butler's and, ironically, a political moderate.

Brooks intended to make good on the threat. Two days later, after the Senate adjourned, all was quiet in the chamber save for a few small conversations among a handful of senators, and the steady scratching of pen on paper: Sumner was sitting in his chair near the center aisle in the back row, busily engaged in writing; actually, he was franking his speech for wider distribution. Deeply absorbed in conversation, Sumner did not notice when two men entered the chamber. One was the youthful Preston Brooks, the other his House colleague Laurence Keitt.

After waiting a few minutes for some people to file out of the chamber, Brooks confronted Sumner directly. "I have read your speech twice over carefully," he declared. "It is a libel on South Carolina, and Mr. Butler, who is a relative of mine." As Sumner began to stand up, Brooks hit him severely on the head using a thick cane adorned with a heavy gold head. Sumner was knocked down, and try as he might to wriggle free, he was trapped under the heavy desk, which was bolted to the floor. Brooks continued to beat him. As the blows rained down, Sumner was soon blinded by his own blood. Brooks hit him again and again until a frantic Sumner managed to rip the desk from the floor. Meanwhile, an elderly statesman, John J. Crittenden from Kentucky, rushed over and lunged at Brooks, calling on him to desist, shouting, "Don't kill him." Brooks did not—yet. Georgia senator Robert Toombs intervened to help as well, but more to protect Crittenden than Sumner. However, Representative Keitt, brandishing a pistol, blocked others from helping, shouting, "Let them be! God damn you!"

Meanwhile Sumner, his clothes now drenched in blood, having wrenched his writing table from the fastenings, finally struggled to his feet. Another blow descended upon him, and this time he fell unconscious. Remarkably, Brooks's cane broke, but Brooks continued to strike Sumner with the remaining stick. Eventually, Brooks decided he had done enough; he left the chamber and drifted out onto Pennsylvania Avenue. For his part, an ailing Sumner was moved to the vice president's room and was later taken by carriage back to his house. There he was examined by a doctor. He was not in good shape.

Badly shaken, still bleeding profusely, Sumner mumbled before drifting off into a dazed sleep: "I could not believe that a thing like this was possible."

But in 1856, it was possible. Indeed, Brooks went so far as to threaten other Northern leaders, writing, "It would not take much to have the throats of every abolitionist cut." Keitt joined him, scornfully remarking, "The city would now float with blood . . . Everybody here feels as if we were upon a volcano."

———————

And that volcano was about to erupt. A million copies of Sumner's "Crime Against Kansas" speech were soon distributed. The affair was an outrage for Northerners, even those who did not much like Sumner or his "vulgarity of language." One Connecticut schoolgirl told her parents, "I don't think it is of very much use to stay any longer in the high school, as the boys would be better learning to hold muskets, and the girls to make bullets." Hundreds sent letters to Sumner expressing their sympathy. "My blood is boiling," cried one. "This murderous outrage," said another. Or as Horace Mann put it, "We are not only shocked at the outrage committed upon you, but we are wounded in your wounds, and bleed in your bleeding."

Overnight, "Bleeding Sumner" became emblematic of the South's inequities, right up there with "Bleeding Kansas." Senator Edward Everett roared that the assault "produced excitement in the public mind deeper and more dangerous than I have ever witnessed." "Has it come to this," wondered William Cullen Bryant of the *New York Evening Post*, "that we must speak with bated breath in the presence of our southern Masters? Are we to be chastised as they chastised their slaves? Are we too slaves, slaves for life, a target for their brutal blows, when we do not comport ourselves to please them?"

The *Cincinnati Gazette* coined it differently. The South, it hollered, "cannot tolerate free speech anywhere, and would stifle it in Washington with the bludgeon and the Bowie knife, as they are now trying to stifle it in Kansas by massacre, rapine, and murder."

As if this weren't enough, Brooks was now a household name, martyred and feted as a hero across the South. To be sure, there were those in the South who were embarrassed by the affair, or who worried about its effect on Northern opinion. But whatever reservations some may have had, they were far outweighed by widespread public approval for Brooks's actions. As the *Charleston Courier* noted, Brooks had "stood forth so nobly in defense of... the honor of South Carolinians." The *Richmond Enquirer* declared, "The truth is, [the abolitionist senators] have been suffered to run too long without collars. They must be lashed into submission." For good measure, it added that Sumner should be "caned every morning."

Brooks himself had a few words to say of his own, boasting that "every southern man sustains me." Evidently this was so. He noted that people were now begging for the fragments of his cane as "sacred relics." In turn, from all over the South, Brooks was sent new canes, some inscribed with such injunctions as "Hit him again." While the House voted 121 to 95 to expel Brooks, Southern opposition prevented the necessary two-thirds majority to do so. However, a resolution of censure passed, and Brooks gaily resigned, returning home to seek vindication. The vindication came soon, as he was unanimously reelected to go back to Washington to the very seat he had vacated. Meanwhile, in yet another insult, dozens of Southern lawmakers made rings out of the cane's remains, which they wore on neck chains to show their solidarity with Brooks.

The disgust in the North was equally loud and vociferous. Rallies in support of Sumner were held across the country, as dense throngs of people, often in the thousands, jammed into city squares and community churches, listening to speeches and prayers. In Sumner's hometown of Boston and in Albany they gathered; in Cleveland and Detroit, too; in New Haven and in New York; and in Providence and Rochester. Ralph Waldo Emerson called Southerners members of a "barbarous community." One old-line Whig turned Republican said that it was not the attack alone ("horrible as it was") that excited him, but the "tone of the southern press [and] of the whole southern people." In the meantime, suffering from multiple head injuries and frequent exhaustion, as well as "psychic wounds" (we know it today as post-traumatic stress disorder), Sumner spent the brunt of the next four years in Europe away from the Senate to recuperate. As a powerful symbol of "free speech," as well as a pointed reproach to South Carolina's legislature, the Massachusetts legislature reelected Sumner.

The effect of all this was to widen the breach between the two halves of the country. To Southerners, Northern justification of Sumner's pointed barbs branded all Northerners with his guilt. At the same time, to Northerners, Southern enthusiasm for Brooks's brutal attack stamped all Southerners as men of violence hardly different from the violent ruffians storming across the fields of Kansas.

And as Sumner was bedridden, reliant on opiates, and "pale and suffering," something else was clearly going on: The two regions, in describing the Sumner affair, spoke the same words but no longer the same language. In indescribable ways, they now had diametrically opposed views of the world.

When Sumner later returned to the Senate, fellow Republicans suggested he take a less strident tone. Sumner answered: "When crime and criminals are thrust before us, they are to be met by all the energies that God has given us by argument, scorn, sarcasm and denunciation."

Then, in a remarkable kaleidoscope of events, at just about the same time would come news of John Brown's brutal murders of five proslavery settlers in Kansas, as well as the sacking of the otherwise little-known town of Lawrence, Kansas, by Missouri border guerrillas, all with fateful consequences.

4

The Mad Prophet

If the vicious caning in the marbled halls of Congress electrified the nation, so would the actions of the fifty-six-year-old abolitionist John Brown. Born in Torrington, Connecticut, in 1800—the same year Thomas Jefferson was elected president—Brown was decidedly a man of his times. A zealot who mesmerized those around him, he was a man who believed he could fire up the nation and start a war. With his haunting looks, long white beard, and bony fingers, he was a lay theologian weaned on the sermons of the Great Awakening preacher Jonathan Edwards, and he lived by the Old Testament injunction of an eye for an eye, a tooth for a tooth. Gaunt and unkempt, he even looked the part of a biblical warrior, a nineteenth-century David who improbably slew Goliath with his slingshot, bringing redemption to the Promised Land. In truth, however, Brown had repeatedly failed in life.

A humble penitent, he was a staunch Calvinist. He was also the father of twenty children by two wives, but his successes ended with procreation. Nine of his children died. None of his roughly two dozen businesses ever panned out, including his sheep business and his wool business. He was bankrupt and frequently a defendant in litigation. Scarred by his own sins and plagued with guilt, he became a justice of the peace. It did little to reverse his fortunes. At the age of fifty-one, he was already a worn-out old man. His health was precarious; he suffered from repeated fevers, changing moods, frequent sweats, and ague.

Yet he realized he had a much greater calling—to strike a blow against the heart of slavery. So it happened that in 1855 he gathered his few belongings, along with a wagonload of guns, knives, and artillery broadsides, and joined six of his sons and a son-in-law to take part in settling Kansas, where a proxy struggle embodied the tensions of the nation at large: whether to be free or unfree, slave-free or slave-ridden. True, this virgin frontier was being settled by a mixed array of speculators, Indian traders, cattle dealers, gun vendors, and riverboat riffraff. But a "save Kansas" movement was now also roaring across the North, as numerous Kansas aid societies solicited guns, money, and men for the free-state cause in the territory, men who hated slavery. As it happened, in this land of undulating prairies, forest recesses, and fertile valleys, some nine thousand people were now settled, most of them Free-Soilers from the Midwestern states. And in covered wagons and crowded riverboats, scores of other pioneers continued to flood in from the Northwest and the border South, too, on their way to this new land: 126,000 square miles of unclaimed wilderness lying west of Missouri in the heart of North America. Brown, seeing himself as a soldier in this holy war to abolish slavery, wanted to be a part of it. He enlisted in a free-state military company engaged in the mounting conflict that was spreading during the spring of 1856.

The winter was hard. Yet, despite subzero temperatures and persistent blowing snow, the Browns survived. Then, amid rumors in May that a human storm was further gathering on the Kansas border, and that an unwashed and hard-drinking band of proslavery border ruffians were massing for an invasion, Brown and company rushed to the town of Lawrence—"a piece of New England set down in the prairie"—to defend it. They arrived too late, only to hear the shocking news. On May 21, the town had already been pillaged and laid siege to by eight hundred men from Missouri, a yelling, howling mob, which for good measure dragged along five cannons and waved banners as if they were a conquering Napoleonic army. For Kansans, it became a horrific scene of despondency and terror. Vowing to exterminate every "God damned abolitionist" in Kansas, the Missouri ruffians plundered shops and houses, demolished its two abolitionist newspapers, and then put the town to the torch. The massive

Free State hotel was burned, as was the home of the elected "free-soil" governor, Charles Robinson.

As this scene played out, dozens had gathered beneath the heated air and the flying pieces of burning wood. All gaped in astonishment at the choking smoke and the flames now roaring out of control. Some of the streets were littered with household items: cooking utensils, heirlooms, and photographs, bureaus and bedding, all gathered in haste and piled randomly on the streets. The residents of Lawrence shuddered as they heard the pounding of the Missourian bushwhackers' feet and their barked commands filling the air. From one house to the next, the streets now shook with the signs of incipient despair. And soon, the gathering night was filled with the sounds of desperation: screaming, swearing, wailing, and the dreadful howls of the Missouri guerrillas, which for the Lawrence residents was the most unearthly sound of all.

Residents wondered, When will the horror end? The suspense was nearly unbearable, and it seemed to keep on, hour after hour. Hard questions arose. How did this happen? What was to become of Lawrence?

And how to fight back?

Few had answers, but Brown had his. Upon hearing of the Missouri guerrillas' attack, Brown flew into a rage at the proslavery forces, leavened by his equal disgust at the failure of the free-state leaders of Lawrence to resist. He lectured his men: This was not how to make Kansas free. Instead, he demanded that they must "fight fire with fire" and "strike terror into the hearts of the proslavery people."

It was then that further word reached Brown that sent him over the edge—the caning of Senator Charles Sumner in Washington. Upon hearing this, Brown "went crazy."

Pacing back and forth, he proclaimed, "Something must be done to show these barbarians that we, too, have rights." Something had to be done, but what? If the caning of Sumner and the acquiescence of Lawrence proved one thing, it was that they couldn't count on the government. There needed to be a different way. By his count, Brown believed proslavery men had murdered at least five Free-Soilers in Kansas. So he instead devised "radical, retaliatory measures" against "the slave power." He and four of his sons, joined by three other men, fanned out near Pottawatomie Creek. They were on their own. Two days after Sumner was beaten in the Capitol Building, on the night of May 24, they broke into five separate cabins, where they abducted unwitting proslavery settlers. The terrified settlers had had nothing to do with the murders in Lawrence, Kansas. No matter. Weeping, mothers frantically begged for the lives of their sons. Several were spared. But Brown had a point to make. An eye for an eye, he dragged men and boys alike out of their cabins and split open their skulls with broadswords. For good measure, he executed one of his victims, shooting him in the head, while cutting off the hand of another victim, whose mutilated body was cast into a creek, where "his brains" floated away.

As if this were the Terror in France, three bodies were hacked into pieces.

News of this massacre quickly spread out across the nation, right into the US Capitol. And as this reign of terror broke out in eastern Kansas, Missouri militia and their Kansas allies continued to murder in cold blood and burn and pillage free-state communities. From Lawrence to Osawatomie, the cycle of violence escalated, and proslavery brigands went on a rampage, flaming the Brown homesteads. Two of Brown's sons were arrested—men who had nothing to do with the affair. Overnight, this bushwhacking war spiraled in Kansas, fueled by the twin nightmares of Lawrence and Pottawatomie and the fact that the population was now divided into two groups, each group armed to the teeth and organized into secret military units. This was in addition to the fact that the pro-slavery faction of the state supported a government at Lecompton, one replete with slave codes and sedition measures that prohibited criticism of slavery, while the antislavery faction supported a government at Topeka, one that pleaded for the Free States to send help for the cause of freedom in Kansas.

The polarization of Kansas, mirroring the nation at large, was nearly complete.

Remarkably, Brown was never indicted for these killings. He moved to a secret camp somewhere in the bush to elude capture. Meantime, free-state men lived in constant fear of a Missouri attack and slept with guns at their sides. And despite efforts by the US Army, the troops were unable to contain the hit-and-run violence that pervaded the Plains. Partisan bands on both sides flamed cabins, assaulted settlements, and seized horses and supplies. In the midst of this "reign of terror," news of the massacre quickly moved eastward, and Brown became as much a legend as Charles Sumner.

A thousand miles from Washington, on a windswept prairie dotted with wildflowers, a mini–civil war was now raging. Its creed was stark: Kill or be killed.

5

The Assemblyman

Watching all this, the forty-seven-year-old Illinois state assemblyman, Abraham Lincoln, was forcing himself to appear in good spirits. To Lincoln, everything seemed so combustible. In truth, he was depressed about whether slavery, which he despised with all his fiber, would ever be eradicated by peaceful means. As he wrote a friend, "Our political problem now is, 'can we, as a nation, continue together permanently—forever— half slave, and half free?'" And further, Lincoln, a lifelong member of the Whig Party, which was rapidly withering away, struggled with where his political home should be.

But one place where he did not struggle was on the question of the Know-Nothings, a burgeoning movement riddled with anti-Catholic, antipope bigotry. He anguished over the bloody anti-Catholic riots smothering small towns and sweeping cities across the North. "I'm not a Know Nothing," Lincoln famously pointed out. "How could I be? How can anyone who abhors the oppression of Negroes, be in favor of degrading classes of white people? Our progress in degeneracy appears to me to be pretty rapid. As a nation, we began by declaring that *'all men are created equal.'* We now practically read it 'all men are created equal, except Negroes.' When the know-nothings get control, it will read 'all men are created equal, except *Negroes, and foreigners, and Catholics.'*"

All throughout the winter, as Lincoln trudged off to his office in the morning, as he undertook his busy rounds of political and legal work, as he went to the state library and studied past congressional debates, he thought constantly about the Republicans, Democrats, Know-Nothings, and Whigs. By February 1856, while tensions were inflaming Kansas as well as Washington, Lincoln came to realize that his once beloved Whig Party, the venerable party of Henry Clay and Daniel Webster, had lost its moorings and seemed "doomed to extinction." Meanwhile, the Democratic Party was increasingly controlled by proslavery Southerners. Conversely, as time passed, Republicans began organizing on a national as well as a state level, and almost overnight they loomed as the major new party of the future. Lincoln, looking forward, prepared himself to help shape a new party in Illinois. And as for the principles that he thought should guide the party? He felt the party must stand with the abolitionists and against the South in blocking the spread of slavery. But in the same measure, it must stand against the abolitionists in upholding the Constitution and the fugitive slave law. In doing so, the party would avoid "dangerous extremes" and occupy a steady "national ground."

Nine days after the sacking of Lawrence, Lincoln joined with other state leaders in gathering at Bloomington, Illinois, to launch this new Free-Soil Party. Post-Lawrence, emotions were at a fever pitch. Though originally called by a host of names—the "anti-Nebraska" party, "the Fusion party," or "the People's Party"—it would soon carry the official "Republican" name.

The "Republican" delegates in Bloomington were appalled by the shocking news of the civil war grinding away in Kansas and the beating of Senator Sumner, which gave them a heightened sense of purpose. Some two thousand people packed Major's Hall: a raucous and emotional crowd, smoking cigars and chewing tobacco. They were old-line Whigs and old-line Democrats, Free-Soilers and abolitionists, and even Know-Nothings. Lincoln seemed to be everywhere at the convention. He was one of the drafters of the party platform. He helped draw up the slate of state candidates. And when all this was done, he was drafted to give the keynote address. Mounting the platform "amid deafening applause," Lincoln delivered a virtuoso performance, one full of "fire and energy and force." He cried out about the "pressing reasons" for the new Republican movement and the need to stem the westward march of the "slave power." He added that the nation must be preserved intact, and that it was the Republicans who would uniquely preserve it.

Normally a poor impromptu speaker, and routinely hamstrung by his "thin, high-pitched" voice, Lincoln had no prepared script. Yet he was uncommonly inspired that day. His speaking touched the soul because it came from the soul. It produced conviction because it came from conviction. He rendered the entire assembly spellbound. Even reporters became mesmerized, tossing their pencils aside or not using them at all. A starstruck Jesse Dubois pronounced it "the greatest speech ever made in Illinois." Remarkably, no record of the speech was ever made, and as a result, it became known in history as the "Lost Speech." When Lincoln finally sat down, the crowd jumped to its feet and cheered him, again and again and again. The Whig Party was dead; the Republican Party had been born.

———————

Back at his desk, Lincoln studied the arguments for slavery—and against it. He tirelessly scribbled; he devised counterarguments on fragments of paper. Day after day, he came to know slavery, its inside and outside. He acquainted himself with the repeated arguments by Southerners that slavery was "a very good thing" (to which he then responded that he never heard of a man who wished to take advantage of this good thing "by being a slave himself"). He examined the issue of slave labor versus free labor. "Why," he said, "even the dumbest animal, even an insect—even an ant—knows it is entitled to the fruit of its own toil."

And he spoke at great length of the illogic of slavery: "If A can prove, however conclusively, that he may, of right, enslave B—why may not B snatch the same argument, and prove equally, that he may enslave A?

"You say A is white, and B is black. It is color, then; the lighter, having the right to enslave the darker? Take care. By this rule, you are to be a slave to the first man you meet, with a fairer skin than your own.

"You do not mean color exactly?—You mean the whites are intellectually the superior of the blacks, and therefore have the right to enslave them? Take care again. By this rule you are to be slave to the very first man you meet, with an intellect superior to your own.

"But, say you, it is a question of interest; and if you can make it your interest, you have the right to enslave another. Very well. And if he can make it his interest, he has the right to enslave you."

But then came the *Dred Scott* case before the Supreme Court, with earth-shattering consequences.

6

The Decision

Dred Scott was an enslaved person involved in a rebellion of the greatest magnitude.

In 1846, on the advice of white friends in St. Louis, Scott sued for his freedom on the grounds that his master, John Emerson, an Army surgeon, had removed him for four years to military posts in both the Free State of Illinois and the free territory of Fort Snelling, the northern part of what is now Minnesota, before returning to the slave state of Missouri. Thus began an eleven-year constitutional drama, one of the most famous cases in American history. The case wound its way through state and federal courts until it finally landed before the Supreme Court in 1856. Here, at last, was a moment of truth for the nation on the question of slavery.

Montgomery Blair, Lincoln's future postmaster general and the son of the renowned diplomat Francis Blair, represented Dred Scott. Reverdy Johnson, who hailed from the slave state of Maryland, represented Scott's enslavers. The court itself was headed by Chief Justice Roger Brooke Taney of Maryland. Taney had once been Andrew Jackson's secretary of the Treasury, helping to destroy the Second Bank of the United States. Now, at eighty years old, Taney was sick and feeble. He was also heartbroken: Two years earlier, his wife and daughter had died in a yellow fever epidemic. At a time when the average life expectancy was fewer than forty years, Taney had little left to live for—little except for the defense of slavery, which had been the overweening theme of his twenty-six years on the court, galvanizing him with an unwavering singleness of purpose. When

Dred Scott came along, it gave him the opportunity to write the opinion for which, in a very real sense, he was hanging on to life. Ironically, even as he was determined to defend his beloved South from the forces of abolitionism, Taney himself had no great love for slavery, having freed those he enslaved. His home state of Maryland actually contained the largest free Black population of any state. But the chief justice was fervently committed to "Southern life and values," which to him seemed organically linked "to the peculiar institution." Taney increasingly railed against what he saw as growing "Northern aggression" against our "own southern countrymen." As he said once, "The knife of the assassin is at [our] throats."

Then on March 4, 1857—after the court had heard arguments in the *Dred Scott* case, but prior to the ruling—James Buchanan was inaugurated president, and he announced in his inaugural address that the US Supreme Court was about to solve the slave controversy "once and for all." Two days later, the Taney court, comprising six Democrats and two Republicans, did indeed hand down that "once and for all," an astonishing opinion that shocked Republicans and lovers of liberty everywhere. Each judge wrote a separate opinion, but the other six Democrats concurred with Taney. For their part, the two Republicans strenuously dissented. As if turning the heavens upside down, or as one historian put it, "juggling history, law, and logic," Taney insisted that free Negroes were not and never had been US "citizens" according to the Constitution. As a result, Scott had no standing in federal court, and no right to sue. In a sweeping reinterpretation, Taney declared further that the Constitution and the language of the Declaration of Independence did not embrace Black people as part of the American "people." Taney contended that upon the framing of the founding documents, Black men were widely seen as "beings of an inferior order, and altogether unfit to associate with the white race, either in social or political relations; and so far inferior, that they had no rights which the white man was bound to respect." To wit: As Taney painted it, Black people were not included in the "all men" who were, according to the Declaration of Independence, "created equal." In short, the Declaration of Independence itself was a white man's document only.

Congress, Taney went on, had no authority to prohibit slavery in the national lands because that would violate the property rights clause of the Fifth Amendment. Thus, the Missouri Compromise, which forbade slavery in territories north of the thirty-sixth parallel, was never constitutional. Moreover, if Congress could not exclude slavery from the territories, then it equally could not authorize any territorial government like Kansas to reject slavery either. All Congress could do was to protect the rights of "property owners." Here, enslaved people were strikingly no different from other property, and a ban on slavery was therefore an unconstitutional deprivation of property.

The ruling spurred waves of discontent, leaving antislavery forces reeling. Republicans hotly answered that *Dred Scott* was "cruel, inhumane, and unfair" and undertook the task of mustering Northern voices against it. The *New York Tribune* was more than willing to comply, arguing that the Supreme Court had forfeited its stature as "an impartial judicial body" and had the same moral weight as the judgment of those congregated in "any Washington bar-room." Meanwhile, Frederick Douglass said the chief justice could do many things, but "he cannot...change the essential nature of things—making evil good, and good, evil." Speaking in Rochester, New York, Senator William H. Seward provocatively cried out that the United States was increasingly divided into two "incompatible" political and economic systems, which had developed radically divergent cultures, values, and assumptions. Standing before an overflowing crowd in Corinthian Hall, he spoke of an "irrepressible conflict between opposing and enduring forces." In his view, the United States must and would, sooner or later, "become entirely a slaveholding nation, or entirely a free labor nation."

Lincoln, his temperament as restless as ever, now scribbled furiously. He had things to say. He worried that if neither Congress nor a territorial government could keep slavery from planting its flag west, then wasn't the effect of the *Dred Scott* case to legalize slavery in all the territories, as many Southerners and Democrats demanded? In addition, *Dred Scott* negated the doctrine of "popular sovereignty," which allowed the people through their territorial governments to vote slavery in or out. As was so often the case, Lincoln was arguing less through a rousing call to arms and more through the relentless force of logic.

As to Black people in the Declaration? Lincoln offered his reply. The founders, he contended, did not intend "to declare all men equal *in all respects*." What they meant was that all men, Black as well as white, "were equal in their inalienable right to life, liberty, and the pursuit of happiness." Soon, the debate included the question of amalgamation, the mixing of races. The Democrats contended that Republicans wanted to "vote, and eat, and sleep, and marry with Negroes." Not so, insisted Lincoln. There was a "natural disgust" among nearly all whites at the idea of racial amalgamation, and the Republican Party opposed it as well. But what the Republicans did not oppose was the fact that a Black person was a human being. "The Republicans inculcate...that the Negro is a man; that his bondage is cruelly wrong, and that the field of his oppression ought not to be enlarged."

In any case, President Buchanan was wrong. Taney and the Supreme Court had not decided the matter of slavery "once and for all." If anything, instead of removing the issue of slavery in the territories from politics, the court's ruling itself became an enduring political issue. And slavery was a national obsession as never before. If this ruling "shall stand for law," said William Cullen Bryant, slavery was no longer the "peculiar institution" of fifteen states but "a federal institution...and shame of all the states." And Republicans, however embittered or disillusioned, pointed to the dissents by Justices John McLean of Ohio and Benjamin Curtis of Massachusetts, who not only upheld Scott's freedom but affirmed Black citizenship and endorsed the right of Congress to prohibit slavery in the territories. Curtis and McLean pointed out that free Black men in 1788 and later had many legal rights, such as to hold and bequeath property, as well as to make contracts and seek redress in the courts. And further, they affirmed that in five of the thirteen states that ratified the Constitution, Black men were legal voters, were included in the preamble's "We the People," and had participated in the ratification process.

But with *Dred Scott*, there were haunting questions. For example, did an enslaver retain power over the people he enslaved while in transit through a Free State? Were they not then free? Most Northern states, excepting New Jersey and Illinois, now had laws on their books offering freedom to any enslaved person brought by an enslaver within their borders. Yet *Dred Scott* took direct aim at these laws. For those with the antislavery view, even the right of "temporary sojourn" from one state to the next was "an ominous foot in the door." The *Springfield Republican* wondered, "If a man can hold a slave one day in a free state, why not one month, why not one year? Why could not his 'transit' be indefinitely lengthened, his visit 'a practical permanency'?"

Why not? And with those words, for many, the country was rushing full tilt into upheaval.

7

The Boundless Future for America

At the time of the Louisiana Purchase, the United States was a minor nation, an obscure fringe republic on the margins of Western civilization with a population comparable to Ireland's. As one European diplomat, the Comte de Montmorin, sneered, the United States was "the laughing stock of all the powers." Yet the majority of Americans were filled with an astonishing sense of optimism and destiny. By settling, conquering, annexing, or purchasing territory that had been occupied for millennia by Native tribes or claimed by Spain, France, Britain, and Mexico, the country had doubled its population every two decades, leaving it behind only Russia and France. It had experienced a dozen years of unparalleled growth and prosperity. It had extended its continental reach from coast to coast and boasted a burgeoning merchant fleet worthy of challenging the leading nations of the Old World for global supremacy. Abroad, it was blessed with uncommon peace. At home, it was a magnet for hope for countless immigrants and for the dreams of Americans migrating along the new roads and fresh railroads into the ever-expanding western territories.

In fact, with an almost religious zeal, Americans felt compelled to press on west. Studding the landscape with balloon-frame homes and hand-hewn log cabins, traveling by oxen and Conestoga wagon, by horse and buggy, Americans were suddenly everywhere over the immensity of the continent's spaces.

Culturally, too, the nation was thriving.

With master painters like George Catlin and Asher Brown Durand,

39

the country was developing an incipient national art; with writers like Walt Whitman, James Fenimore Cooper, and Louisa May Alcott, it was developing a national literature; it was also developing a thriving, rancorous press, and even a new national idiom. Though it was still a rural land, major cities were increasingly blossoming.

On the East Coast these years became a period of glittering political and intellectual achievement, an unrivaled ferment of activity that included not only politics but economics and philosophy and science. Economically, over the previous ten years, the number of banks had increased by 50 percent. Wall Street thrived and stocks and bonds rose rapidly. The country weathered a major depression from 1837 to 1843 and a lesser one in 1857–58. Average income rose more than 100 percent, while real wages for workers increased by some 65 percent. Textile mills, foundries, and factories ran from sunup to sundown to meet the vast demands of consumers. California gold pumped millions of dollars monthly into the economy. Construction was running at full force, crop prices were steady, and new factories were being built. And perhaps most significantly, it suddenly became an age of instant communication; newspapers and financial markets in most parts of the country were now connected by copper wires: the telegraph. The "latest news" was no longer weeks or days old, but hours. And in 1848 several major newspapers made a quantitative leap in news, with vast implications; they pooled resources to form the Associated Press for the handling of telegraphic dispatches.

Meanwhile, beyond the information revolution another wonder profoundly altered American life—the transport revolution—the "iron horse," racing at breakneck speeds. By 1850 some 9,000 miles of rail in the United States had been laid down, which was then dwarfed by the 21,000 additional miles laid during the 1850s, providing the United States with the largest rail network in the world, more than all the rest of the nations combined.

While many Americans still lived in a rural world not much different from what their forebears had known, the United States had the world's highest standard of living and the second-highest industrial output, coming fast on the heels of the British. By most indices, the modern American economy was characterized not by individually made items but by mass consumption, mass production, and capital-intensive agriculture. Suddenly, consumer goods at reasonable prices were widely available. Most Americans were now able to buy furniture, ready-made women's shoes, handsome men's shirts and soft woolen pants, and watches and rifles.

To be sure, many people still lived in insufferable poverty. And there were those who lived in great opulence. But what observers increasingly saw in the United States was the vast "middling classes."

Another area where America raced past the other nations of the world was in breakthroughs for women. Where in much of the world it was common for women to have less formal education than men, and a considerably higher proportion of illiteracy, by 1850 that had changed. Girls now routinely went to elementary school and achieved literacy at virtually the same level as boys—the only country in the world where this was true.

America was hailed for its educational system in general. Even counting enslaved people—only about one-tenth of them could read or write—nearly four-fifths of the American population was literate in the 1850s, which was greater than the two-thirds of northwest Europe and Britain, and considerably more than in eastern Europe. A public school system was created, becoming the envy of the world and extending to the secondary level. And, too, there were schools to train teachers; there was the introduction of standardized graded curricula; and there was the evolution of various kinds of rural district schools as well.

Increasingly sophisticated and wealthy, America was envied and admired in much of the world. And for many Americans, the future seemed boundless.

This is not to say that the growing economy was free of problems. Notwithstanding the rising trends of real wages, laborers at the bottom of the scale worked their fingers to the bone in sweatshops or filthy, airless factories for a pittance. Against the improvements being made by many Americans, poverty was still widespread and even intensifying among workers in large cities where there were substantial immigrant populations. In New York, for one, an immense populace was packed into unthinkably disgusting, smoke-filled tenements, and the death rate was twice as high as London's.

More and more across the American landscape workers were separated into haves and have-nots, that is, "employers" and "employees," often with different and conflicting interests. The employer wanted to maximize profits, while the employee was woefully dependent upon his "boss." The emergence of this new industrial capitalism led some to argue that wage labor was no better than slave labor—hence the term "wage slavery." The boss, it was argued (mainly by Southerners), was like an enslaver. It was he who determined the hours of work. It was he who determined the pace of the work. It was he who determined the division of labor and the level of wages. And of course it was he who could hire and fire at will. This was in contrast to the preindustrial artisan who had once worked as much or as little as he pleased, working not by the clock, but by the job.

Yet as Lincoln and others pointed out, it was the genius of the free labor system that there was no permanent class of hired workers. Northerners were free to move up, to progress, and to enjoy social and economic mobility. In the free labor system, the hired labor of today would hire others to labor for him tomorrow. As Lincoln further noted, the free labor system "gives hope to all, and energy, and progress, and improvement of conditions to all." The laborer goes into business for himself, and in time has enough capital to hire another. In short, the free labor system "opens the way for all."

The core of Republicanism, however, remained not simply the abundant (albeit imperfect) economic and social progress, but liberty, a precious if not precarious birthright. And for many Americans, the mid-century was a time of hope and progress. The nation remained a land of limitless opportunities, extending its continental reach from coast to coast. Here, civilization was brilliantly sweeping from east to west, as Thomas Jefferson once put it, "like a cloud of light." And also as Thomas Jefferson once said, America remained the "world's last hope."

For many Americans, it was to be their last hope forever.

8

The Dilemma

When the founders first gathered in Philadelphia, few words could capture the boldness of their enterprise—a country not forged by a thousand years of shared history, but conceived in the minds of a handful of men over a handful of months. With imagination, pluck, daring, and iron will, and a brilliance almost unsurpassed in history, the founders begat a national idea unlike any since the beginning of time. But fateful questions lingered then, just as fateful questions lingered in the 1850s. What ultimately would knit the country together? Was it to be one country and one nation—or perhaps two, or even several? And was it to last in perpetuity, or be a brave experiment in democracy that could yet founder?

Whereas in most countries a sense of nationhood spontaneously arises over centuries, the product of generations of common kinship, common language, common myths, a shared history, and the mutual ties of tradition, America was born as an artificial series of states, woven together by negotiated compacts and agreements, charters and covenants. It was not born out of ancient custom or claim, nor did it arise naturally but out of ink set to parchment paper, crafted by statesmen.

Even the Declaration of Independence in 1776, the contract to become American, did not make them a nation. The very word "nation" was explicitly dropped from the Declaration, and all references were instead to the separate states. Thus, the very heading of the final version of the Declaration, which was to become the DNA of Americans, described the document as "the unanimous Declaration of the *thirteen* united States of

America," and the momentous resolution introduced at the Continental Congress on June 7, 1776, declared "that *these* United colonies are, and of right ought to be, free and independent *States*." As one historian noted, "Independence had not created one nation but thirteen."

At the outset, there was more than a dose of truth to this. Like the colonies that preceded them, and long before the North-South divisions, these new states were as dramatically different from one another as they were from England itself. Each jealously guarded its own sovereignty. Each oversaw its own postal routes and commanded its own military actions. Each had its own legislatures, courts, taxes, and in time, individual constitutions. And too often forgotten is a simple but revealing fact: Before independence, Americans were British subjects as well as citizens of Virginia or Massachusetts, New York or Connecticut, or some other home colony. After independence, they were no longer Britons, but neither were they Americans. There was, as yet, no American country to which they could affix their loyalties. And so they remained proud members of their sovereign states. To the extent there was an American national identity, it was an artificial creation of the Revolution.

For all its genius, the US Constitution provided little firm resolution. Until this point, constitutions were not generally written down, but existed almost intuitively, the sum of the whole country's charters, statutes, declarations along with informal understandings, habits, and traditions. Yet what started out as an exercise to do little more than revise the existing Articles of Confederation—a loose system designed for the exigencies of the Revolutionary War—instead produced a far more audacious gamble, an entire new body of laws. Nowhere on the planet had anything like it been devised before. It was at once a central government with the authority to tax and maintain an army, and at the same time, a Republican government with its power divided among a president, a House of Representatives, a Senate, and the Supreme Court—not to mention among the states themselves. But when it came to articulating America as a nation, the men of Philadelphia did not have an answer.

Neither the word "nation" nor the word "national" appears in the

Constitution. Unable to reconcile the gnawing tensions between the proponents of the states, the anti-Federalists, and the proponents of the new federal authority that would come into being, the Federalists, the founders resorted to the more ambiguous phrase, "the United States." (Even the very use of the word "federal," or "*foederal*," as it was more often written, was meant to describe a relationship resting in good faith, *foedus* in Latin being the cognate of *fides*, "faith.") When it was all done, an elated George Washington recognized not just the historic import but also the precariousness of the whole enterprise. It was, he maintained, "little short of a miracle" that delegates from "so many different states" should have united to form a national government.

In Washington's parting speech, he used the word "nation," but only prescriptively: "The name of AMERICAN, which belongs to you in your national capacity, must always exalt the just pride of patriotism more than any appellation derived from local discriminations." In other words, in the architecture of nationhood, the United States erected their constitutional roof before they put up national walls.

The result? Americans had a country before they had their nation. And in turn, the Constitution did something unique in the annals of human history: It substituted as a national identity, and in doing so sidestepped the price of hate and blood normal in the making of nations. But the question remained: Were the seeds of discord there long before the rancor over slavery? In the absence of a common national identity, they were always there.

The generation that wrote the Constitution was consumed by the thought that a Republican government could not survive across a vast domain. Why was this? For one, tradition was against them. In the mid-eighteenth century, the great French philosopher Montesquieu had pronounced that a republic could function only in a small territory, and the thirteen original states together—even some of the larger states individually—were already considered too large. And as Americans traveled farther south and trekked farther west, the wilderness and the mountains rapidly created breathtaking differences—differences in culture, differences in economics, differences in lifestyles, and differences in political outlook.

It remained a fact that the flip side of America's remarkable birth was not union, but secession, a tradition that was older than America, older than the Revolution, as old as the earliest colonial settlements. Indeed, from the very beginning, the vastness of the New World made major secessions and withdrawals, separations and dissolutions, practicable across a full hemisphere. And from its very beginnings, American life was not just about relentless growth or the solidifying of union, but countless efforts to secede. Of course, the pilgrims were the first American secessionists, coming to Plymouth only after their failed efforts to extrude themselves from England and the Netherlands. Too often forgotten is that the colonies themselves acquired their varied characters by secession. Roger Williams and Anne Hutchinson, themselves separatist fanatics, were driven from Massachusetts Bay and founded Rhode Island. Thomas Hooker seceded to his Connecticut. Lord Baltimore helped provide space for Catholics to secede from English life into a community they could call their own. So, too, William Penn provided Quakers with a refuge. Vermonters conspired with Britain to join Canada. And, of course, the American Revolution was itself a monumental act of secession.

Nor did this change after independence. However much Americans increasingly embraced union, for some two hundred years the American ethos was characteristically secessionist. In the 1780s, for example, Americans solemnly believed the nation would inevitably divide into two countries, and by 1794, they seemed to be right. It was as though Montesquieu's dire predictions were coming true.

The very first spark assaulting national unity was not between North and South over slavery, but between West and East over taxes. Americans living in towns hewn from the wilderness wouldn't countenance taxation without representation. They refused to pay the "infernal" whiskey tax emanating out of the federal government. More than that, they set fire to the homes of George Washington's representatives, and tarred and feathered his federal officials. Then, after a chaotic military encounter between frontiersmen and federal representatives, war fever swept the country in July 1794. Soon, these "whiskey rebels" began to gather, hoisting their own flag and openly flirting with independence. The rationale of their rebellion was the same as that of the Revolution; just as the ocean that divided England from America mandated there be two countries, the mountains that carved East from West cried out for two nations, not one.

But it didn't happen. Washington personally reviewed an army of volunteer troops to quell the rebellion, and the famous soldier-politician Light-Horse Harry Lee—Robert E. Lee's father and Washington's best friend—led the troops. The show of force worked, and the leaders of the rebellion fled down the Ohio River, thus ending the threat of secession, at least momentarily. Nonetheless, other secessions loomed. The next direct threat came not from settlers, but from two of the Founding Fathers themselves, Thomas Jefferson and James Madison. They secretly authored the Virginia and Kentucky resolutions of 1798–99, only a decade after the adoption of the Constitution. These resolutions held that the states and the federal Union could nullify acts of Congress as a "rightful remedy" in state and federal disputes. In doing this, Jefferson and Madison laid the conceptual foundations for national dissolution as well. The resolutions were never tested, but they were certainly a danger to the country. If invoked, both could have been fatal to the ten-year-old Constitution, if not the very existence of the United States.

The next controversy occurred during the War of 1812 against Great Britain, this time with the advocates of disunion coming from the North, in Federalist New England. Disgusted with the iniquity of "Mr. Madison's war," fed up with the folly of Thomas Jefferson's Louisiana Purchase as endangering the "world's last hope of a republik," and fearing that their own voice was now under permanent eclipse, New England exclusivists let out a resounding cry for unified protest. To the horror of Southerners, not to mention their disgust, New Englanders talked not only of forging a separate peace with Great Britain, but more ominously of outright disunion itself. Massachusetts, Connecticut, and New Hampshire flatly refused to send their militias to fight, and New England even went so far as to collude with the enemy by investing money in London securities as well as selling supplies to the British forces.

It was Timothy Pickering of Massachusetts who aptly summed up the bitter feelings of the disgruntled New Englanders: There was "no magic in the sound of Union, if the great objects of Union are utterly abandoned... Let the Union be severed."

By early 1814, that seemed to be a real possibility. Massachusetts, with its socially conscious aristocrats and grassy residential squares, teetered on the verge of rebellion, and there were some, like the cleric Elija Parish Lovejoy, who now urged New England to "cut the connexion with the southern states." So the call went out from Massachusetts for a winter convention in Hartford, Connecticut. Ultimately, cooler heads prevailed that fateful December, and the Hartford Convention did not urge secession as many feared. It did, however, endorse the next strongest thing: nullification.

Nullification and its logical extension, secession, formed the bricks of separation, if not of a civil war itself. After the government had been in operation for more than forty years, at the end of the 1820s and into the early 1830s, the language of state sovereignty and nullification, and the notions of self-governance and regionalism, had become indelibly embedded in the American vocabulary. Thus, even as Americans spoke of the Union with boundless affection, they also spoke of "our Confederacy," or more simply of "the Republic." The United States was just as often "the states United," or "the united States," or even "a league of sovereign states." Invariably, it was spoken of as a plural noun. Meanwhile, state legislators took for granted the right to "instruct" their United States senators on how to vote in Congress. And the term "sovereign" was associated every bit as much with the individual states themselves as it was with the "general government."

To be sure, a crucial question was raised: Did the Constitution create a Union from which no state, once having joined, could escape except by extra-constitutional acts of revolution? Or did it create a union of sovereign states, each of which retained the right to secede at its own discretion? On and off Americans wrestled with this issue, but it quickly became apparent that there was no clause in the Constitution that established the

Union's perpetuity. Where the Articles of Confederation contended that "the Union shall be perpetual," the Constitution only spoke of "a more perfect Union." Indeed Charles Pinckney's draft resolution asserting that "the Union shall be perpetual" was never even brought before the general body for consideration. And in another studied ambiguity, where the Constitution was framed in the name of "We the People," Article VII firmly declared that it would be ratified "between the States." In the end, there was no consensus about the perpetuity of the Union. James Madison himself wrote, "Each state...is considered as a sovereign body independent of all others, and only to be bound by its own voluntary act." And the new Constitution was not a national Constitution but a "federal" one.

Where for many the Union was much beloved, for many others, it was an experiment valued for its defense of people's liberties and protection against enemies abroad. If the wording of the Constitution gave neither the believers in the right of secession nor the early advocates of perpetual union a decisive case, the most common perception of the Union was that of George Washington: America was "worth a fair and full experiment."

Between 1830 and 1833, once more the pendulum swung from union to secession, this time in South Carolina. Seeking to nullify the collection of federal tariff duties, South Carolina insisted upon nullification and invoked the principles of regional self-rights. Here was a distinct threat to the nation. But the crisis was averted by President Andrew Jackson's firm response—he proposed to raise an army and hang the Southern insurgents—and an ingenious compromise crafted by Henry Clay. And once more it seemed that Northerners and Southerners alike would still march forward together in forging one nation.

But with each passing year, even as attachments broadened and deepened toward the prize of perpetual union, the strains of secession remained, hardening into a new fierce debate that would at first consume the country, then threaten to divide it: the debate over slavery.

From 1820 onward over the next four decades, the country continued to lurch from one confrontation to another. Too often forgotten is that New Jersey, for its own parochial reasons, flirted with withdrawal, as did

California, which, with Oregon, considered creation of a separate Pacific nation. Meanwhile in Utah, the Mormons fought a handful of bloody skirmishes with the federal government, and they also sought freedom. And even New York City, on and off, talked about its independence, if not confederation with the South. Yet as Daniel Webster once thundered, speaking for the majority of Americans, "liberty and union, now and forever, one and inseparable." He added later, "The people of the United States are one people. They are one in making war, and one in making peace; they are one in regulating commerce, and one in laying duties of imposts." However, John Quincy Adams, son of the second president, spoke a different refrain: "I love the Union as I love my wife. But if my wife should ask for and insist upon a separation, she would have it though it broke my heart." And some Americans continued to speculate about the country splitting into three or four "Confederacies," with an independent Pacific Coast thrown in to boot.

As Americans wrestled with these unsettled questions gnawing away at the country, some looked to the rest of the world for guidance. These examples were not encouraging. In Latin America, wars for independence produced not one, but some twenty-two separate nations from a few viceroyalties. Meanwhile, across the Atlantic, the specter of the "contagion" emanating from the French Revolution and the dreaded Terror hovered. Taking place in the most advanced country of the day, it threatened to plunge Europe into an ongoing cycle of terror and violence. From Denmark to Bohemia, Sicily to Hungary, no country was immune. And the problems of France were not dissimilar to those of the United States—the task of bringing the people into some kind of rational relationship with their government, and some form of mutual relationship with their sovereign states.

And of course, back in America itself, to stem the secessionist tide, there were the compromises of 1820, 1833, and 1850; the prelude of the Kansas-Nebraska Act of 1854 and of the Wilmot debates; the shock of the *Dred Scott* decision and the terror of Lawrence and Pottawatomie; and last but not least, the fearsome spark led by a refugee from Kansas: John Brown.

Part III

THE UNRAVELING

9

The Spark

Who was John Brown?

Was he an instrument of God to free the enslaved people? Or was he merely a poor self-deluded old man? Was he the fuse that would ignite a powder keg that might explode into civil war? Or was he a rambling old man who was "insane"? We do know this: Photos from the time capture a man who aged considerably after the Pottawatomie massacre. Fifty-six years old, he easily could've been taken for seventy. He was stooped and emaciated, often tired, and frequently sick. A daguerreotype made at the time shows him clad in an old black suit, with a high collar wrapped around his leathered neck. He looks drawn and unhappy, yet what is most striking are his eyes, eyes that seem locked on an adversary looming off on the horizon. It was difficult to resist the power of Brown's steady gaze. If "his piercing gray eyes" were irresistible, so was his slow, masculine, "deep...metallic" voice." He went by the aliases of "Shubel Morgan" and "Isaac Smith"; friends referred to him as "the old man"; and Julia Ward Howe, the noted intellectual, called him "a Puritan of the Puritans."

It was apparent from the start that Brown was different from other abolitionists seeking an end to the brutal institution of slavery. His head was filled with Scriptures, and the old spiritual was frequently on his lips, "Go down, Moses / Way down in Egypt land / tell ole Pharaoh / let my people go." Where previous abolitionists were committed to nonviolence, Brown's favorite New Testament passage read "Without shedding of blood there is no remission [of sin]" (Heb. 9:22). Where abolitionists embraced the Christlike martyrdom of Uncle Tom, Brown's God was instead the Jehovah who angrily drowned Pharaoh's mercenaries in the Red Sea. Where moderates eschewed a revolution in favor of the soft cadences of reason, Brown insisted that all abolitionists do is "Talk! Talk! Talk!" As Brown boomed, victory over enslavers—"the thieves and murderers"—could be won only by "ACTION!"

In 1856, he took part in the bitter Battle of Osawatomie. When it was all over he surveyed the wreckage, watching the town smoke and blazes lighting up the Kansas sky. With tears running down his cheeks, he saw the homes of free-state Christians going up in flames. He saw the body of his own son lying limp in the dirt with a proslavery bullet through his heart. Trembling with grief and rage, Brown promised, "I have only a short time to live—only one death to die. And I will die fighting for this cause."

He set out for Nebraska, headed across Iowa to the northwestern states, but then took sick. As he lay curled up on a makeshift pallet inside a wagon, his feverish brain was filled with visions of an abolitionist guerrilla force striking in the Appalachian foothills of Virginia. It was here, he decided, in mountain passes and wooded ravines, that he would carry out a raid to liberate the enslaved people. After recuperating, the "old man" visited Governor Salmon P. Chase (Lincoln's future Treasury secretary) in Ohio, then caught a train for Boston, where he linked up with Franklin B. Sanborn, a twenty-five-year-old schoolteacher and activist from nearby Concord. Sanborn, Harvard-educated and well-connected, thought Brown the very embodiment of a fire-and-brimstone Calvinist, or even a latter-day "Oliver Cromwell."

In Boston, Brown was a sensation. He met the forty-seven-year-old Theodore Parker, the most eloquent and controversial Unitarian minister of his day, whose radical sermons were filled with moral outrage over slavery, wars, and the mistreatment of criminals and the insane. He met the great William Lloyd Garrison, the bald, bespectacled sage who was the crusading editor of the *Liberator*. From Boston, Brown then took a train to New York, where he met yet more prominent intellectuals. Later, he and his caravan traveled by train with protection from no less than the vaunted detective Allan Pinkerton.

With snow blanketing the fields and mountains, Brown continued on the move, taking slow, rattling trains all over New England and New York, where he spoke before antislavery audiences. He met Henry David Thoreau as well, and Ralph Waldo Emerson, to whom Brown made the telling comment that he believed in two things—"the Bible and the Declaration of Independence—and that it was better that a whole generation of men, women and children should pass away by a violent death than a word of either should be violated."

Egotistical and imperial, he tried to raise money for his cause but failed miserably, leaving him "sullen and embittered." He despaired at President Buchanan's support for the proslavery government in Kansas. He penned an autobiographical tract, *A Boy Named John*, probably the most revealing document Brown ever wrote. It afforded rare insights into his childhood, not to mention his shifting belief in the "eternal war with slavery." Then one night, as a cold November wind howled, Brown sat around a fire with a host of new recruits discussing his most ambitious scheme yet: an "incursion into Virginia," for, as he revealed, "God had created him to be the deliverer of the slaves the same as Moses had delivered the children of Israel."

Shortly thereafter, Brown headed for Rochester, New York, to see his old friend Frederick Douglass. Brown unfolded his plan to raise a guerrilla army that employed the Southern mountains as its base of operations. By his calculation, there were 128,000 free Blacks living in New York, New Jersey, and Pennsylvania, and another 23,000 in New England; Brown hoped to persuade a substantial portion of them to enlist in his guerrilla force. Douglass shuddered at the boldness of the plan. Brown planned to have a president and vice president, a Supreme Court, and a one-house Congress, along with a commander in chief. But on one matter, Brown was uncompromising: In the course of the anticipated massive slave uprising, the blood of enslavers would have to be spilled. Pacing back and forth, Brown insisted, "If God be for us, who can be against us?"

In May 1858, Brown met secretly with thirty-four Black men ("true friends of freedom") in Chatham, Canada, which was a terminus of the famed Underground Railroad and home to more than a thousand Black people, most of whom were former enslaved people. There they convened a latter-day constitutional convention, nothing less than the creation of a new American government. Under Brown's guidance, they adopted a "Provisional Constitution" for the Republic of liberated enslaved people, which would be established across the Southern foothills. In the darkened rooms of an old Baptist church, the delegates also elected Brown commander in chief of the army of this "new nation." Brown accepted.

Throughout the year, Brown continued to refine his plans. At the peak of his frenzy, he purchased a thousand pikes to arm the enslaved people whom he expected to join the cause, and four hundred guns to arm his fledgling army. Then, under an assumed name, he rented a farm in Maryland across the Potomac River from Harpers Ferry, Virginia. His goal: to take hold of the federal arsenal there, then fan out to invade slave territory while assaulting US property along the way. In particular, he would seize the US Armory and distribute its arms to the enslaved people as they joined up with him.

Was the plan viable? There were those who thought Brown was "insane." But then there were others who looked at Brown's "thin, worn, resolute face" and saw "signs of fire." In turn, Samuel Gridley Howe, one of his aides who had fought in Greece, had seen Turkish armies defeated in the Greek mountains by small guerrilla bands and believed the same could be done against Southerners in the Alleghenies. And Brown himself had already studied Roman warfare, the Spanish uprising against the Romans, and Toussaint Louverture's slave war in Haiti in the 1790s. His plan? After he invaded Virginia, he would march into Tennessee, then northern Alabama, where the enslaved people would rally to his standard. They would then wage war upon the plantations of the plains west and east of the mountains, which would serve as his base of operations. Had they reached the point of no return? Some, like Hugh Forbes, may have thought that "firmness at the ballot box" might avert the storm, but Brown insisted that "only bullets and bayonets could settle anything now."

Brown was tireless. He met secretly with Harriet Tubman in Chatham, and then in August 1859 again with Frederick Douglass in an old rock quarry near Chambersburg, Pennsylvania. He had wanted to enlist Tubman, famed for her Underground Railroad and known as the Moses of her people, but she declined. And he wanted Douglass to serve as a liaison officer to the enslaved people. Douglass, himself a former enslaved person and the most eminent Black spokesman in the North, had endured his own personal odyssey from peace to war. Before 1850 he had been a pacifist, once saying, "Were I asked the question whether I could have my emancipation by the shedding of one single drop of blood, my answer would be in the negative." But then as the slave states increased in power and force, as slave sales and fugitive slave hunting showed no signs of diminution, an angry Douglass changed his tune. "Slaveholders, tyrants and despots have no right to live," he bellowed. One of his favorite sayings became "Who would be free must himself strike the blow."

An anxious-looking Brown, wearing an old hat and carrying a fishing rod to mask his identity, sat down among the rocks with Douglass; they were joined by a fugitive slave whom Douglass had sheltered in his home. There the two men debated the raid throughout the day and part of the next. This time, Brown held nothing back; he sketched out the entirety of his plan for seizing Harpers Ferry. Douglass had his reservations, arguing that an attack on the federal armory "would array the whole country against us" rather than rally Americans to the antislavery cause. Undeterred, Brown nodded, then said in a commanding voice, "Come with me, Douglass. I want you for a special purpose. When I strike, the bees will begin to swarm, and I shall want you to help hive them." But Douglass, convinced that this was a suicide mission, ultimately demurred.

He warned Brown, "You will never get out alive."

Yet then, to Douglass's surprise, his enslaved friend Shields Green, who had been quiet all along, averred: "I b'leve I'll go wid de old man." With such trickles do tidal waves begin.

As fall came, Brown and his men hid out in an old farmhouse. They occupied themselves with playing checkers and learning about warfare.

Humming to themselves, they buffed their rifles. They scoured the *Baltimore Sun* and devoured Thomas Paine's *The Age of Reason*. They wrote letters to their families. And they waited for fresh recruits to join the cause; however, few did. Brown decided to proceed anyway. The sage of the abolition movement, now he was swept away by a sort of fatalism. Sitting at an old wooden table in his kitchen, he wrote a "Vindication of the Invasion" as well as a companion piece to his constitution titled "A Declaration of Liberty by the Representatives of the Slave Population of the United States of America."

The original date for the attack was July 4, Independence Day, but it was shifted to October 16.

In the meantime, Brown worried that a mob would one day discover them, torch the farmhouse where they were staying, and string them all up. Curiously, during this time, Brown made no reconnaissance of Harpers Ferry itself. Nor did he work out an escape route from Harpers Ferry—it was sixty-one miles northwest of Washington, DC—or places of refuge should federal troops or state militias come to the town's defense. Was this sloppiness? An overreliance on the Almighty, who would guide them? Or was it a mission designed less to succeed than to confer upon Brown everlasting martyrdom? In one of his final acts, he stored all his vital documents—his "Vindication of the Invasion," his maps, and his constitution—in a trunk in the downstairs of the farmhouse. Then, on October 15, three late recruits straggled onto his farm. For Brown, this was an unimpeachable sign from the good Lord. On Sunday, October 16, the revolution would begin.

Brown assembled his eighteen recruits, five of whom were Black, and enjoined his little ragtag army, "Men, get your arms."

It was a chilly, overcast night. A soft rain began to fall.

———

With a wagonload of guns, knives, and artillery broadsides, Brown's men marched past farmhouses and down wooded hillsides until they came to Harpers Ferry itself. They quickly cut telegraph lines east and west of town and overwhelmed the single watchman. Wasting no time, they captured the armory complex, which held several million dollars' worth of federal munitions and arms. Brown then sent a patrol into the countryside with a stark message: Pass the word among the enslaved people in the area that the "day of liberation" was here. And take hostages. They did, thirty all told, including Lewis Washington, a local enslaver and the great-grandnephew of George Washington; Brown also seized the pistol given to George Washington by the Marquis de Lafayette, as well as the historic sword once reportedly given to Washington by Frederick the Great. Then, in Brown's war against slavery, blood was finally shed: Ironically, the first casualty was a free Black man at the railroad station who was killed by Brown's men in the dark.

Brown announced to the frightened onlookers, "I came here from Kansas and this is a slave state. I want to free all the Negroes in the state. I have possession now of the United States armory, and if the citizens interfere with me, I must only burn the town and have blood."

Within hours, Harpers Ferry descended into bedlam. Tense and confused, townspeople gathered in the streets brandishing knives, axes, clubs, even squirrel rifles, any weapon they could get their hands on. At the same time, the bell began to ring at the Lutheran church, tolling the alarm for all farmers in the countryside. The word went out that it was a slave insurrection, that "hundreds of n***ers" with "bloodthirsty" abolitionists were "raping and butchering" in the streets.

By eleven o'clock on Monday morning, a pitched battle raged at Harpers Ferry. Armed farmers and militiamen poured into the town. Yet Brown stuck to his plan. Monday, at 1:25 a.m., Brown stopped the eastbound B&O midnight train. He held it hostage for several hours—in terror, passengers openly wept—only then to let it proceed. Why let it go? So it could spread the alarm. Brown warned the Southerners that God had appointed him to liberate the people they enslaved "by some violent and decisive move."

As the train lurched eastward in the darkness, the startled train passengers scribbled notes announcing the insurrection and flung them out the train windows to warn residents of the Maryland countryside. By the time the train pulled into the Baltimore station, a clamoring throng had amassed in the street, eager for any bit of news about the uprising. Journalists quickly telegraphed the news to papers in New York and Boston and elsewhere. In a matter of hours, the news had coursed across the country. Just as he had predicted, Brown had sown confusion and panic.

In Harpers Ferry itself, rumors flew that Brown had an army of some 750 men. Shrewdly, Brown repeatedly shuffled his tiny band of 18 men around, keeping them in constant motion, thereby obscuring the actual size of the paltry force he brought to Harpers Ferry.

At the same time, Brown made it clear to his hostages that he meant them no harm. He added that his goal was "to free the slaves—not to make war on the people." At this point, the townspeople didn't realize that he was actually *the* John Brown; they knew him only as "Smith" or "the captain." Brown was still convinced that his men would succeed in staving off his adversaries. For one thing, he knew that the nation's standing army numbered less than twenty thousand men, the majority of whom were hundreds of miles away stationed at posts west of the Mississippi, with the rest scattered across a string of countryside forts.

Brown believed that it would take days, perhaps even longer, for federal troops to mobilize and make their way to Harpers Ferry.

He was sorely mistaken.

———————

Brown's plan began to unravel, slowly at first, then quickly. He didn't realize that a number of people had gathered on a steep rise overlooking the town and plotted how to fight back; while he waited in vain for enslaved people in the area to join him, the people of Harpers Ferry quickly set about arming themselves. Nor did he realize that a young doctor from Harpers Ferry had jumped on his horse and ridden off to seek reinforcements in the county seat of Charleston, eight miles away. In truth, Brown had sent deeply confusing messages; what the people saw was not a peacemaker but a grizzled, menacing figure who forcefully seized the town at night, took hostages at gunpoint, and claimed command of a vast army. Not unsurprisingly, the people of Harpers Ferry doubted Brown's peaceful overtures.

By midmorning on October 17, the fight had been joined. Brown's men were suddenly pinned down by sniper fire as the Maryland and Virginia militias, eventually a total of some eight hundred troops, converged on the town. One of Brown's men was cut down by a sniper's bullet, and as if this were the storming of the Bastille, angry townspeople used pocketknives to cut off pieces of the dead man's ears for gruesome souvenirs. Another of Brown's men was shot at point-blank range, and his body slipped into the river nearby. Still another, Will Thompson, was carried by a mob kicking and screaming down to the Potomac, where they shot him in the head.

Brown, who hadn't eaten or slept in more than twenty-four hours, now faced a series of fateful decisions. Should he continue fighting? Negotiate his way out? Surrender? He first sought to negotiate. He was rebuffed. Indeed, two of his men who were carrying a flag of truce were gunned down by a mob in the streets. He was offered surrender; he scornfully refused. So instead, he chose to fight.

He was dangerously outnumbered, and he knew it. That afternoon eight of Brown's men, including two of his sons, were killed or lay dying. Lewis Washington recalled that Brown "was the coolest and firmest man I ever saw in defying danger and death." Washington watched while Brown felt the pulse of his dying son with one hand as he gripped his rifle at the ready with the other. Then Brown and his surviving comrades frantically retreated with the hostages to the local firehouse, where he prepared to make his last stand. Now he yelled to his remaining band to "sell" their lives "as dearly as they could!"

Brown's son who had been injured begged to be shot, to be put out of his misery. Brown refused. "If you die," Brown told him, "you die in a glorious cause."

The mayor of Harpers Ferry, Fontaine Beckham, a gentle soul and "the best friend the Negroes had in the country," was shot to death by one of Brown's men, who happened to be a young Quaker boy. With that, the melee intensified. When five militia companies in Baltimore boarded a special train for Harpers Ferry, thousands of citizens waved their caps and handkerchiefs and cheered boisterously around Camden Station.

Meanwhile, Washington was in a state of panic. Leaders wondered: Was this a grim prelude to other cities and towns being attacked? Was this but the first of a series of coordinated insurrections? The mayor of Washington mobilized the entire police force and blocked all routes into the capital. And upon hearing about the invasion, President Buchanan himself ordered three artillery companies to Harpers Ferry and instructed some ninety US Marines to move in as well.

As more militias arrived, Brown once again tried to negotiate. He offered to release his hostages if he and his men could escape across the Potomac and Maryland. Once more he was rebuffed. It was pitch-black inside the enginehouse as Brown paced back and forth, muttering to himself and calling out, "Men, are you awake?"

Meanwhile, Oliver Brown, still writhing in pain from his wound, begged his father over and over to be shot. Brown angrily retorted, "If you must die, die like a man."

Outside, the drizzling continued.

———————

Later that day, Brown's fate would be sealed and two names forever joined in history: John Brown of Kansas and Colonel Robert E. Lee, whom Buchanan had tapped to take command.

10

The Soldier

If ever destiny were knocking for a soldier, it was knocking for Colonel Robert E. Lee. Fifty-two years old and uncommonly handsome, he lived in the family mansion high up on Arlington Heights in Virginia, south of the Potomac. Lee was proud of his lineage; he was descended from two signers of the Declaration of Independence, and his father was a Revolutionary War hero. Determined, willful, and quietly but fiercely ambitious, Lee was one of the nation's most gifted fighting men. Appointed to the prestigious Corps of Engineers, he graduated second in his class at West Point (without a single demerit), was brevetted three times for valor in the Mexican-American War, and served with distinction as head of the US Cavalry against the Comanche Indians on the Texas border. Later, he ably ran West Point as its superintendent.

By all accounts, Lee was driven by an antique sense of honor nearly unfathomable by the standards of today. Underneath his thick skin, he was a dreamer. Indeed, it is tempting to say that he lived less by the dictates of the Army hierarchy than by the chivalric code, melding humility with bravery, quaintness with toughness, personal loyalty with ruthlessness, and above all, a gentle heart with devotion to God. Yet in battle his eyes would be gleaming, his face flushed with anticipation. As much as any other officer in the US Army, he had a true killer instinct; once fighting began, his audacity and aggressiveness were second to none.

All his life he was haunted by a sense of destiny, and by birth and inheritance, he was tied to the Union. Southern history ran equally deep in his blood; he was related to most of Virginia's first families, the Lees, Carters, Randolphs, and Fitzhughs. For more than a century his family had played a leading role in the history of Old Dominion. His father was not just the Virginia delegate to the Continental Congress, but three times its governor, and then one of its congressmen. And Robert E. Lee himself was born at Stratford, a grand mansion overlooking the Potomac, and one of the most famous estates in all of Virginia. It once belonged to George Washington's adopted son.

Destiny stalked Lee in one other way: the lingering black mark upon his family's name. For all his exploits, his father was also a compulsive land speculator and, like John Brown, frequently in debt and repeatedly in flight from his creditors. He was jailed twice and subsequently left for the West Indies, deserting his family when Robert was just six. Robert never saw the elder Lee again. So in his youth Robert was left fatherless, nearly broke, his once pristine family reputation soiled.

Yet his family made do. Lee's mother, Anne, raised him in genteel surroundings, teaching him to revere George Washington and to lead an exemplary life that would redeem the family's honor. Central to these teachings was emulating not simply Washington's dignity, but his practice of "self-denial and self-control." Lee learned these lessons well, and they would stick with him all his life. His separation from his mother was not easy when he went to West Point at the age of eighteen. "How can I live without Robert?" Anne Lee mourned. "He is son, daughter, and *everything* to me."

Later, Lee married Mary Custis, the daughter of George Washington's adopted son. Austere, ascetic, devoted, he neither drank nor swore nor smoked, yet he delighted in such little pleasures as music, dancing, and food, especially fried chicken. Forever faithful to his wife, he was a constant flirt with other women and maintained a sensuous and lifelong correspondence with several of them. Rarely self-righteous, he was a pious man, praying regularly and long. And despite his legendary self-control, his foul moods and temper were equally well-known. Physically he was impressive, and again paradoxical. Nearly six feet tall with a powerful, imposing frame and a striking barrel chest, he nonetheless radiated beauty and grace, accentuated by his unexpectedly tiny feet (4-C) and a beautifully shaped mouth. His eyes could be large, sad, and brooding; at the same time, when angered, his cold stare was unforgettable.

Whenever he heard talk of secession, he shunted it off, dismissing it as "anarchy, nothing but revolution." He despised the thought of civil war as well. As to slavery, while he regarded the peculiar institution as a "moral and political evil," as a creature of his age he enjoyed the benefits of the plantation life and managed some two hundred enslaved people (whom he would free in 1862). He also harbored a quiet antipathy toward incessant abolitionists, whom he derided as "fanatics," and he believed, not unlike Lincoln, that emancipation would one day be carried out not by congressional dictates or constitutional changes, but by "a wise and merciful providence."

Following his service in the Mexican-American War, Lee, ever the picture of moderation and restraint, grew dissatisfied. He cherished the military, but after years of service, he was tired of the constant intrigue, the backbiting politics, and the daily pettiness. Once he confided to his son, "I wish I was out of the Army." This was cant. And while he had already achieved considerable fame and glory in the field, he still craved more active duty befitting a great soldier, not postings that smacked of an administrator or a bureaucrat pushing paper. He brooded that the years were slipping away, that he was growing old, rusty, and unappreciated in the service of his country.

Then came a call from the secretary of war about a fanatic they quickly learned was named "John Brown."

11

The Counterattack

After Lee got the call, he hurried to the capital, where he was put in command of the Navy Yard Marines, which numbered ninety. As a light rain fell, Lee marched them to Harpers Ferry, reaching the town somewhere around midnight.

It was rapidly clear to Lee that far from being an army of 750 fighters, Brown's force was only "a party of banditti" huddling for its life in the armory. It was equally clear that there was no mass uprising. Rather than endanger the hostages with a nighttime assault, Lee decided to wait for daybreak before moving in. Lee promptly composed a communiqué to "the persons" inside the enginehouse—he didn't yet know who they were—which informed them that the armory was surrounded on all sides by troops, that it was "impossible" for them to escape, and that if he were left with no choice other than to take the enginehouse by force, he could not "answer for their safety."

Lee had few illusions about the insurgents accepting the demand for surrender. He expected they wouldn't. His plan, then, was to attack immediately with overwhelming force so the gunmen inside the enginehouse wouldn't have additional time to prepare, let alone harm the hostages. To further minimize risk to the hostages, he intended for his Marines to attack with only battering rams, sledgehammers, and bayonets.

No one was to fire a single shot.

Soon after sunrise on Tuesday, October 18, the dashing J. E. B. (Jeb)

Stuart, a lieutenant from Virginia, approached the enginehouse carrying a flag of truce. A gunman cracked open the door, and Stuart immediately recognized him from his time serving in the US Cavalry out west. "You are Osawatomie Brown of Kansas?" Stuart asked. Brown replied laconically, "Well, they do call me that sometimes."

Stuart replied, "This is a bad business you are engaged in," adding, "The United States troops have arrived, and I'm sent to demand your surrender."

Stuart delivered Lee's missive that promised protection to Brown until the government determined his fate. Brown refused, instead retorting with his own request: that he and his men be granted escape across the river. As this exchange took place, the hostages, who feared for their lives, became greatly agitated. Shouting, they begged to involve Lee himself. But Stuart demurred. His orders were to avoid negotiations.

Stuart asked tersely, "Is that your final answer, Captain?"

Brown: "Yes."

Stuart stepped back and waved his cap. For Robert E. Lee, looking on from a slight rise about forty feet away, this was the signal to unleash hell. Wasting no time, the storming party now began to batter the heavy wooden doors with sledgehammers and then a ladder. Just as Lee had predicted, the speed of his assault took Brown by surprise. The Marines charged three times, finally opening a breach in the enginehouse, just enough for the US forces to pour through. It was pandemonium. Outside, spectators were waving their arms and cheering wildly. Inside, men were screaming or whimpering or swearing. Brown's men began firing, and despite instructions not to use their guns, some of Lee's men fired back.

One of Lee's officers, Lieutenant Israel Greene, found a desperate Brown and struck him with his dress sword. One of his thrusts was deflected by a strap or buckle, but Greene continued to stab Brown and savagely beat him over his head with the sword's hilt. At the same time, two of Brown's men were bayoneted. Amid the rancid odor of sweat and random shouts, blood soaked through Brown's shirt and pants and spurted on the floor. His long white beard was caked with blood as well. His men had been subdued, the hostages rescued, and Brown himself was unconscious.

Outside, a hostile crowd called for the remaining insurgents to be lynched or shot. Less than thirty-six hours after the raid started, Brown was a hostage, his bold effort to start a major slave uprising inauspiciously concluded. As Lee wrote in his report to the secretary of war, "The whole business was over in a few minutes."

Not a single enslaved person had come to Harpers Ferry to join Brown. And the handful Brown had forcibly liberated refused to fight back once shooting began at the enginehouse. Seventeen men had died, including two of John Brown's sons.

Upon closer examination, a surgeon said that Brown's wounds were not "mortal." When he regained consciousness, Brown was interrogated for three hours by the governor of Virginia, Henry A. Wise, soon joined by Lee, Jeb Stuart, and three proslavery congressmen, including Senator James M. Mason of Virginia, the author of the Fugitive Slave Act. Several journalists for pro-Southern newspapers were there as well.

Brown was still bleeding and suffering, yet all were struck by his remarkable composure. Even Governor Wise was impressed by Brown, later admitting that he was "the gamest man I ever saw." When Mason asked, "How do you justify your acts?" Brown replied, "My friend, you are guilty of a great wrong against God and humanity." When someone else said to Brown, "I think you are fanatical," Brown responded in his husky voice, "And I think you are fanatical. Whom the gods would destroy they first made mad, and you are mad."

He later added prophetically for the reporters, "You may dispose of me very easily; I am nearly disposed of now. But this question is still to be settled—this Negro question I mean—the end of that is not yet."

Lee's intention was to return to Washington, where he would write his report underscoring the relative insignificance of Brown's actions, actions that were the efforts of "a fanatic or madman, which could only end in failure." But when Lee sent a special detachment of his men into the countryside, including to the Kennedy farm, where Brown's men had been holed up, his soldiers made a series of heart-stopping discoveries. They found sixteen heavy boxes of rifles, revolvers, bayonets, swords, and ammunition. They found tents, blankets, axes, knives, boxes of clothing, and almost a thousand pikes, which were to be used by the liberated enslaved people. They found hundreds of carbines and revolvers, fourteen pounds of lead shot, and sufficient clothing, tools, and other supplies to arm a large mountain army, "all the necessaries for a campaign," Lee wrote. As if that weren't enough, they found that Brown's ambitions confirmed their worst fears, as evidenced by the thousands of copies of his "Provisional Constitution," the hundreds of copies of the Forbes *Manual* on guerrilla tactics, the presence of his "Vindication of the Invasion," the carpetbag filled with letters to and from Brown's secret backers, and perhaps most striking of all, the large maps of Southern states with cross marks and census figures denoting counties where Blacks significantly outnumbered whites.

All this, clearly, was a manifesto for war and rebellion.

12

Martyrdom

The news of Harpers Ferry quickly sent a wave of shock and rage throughout the region as well as the country. In Harpers Ferry itself rumors flew that enslaved people had been "seen in the mountains" and that thousands of abolitionists were "coming down" to slaughter the townspeople. Meanwhile, across Virginia, mobs clamored for Brown's head. Even though Brown had attacked and seized federal property at Harpers Ferry, Governor Wise decided to prosecute him in a Virginia court rather than turn him over to federal authorities.

The trial began on October 27. Lying on a cot in full view of the crowded courtroom, Brown remained the very picture of composure. He was at first labeled a "madman" for thinking he could start a slave uprising under conditions where there were "not abundant Negroes." Yet Northern readers quickly came to agree with the sentiments of the *New York Tribune*, which maintained that Brown "dared and died for what he felt to be right." Brown's exemplary behavior during his trial quickly led to the view that he was a martyr with a noble cause. In his closing speech to the court, he rose slowly to address an audience far beyond the room—the nation, if not the world. Still suffering from his wounds, his eyes purple and swollen, Brown masterfully calibrated his words, maintaining that he did not want to incite insurrection (not true), but only to free the enslaved people and arm them in self-defense (true). The eloquence of his closing speech would echo down through the years: "Now, if it is deemed necessary that I should forfeit my life, for the furtherance of the ends of justice, and mingle my blood further with the blood of my children, and with the blood of millions in the slave country, whose rights are disregarded by wicked, cruel, and unjust enactments—I say, let it be done."

No less than Ralph Waldo Emerson prophesied that Brown would "make the gallows as glorious as the cross." For his part, Theodore Parker pronounced Brown "a SAINT."

Meanwhile, fearing he would be arrested—Wise had requested that President Buchanan bring him to trial—Frederick Douglass fled to Canada and then sailed for England. From his safe perch abroad, Douglass compared Brown to Samson, who laid his hands upon the pillars of "this great national Temple of cruelty." Meanwhile, several of Brown's conspirators who were willing to give guns and money for Brown's cause, but did not want to hang for it, went into hiding. But that was simply a sideshow for now. Just six days later, on November 2, Virginia convicted Brown of treason, murder, and fomenting insurrection. His sentence was never in doubt: He was slated to hang one month later, on December 2.

Although many urged Brown to plead insanity and thereby cheat the hangman's rope, he refused. "I am worth inconceivably more to hang," he told his brother, "than for any other purpose."

Was Brown mad? We know this: He did not hear voices, he was not clinically depressed or beset by hallucinations, and he never had a breakdown. To be sure, he was angry. To be sure, he was unusually messianic. He was also egotistical and at times incompetent, often cruel to his sons and a cold-blooded killer to his would-be enemies, a man of powerful religious convictions with delusions that he would somehow become an American Moses leading a slave army to their freedom. He was, too, beaten down by a lifetime of hardship. But he almost uniquely understood that his raid, however ineptly carried out, would affect the tensions already reverberating between North and South.

The *Boston Post* perhaps had the last word on this matter. It insisted that "John Brown may be a lunatic, [but] then one fourth of the people of Massachusetts were madmen" and so were "three fourths of the ministers of the gospel." And what of the legions of Christians and politicians who lauded slavery as "inevitable" or "enlightened"? Or of the enlightened millions who were indifferent to the contradictions between slavery and a free republic? Or of the thousands of Southerners plagued by terrifying visions of Negro hordes raping "our wives and daughters"? Or of those cringing in the South, barricaded in their homes, at the thought of an impending Black Republican invasion? It was, in light of all this, as the *Post* pointed out, "hard to tell who's mad."

In the meantime, the nation was in an uproar over Brown, especially in the South when newspapers reported that among Brown's notes were maps of the seven Southern states designating additional targets for insurrection. For weeks afterward, wild rumors circulated that armed abolitionists were marching in the North, that slave uprisings were poised to explode, and that a Northern abolitionist Republican juggernaut was ready to plunge the South into a never-ending racial bloodbath. In Virginia itself, an estimated four thousand men were under arms, and thousands more in the other Southern states. It was further pointed out for millions of readers that Brown's raid had taken place not in far-off Kansas, but within a few miles of Washington, DC. Innocent people were butchered, and no one could tell when or whether a slave uprising would follow. Accurate or not, the uncomfortable truth was that the images of Brown's style of revolutionary violence were now indelibly etched into the Southern mind. Reminiscent of the 1789 haunting Great Fear in France, it was to be the French Revolution all over again, yet perpetrated not by the king's menacing brigands but by Black men and fanatical abolitionists.

The majority of planters in the South, as well as vast numbers of nonenslaving whites, had for more than a decade opposed secession, let alone the idea of a cursed planters' war for Southern independence. Yet now they were crying out that the only solution for the South was, as *De Bow's Review* pithily wrote, "secession and an independent southern Confederacy."

Distinguished intellectuals quickly rushed to Brown's defense. True, there were those like William Lloyd Garrison who initially denounced Brown, hysterically calling the raid "misguided, wild, and apparently insane." But even Garrison soon changed his tune. Had Brown's career as a prophet tumbled into the dust? No, for perceptions began to change. Brown's exemplary behavior during the trial quickly cemented the view that he was a saint with a hallowed cause. Garrison now saw Brown as a martyr for the fight, declaring, "Let no one who glories in the revolutionary struggle of 1776 deny the right of the slaves to imitate the example of our Fathers." He added, "It will be a terribly losing day for all slavedom when John Brown" is brought to the gallows. Wendell Phillips grandiloquently declared that "Harpers Ferry is the Lexington of today" and further maintained that Brown "has twice as much right to hang Governor Wise, as Governor Wise has to hang him." And Ralph Waldo Emerson spoke of Brown in lectures in Concord and Boston, calling him "that new Saint...awaiting his martyrdom."

For his part, Henry David Thoreau wanted Brown to hang, so that the entire North could recognize "the eternal justice in glory" of Brown's vision. And the abolitionist minister Theodore Parker predicted that Brown's death would detonate a civil war that would run "from man to man, from town to town" across a South drenched with the "white man's blood!"

From his cell in Charlestown, Brown, a picture of repose, wrote almost daily to his supporters—friends and family, varied activists and assorted scientists, and prominent thinkers across the country. Time and again, he said that he felt the presence of God in his cell, guiding his pen across the paper. "I have fought the good fight," he said, "and have, I trust, finished my course." At the same time, hate letters from all over the Union piled up on Governor Wise's desk, deriding Brown as "a maniac," "a murderer," and "a killer."

Just before 4:00 p.m. on December 1, with hundreds of soldiers assembled outside, the jailer opened Brown's cell door. Lost in thought, Brown saw he had a visitor: his wife, Mary, whom he hadn't seen in six months. Back in Philadelphia, after Governor Wise had rebuffed her pleas to spare

Brown's life, Mary had wrestled with her uncontrollable anguish about her husband's imminent hanging. She now knew it was final; there was no hope. In the cell, she sat slowly, gathering close to Brown for the last time, and broke down. Both began to cry.

They discussed his will, the uncertain future, and the education of their daughters. They talked about what he wanted to leave behind: a compass to one of his sons, and to his eldest daughter his old family Bible, in which Brown had marked a number of passages of particular significance to him. They picked at their food—it was "supper"—in the jailer's room. Brown wanted her to spend the night with him, but the governor had given explicit orders that Mary had to return to Harpers Ferry that evening. Hearing this, for the first time, Brown lost control of himself, flashing his temper and openly railing against such a punitive, seemingly arbitrary decision. Then, as if realizing he didn't want the world to see him like this, he straightened himself up and regained his composure.

They had been together for four hours. Now it was time to say goodbye. Trembling, Mary wept as he hugged her. They had been married for twenty-six years and had endured years of privation and struggle. With tender sobs and saddened glances, he prayed that God would give her strength and watch over her. Finally, she had to leave, back to Harpers Ferry to wait for his black walnut coffin, which the governor had agreed to send to her after Brown's death.

Brown returned to his cell and for the longest time tossed and turned on his cot. He couldn't get his mind off his visit with Mary. So instead, he composed a short letter to his brother Jeremiah, in which he declared that he was "quite cheerful and composed."

He lay down again and closed his eyes, prepared to spend his last evening on earth. Sometime later that night, he fell asleep.

———————

At dawn he woke up to the first rays of daylight and opened his Bible. He read the passages that had had a powerful effect on his life: from Genesis and Exodus, Leviticus and Deuteronomy, Job and Proverbs, Ecclesiastes and Isaiah, and Matthew and Revelation. He wrote one final letter to Mary, enclosing his will, which he had forgotten to give her the night before.

It was almost time. Now he gave his Bible to the guard, and a silver watch to the jailer, both of whom had treated him with dignity and even measured friendship. As he walked down the corridor, he said his good-byes to his fellow conspirators, also imprisoned. One of them shouted out, "Goodbye, Captain, I know you are going to a better land."

"I know I am," Brown replied softly. At that, the guard escorted him down the corridor and into the street. Brown paused, taking in the sight of his jail for one last time. Then he stared at the wagon that would carry him to the gallows, stared at the streets around the jail, stared at the armed guards and soldiers. Overhead, there was an immense dome of sky, and below, there was a vast sea of faces in every direction. He was wearing "blood red" slippers, a broad-brimmed hat, and sweat-soaked, disheveled clothes. Asked for his autograph by a jailor, Brown instead scribbled a terse note:

Charlestown, Va, 2d, December 1859.

I John Brown am now quite *certain* that the crimes of this *guilty, land*: will never be purged *away*; but with Blood. I had as *I now think: vainly flattered* myself that without *very much* bloodshed; it might be done.

Brown then climbed into the wagon and, in a macabre scene, sat on his coffin. One of Brown's jailers tied him up by wrapping a cord around him.

It was a warm, almost springlike December day, with the famed actor John Wilkes Booth in attendance, as well as Thomas J. Jackson (one day to be known as the great general Stonewall) of the Virginia Military Insti-tute, and Lee. The gallows had been erected just outside the town in a forty-acre open field. In the distance were the shimmering Blue Ridge Mountains, and in the foreground the hills were dotted with white farm-houses and leafless trees and stalks of corn. Dozens of spectators had gathered to see the execution, and in a sign of the historic event about to take place, there were members of the press as well as fifteen hundred cavalry and militia.

Brown was taken in slow time to the gallows, the carriage clicking monotonously on its way. Once there, with a confident stride, he climbed the platform. The noose was slipped around his neck, and his hands were tied behind his back. For the barest of moments, there was a perfect stillness. Soldiers placed a white linen bag over Brown's head, then had to pin it so it wouldn't blow away in the stiff wind.

In a firm voice, the sheriff ordered Brown to "move ahead." "You will have to guide me," Brown responded. The sheriff tied Brown's ankles together and guided him to the trapdoor.

There was then confusion on the scaffold, as a retinue of soldiers nervously milled about trying to find their precise appointed positions. After about ten minutes of the troops shuffling into position, all the civilian officials made their way off the scaffold. Motionless "as a statue," and standing "upright as a soldier," Brown now stood there alone.

All was quiet. It was just after 11:00 a.m.

On the ground below, the sheriff cut the rope with his hatchet, then Brown took a last step, slipped through the trapdoor, and wriggled wildly as if he were "hanging between heaven and earth." As it happened, the rope was too short. This was not just a hanging; it was inadvertently torture. Brown's body continued to struggle for about five minutes, until his spinal column finally broke.

13

The Aftermath

As John Brown swung back and forth in the wind, in the North church bells rang and minute guns fired solemn salutes. Brown was dead, but his name would live on. In Albany, New York, a 100-gun salute was fired to honor Brown's martyrdom, and across the nation a river of supporters flooded into churches to hear commemorative services. In Akron, Ohio, banks, business establishments, and public offices closed for the entire day, and public prayer meetings took place across New York and New England. In Hartford, the Statue of Liberty atop the statehouse dome was draped in black. In Boston, four thousand people gathered to pay tribute to Brown. A tearful Henry David Thoreau pronounced Brown "a crucified hero," while Henry Wadsworth Longfellow noted in his diary that this event marked "the date of the new revolution—quite as much-needed as the old one."

In the days and weeks that followed, Brown was enshrined in an almost never-ending cascade of public addresses, songs and poems, letters and essays. Herman Melville and Walt Whitman composed poems immortalizing Brown, and even a Polish poet named Cyprian Kamil Norwid wrote, "Thus, ere the ropes will test your bare neck / to find it remains unyielding," while in France, the famed Victor Hugo praised Brown as "the champion of Christ."

For all the encomiums, it was Frederick Douglass who perhaps best captured the meaning of John Brown: "I could speak for the slave," he said. "John Brown could fight for the slave. I could live for the slave, John Brown could die for the slave."

As for the Republicans? They did everything they could to separate themselves from the sedition and bloodshed of Brown's attack. Their policy was, and always had been, or so they insisted, leaving constitutionally sanctioned slavery untouched in the South. They had never condoned nor called for invasions of the South. Never condoned nor called for a mass slave uprising. They said again and again that Harpers Ferry was the result of a lone madman, or as one Chicago editor put it bluntly to Lincoln, "We are damnably exercised here about the effect of Brown's wretched fiasco in Virginia upon the moral health of the Republican Party. The old idiot—the quicker they hang him and get him out of the way the better."

Back in Illinois, working in the Urbana Circuit Court, Abraham Lincoln was also chagrined about Harpers Ferry—chagrined at how Southerners wrongly blamed it on the still-almost-infant Republican Party, and chagrined about the prospects of strife and bloodshed to follow. Publicly, Lincoln maintained that Brown was "mad" and that he would never approve of such a raid based on violence and terror. The day after Brown was hanged, on December 3, Lincoln traveled to Leavenworth to give a speech. While wintry winds lashed outside, he told a crowd that sending the aging warrior to the gallows was appropriate, even if Brown agreed with Republicans in "thinking slavery wrong." Lincoln added, "That cannot excuse violence, bloodshed, and treason." Privately, though, it was a different story. He thought Brown a man of "great courage" and "rare unselfishness."

Conservative Democrats, in the North as well as the South, weren't buying it. They saw matters differently. They blamed the raid not on Brown, for he was "mad," but on Republicans who "induced him to resort to arms to carry out their political schemes."

Meanwhile, all along the route taking Brown's body back home, large and boisterous crowds gathered to take part in the procession. They sang in Philadelphia and in New York, and they continued to sing until he reached Elizabethtown, where a sole sentry—an honor guard—stood watch over the coffin until dawn. It was a chill winter day in the mountains on the afternoon of December 8, when final services for Brown were held at his family farmhouse. Mourners, knee-deep in slushy snow, stood shivering around the graveside; the Reverend Joshua Young read from the Bible, and the coffin was slipped into the earth.

Three days later, the 36th Congress opened a new session. Congress quickly degenerated into an unending cycle of accusations and counteraccusations regarding Harpers Ferry.

Just as John Brown had predicted, the nation was beset by paroxysms.

14

Debate

The South continued to be in an uproar. One Richmond newspaper bellowed that "the Harpers Ferry invasion has advanced the cause of disunion more than any event that has happened since the formation of the government." *De Bow's Review* asked if the South could afford any longer to live "under a government, the majority of whose subjects or citizens regard John Brown as a martyr and a Christian hero." Another paper observed that thousands of men who just a month ago scoffed at the idea of the dissolution of the Union "now hold the opinion that its days are numbered."

To quell the ire of the South, and to demonstrate antipathy for Brown and his noisy rabble, conservatives in the North circled the wagons and organized large anti-Brown rallies. "We are," they bellowed, "ready to go as far as any southern man in putting down all attempts of northern fanatics to interfere with the constitutional rights of the South." And as the election year of 1860 opened, Democrats sought to take political advantage of the strife. Convinced that Senator William H. Seward would inevitably become the presidential nominee for the Republicans in the upcoming election, they singled him out for special contempt.

But far more than politics were at work. After Harpers Ferry, Southerners increasingly saw matters as an issue of "capitulation or secession." Whether they were faced with the moral ethos of Republicans, or Brown's murder and mayhem, the result for them was almost always the same. At this stage, John Brown's ghost—and the visage of Kansas—cast a shadow over almost every debate, every discussion, and every national issue.

On the floor of the Senate, the soaring sentiments of moderates like John J. Crittenden seemed hopelessly overtaken. Crittenden, one of the nation's most vaunted statesmen, had exclaimed, "What a magnificent country is made when we put it all together," a country "as the Almighty never gave to any other people, and never before placed on the surface of the earth." He pointed out that "the very diversity of our resources is the natural cause of union between us"—in other words, it would not do for us all to make cotton, nor would it be wise for all of us to work in manufacturing. Nature herself had sanctioned the Union.

He closed with an eloquent plea for a return to the spirit of tolerance and moderation that had been demonstrated by the Founding Fathers. Over and over, he stressed that the bonds of Union—language, blood, country, memories of the past, and dreams for the future—were much stronger than the forces attempting to divide the sections. As Crittenden sat down that day, senators jumped to their feet and there was a spontaneous, deafening burst of applause, so deafening that the president of the Senate threatened to clear the galleries.

The tug for an enduring Union was still strong.

Now, after Harpers Ferry, it was as though the heavens were turned upside down. Representatives, fearing for their lives, came armed into the ornate Senate chamber, some with revolvers, some with bowie knives, some with both. Then there was the rash of resolutions introduced into the Senate by former secretary of war Jefferson Davis, now elected to the Senate from Mississippi. Davis denied that the United States was a government of "one people." On the contrary, it was a "compact between the sovereign members who formed it." The colonies in 1776 had not declared their independence as a people but separately as independent sovereignties, just as they had ratified the Constitution separately and over a period of several years. Davis quoted from James M. Mason, James Madison, Alexander Hamilton, and other framers to show that the United States had sovereignty over the territories but stressed that the federal government was not the United States. It was merely "its agent." The government had only such powers as the Constitution gave it, and it had not been given power to legislate slavery "out of a territory."

The South was increasingly on edge by the day, readying itself for a war that existed more in their fears than on any battlefield but was real to them nonetheless. Also real was the fact that for them John Brown's nefarious plot seemed to be the inevitable fruit of seeds long ago sown by abolitionists. State legislators appropriated funds for purchases of arms to ready themselves for impending battle; thousands of men joined military companies. If a house somehow burned down, it would be whispered that a slave insurrection was the cause. If a cotton farm crop for some reason spoiled, it was rumored that it was a result of terrorism by abolitionist invaders. Northerners, even family or old friends, were treated like hostile alien beings, rather than heirs to the common rebellion that valiantly fought fearlessly together against the British Empire for independence. Yankees were routinely hissed and booed; down south, some were tarred and feathered, as if it were the Whiskey Rebellion all over again. Others were angrily driven out of town. And a few were even lynched.

It was in this atmosphere of terror and hostility that the Democrats and the Republicans now began to prepare for the 1860 presidential election.

The presidential election really began with the 1858 Illinois senatorial election, pitting the nationally renowned Democrat Stephen A. Douglas against a lanky political unknown, Republican Abraham Lincoln.

Douglas did not take the challenge lightly. Upon being told that he would run against Lincoln, he said to a fellow Democrat, "I shall have my hands full. He is the strongman of the party—full of wit, facts, dates—and the best stump speaker, with his droll ways and dry jokes, in the West." Sensing an opportunity to boost his name, Lincoln challenged Douglas to fifty official debates around the state of Illinois. Having nothing to gain, Douglas agreed to meeting only seven times—once in each congressional district. That he consented to any debates was more due to his ego-driven sense of competition than to his good political sense.

For Americans of that day, debates were akin to carnivals. It was not uncommon for these contests to go on for hours as a form of open-air entertainment; metalworkers and farmers, clerks and shopkeepers, and citizens from every walk of life would come to sit or stand outdoors for hours, milling around with friends and neighbors in sunshine or rain, heat or cold, dust or mud. They were active participants as well, stomping their feet and shouting out rambunctious comments or sharp questions, pointed huzzahs or wild cheers. In each debate the opening speaker would talk for an hour, followed by an hour and a half of rebuttal, and that was just the beginning.

These debates between Douglas and Lincoln would become the most famous in history, perhaps rivaled only by those that took place during the US Constitutional Convention. Yet they wouldn't say a single word about homestead or economic policy, what would eventually be the Land Grant College Act, banks, railroads, public education, tariffs, corruption, Native Americans, Cuba, Russia, France, or war and peace. The single topic was slavery and the future of the Union.

Neither side was above a bit of demagoguery or exaggeration. In the summer of 1858, in a public square in northern Illinois, approximately twelve thousand people came from miles away to witness this great contest between the two political warriors. As the two men stood on a lumber platform, it was dusty, hot, and the sun was shining. Known as the Little Giant, Douglas was a spellbinding speaker, a veritable whirlwind of gestures and frowns punctuated by a booming voice that had captivated people for years. Where he was outfitted in a dark full coat with shiny buttons and a white felt hat, Lincoln listened assiduously, with his eyes half closed, knees raised, and holding a rumpled bag stuffed with notes. Where Douglas had a mammoth head and a duck-like walk and was uncommonly short (five foot four), Lincoln was a foot taller, a tangle of Gumby-like arms, clownish legs, and, as the press noted, "ape-like gestures."

Shouting and waving his fists, Douglas contended that Lincoln was at once an abolitionist and a "black Republican," who would destroy the Union with civil war as well as overwhelm Illinois with thousands of "thick-lipped, degenerate" Black people. Pandering to the prejudices of the day, he contended that Lincoln wanted to make Blacks the political and social equals of whites. "Lincoln believes that the Almighty made the Negro equal to the white man. He thinks that the Negro is his brother. I do not think the Negro is any kin of mine...This government...was made by white men, for the benefit of white men and their posterity, to be executed and managed by white men. But Lincoln wants Negroes to vote on an equal basis with you!"

"Are you for this?" Douglas asked the crowd.

"No! No! Never!"

Are you for letting Negroes flood into Illinois "and cover your prairies with Black settlements?"

"NO! NO!"

"Do you want Illinois to become a free Negro colony?"

"NO!"

"I do not question Mr. Lincoln's conscientious belief that the Negro is made his equal, and hence his brother"—there was great laughter—"but for my part, I do not regard the Negro as my equal, and positively deny that he is my brother or any kin to me whatever."

Then it became time for Lincoln to reply. He stood. Out came thunderous applause—this area was, after all, Republican. Lincoln was all frenetic action; his long arms swung awkwardly, his voice was reedy and high-pitched, and for emphasis he crouched down, only to spring up to his toes. Again and again he insisted that Douglas was distorting his views, to the point that he was demonstrating that a man "can prove a horse chestnut to be a chestnut horse." Negroes were not his equal, Lincoln maintained, nor the equal of Douglas in moral and intellectual facility. And as long as there were differences, the whites would have the superior position. But—and it was a big but—he maintained that Negroes were equal to Lincoln, Douglas, and "every living man" in their right to life, liberty, and the pursuit of happiness, which, as he said, included "the right to the fruits of their own labor."

Then there was the central issue of this senatorial contest: the great moral question of whether slavery would ultimately triumph or perish in the American Union. Douglas, Lincoln noted, repeatedly evaded this issue. Why? Whereas Lincoln maintained that the country could not exist forever half-slave and half-free, Douglas, he insisted, looked not only to *"no end of the institution of slavery"* but to the *"perpetuity and nationalization"* of slavery. The crux of what Lincoln was saying was that Douglas had departed from the position of the Founding Fathers, while Lincoln was upholding it.

Lincoln tried to trap Douglas in a verbal cul-de-sac. He asked if the people of the western territory could exclude slavery if they wished to do so. There was no winning for Douglas on this issue. If he answered no, he jeopardized his reelection to the Senate and alienated Illinois voters. If he answered yes, he alienated the South and lost their support for the presidency in 1860. Lincoln knew that Douglas would retreat to the issue of popular sovereignty, a concept that he devised himself, that slavery cannot actually exist in territories unless people desire it.

Douglas had his own counterattack against Lincoln's house-divided metaphor. Why, he wondered, could the country not continue to "exist divided into free and slave states"? He noted that the Founding Fathers left each state free to do as it pleased on the subject, whatever their personal views were toward slavery. If the nation couldn't "endure thus divided," then Lincoln was striving to make them all free or all slave, which, if that meant anything, it meant "warfare between the North and the South, to be carried on with ruthless vengeance, until one section or the other shall be driven to the wall and become the victim of the rapacity of the other." No, screamed Douglas. "I would not endanger the perpetuity of this Union. I would not blot out the great inalienable rights of the white men for all the Negroes that ever existed."

Wherever the two candidates met, whether in blistering cold or oppressive heat, the debates bulged with thousands of people, buzzing and humming and wanting to get a glimpse at history being made. The debates were a blizzard of activity: Flags flapped grandly from buildings and banners were strung across country roads. Reminiscent of revolutionary times, there was the rhythmic thump-thump of drums and the whistle of fifes being played by armed cadets, not to mention the spectacle of glee clubs singing, welcoming the two candidates. Of course, partisans flapped their caps or raised their signs.

Emotions were high. One typical Democrat sign portrayed a Republican domestic scene with a white man spending time with his "n***er" wife and "n***er" children, while a typical Republican sign showed a train called "freedom" careening toward Douglas's oxcart. The Black driver was saying, "Fore God, Massa, I b'lives we're in danger." All this was dutifully recorded by partisan journalists. The Republicans invariably ridiculed Douglas's swagger and just about everything else about him, while the Democratic journalists invariably mocked Lincoln just as viciously. It was not uncommon for Lincoln to be depicted as a baboon.

The election was held on November 7, a day that was cold and drizzly. Historians have judged Lincoln to be the winner of the debates, but the voters thought differently. The Democrats still held the majority in the legislature, and so Douglas won the senatorial election. In the end, however, this was more than a senatorial election. It was a crucial victory for Douglas, affirming him as a leader of the Democratic Party in the North and its strongest candidate for the next presidential nomination. Lincoln, meanwhile, had successfully held his own against the venerated Little Giant, while emerging as a national spokesman for the Republicans. This didn't mean that the loss didn't sting. Back in his legal office in Springfield, a depressed Lincoln lay on his couch and muttered quietly to his friends, "I feel like the boy who stubbed his toe. I am too big to cry and too badly hurt to laugh."

But in a turn of events that would alter the political history of America forever, Lincoln wrote to a friend soon thereafter, "The fight must go on."

15

Lincoln

So who was Abraham Lincoln? We know that one day he would become an American original, and that his genius would be unquestioned. The same for his niche in history. In truth, he was always a riddle of quirks and impenetrable eccentricities. And from his earliest years it seemed as though this stage of his life was always set for high drama, if not towering tragedy.

It wasn't always this way, however. Lincoln was born in a log cabin in Kentucky, where ironically his father, Thomas, once did a stint on the Hardin County slave patrol, and spent his early life on a succession of frontier farms as his family, like thousands of others at the start of the nineteenth century, chased their futures west. His father knew enough to sign his own name—though scarcely more than that—so it was his mother who taught Lincoln to read. But she died when he was nine. After that, he largely taught himself; he had one year of formal school-ing. In the years that followed, Thomas Lincoln hired his own son out for wages, until Abe was finally able to work for himself. In the backwoods of Kentucky, Indiana, and Illinois, and also along the Ohio and Missis-sippi Rivers, Lincoln grew to be unusually tall and learned a myriad of trades: rafting, carpentry, boating, forestry, butchering, throwing, distill-ing, plowing, storekeeping, and, naturally, rail-splitting. But he would shrewdly turn these modest beginnings into political assets later on. As local settlers once gibed, he was a "wild, harumscarum kind of man, who always had his eyes open to the main chance."

That main chance came, of course, first in education. Whatever the shortcomings of his formal education, Lincoln's innate intellect was apparent from his earliest years. He delved into the great works of history, literature, and biography, devouring the works of Edward Gibbon, Thomas Paine, and C. F. Volney; he enjoyed reading *Robinson Crusoe* and *Aesop's Fables*, as well as *The Pilgrim's Progress*. Unsurprisingly, he ensconced himself in Parson Weems's lives of Washington and Franklin, too. Crucially for his later career, he was deeply inspired by Thomas Jefferson, Henry Clay, and Daniel Webster, three giants of American politics and history. He constantly sought to improve himself, reciting poetry, practicing "polemics," and teaching himself mathematics.

Physically, he was a strong man. He was stoop-shouldered and flat-footed, with a peculiar rambling gait, until he decided to stand tall for effect, holding his head high and regal. His trademark stovepipe hat only accentuated a stature that was already outsized.

Despite his modest station in life, he traveled a fair bit, which gave him insights into the country that a number of his more refined colleagues sorely lacked. The majority of Americans knew little about the state of society beyond the nestled confines of their own towns or cities, let alone their region. Senator Charles Sumner saw Paris and London but never once set foot in the South; Jefferson Davis, a graduate of West Point, visited New England only once. By contrast Lincoln once rafted down to New Orleans and worked his way back on a steamer; he visited the South several times.

Early on, his life was checkered, and he had his run of bad luck. He opened a store, which failed, then became a postmaster, and failed at that as well. When a circuit court issued a judgment against him for overdue notes—recalling John Brown—the sheriff attached his personal possessions, including his horse. Compounding matters, his store partner died. Lincoln was forced to shoulder the hefty $1,100 burden of remaining debt, which took him fifteen years to pay off. His personal life was little better. His first lady friend, Ann Rutledge, died abruptly of an attack of "brain fever." His first great love, Mary Owens, turned him down. Subsequently, like many ambitious politicians, he eventually did marry, and marry well: Mary Todd, who came from an aristocratic, wealthy, and educated Kentucky family. She was ambitious, cultured, plump, and witty; she also spoke French. And she was as determined as Lincoln himself, having handpicked him as destined for the White House. "Mr. Lincoln is to be president of the United States some day," she said. "If I had not thought so, I would not have married him, for you can see he is not pretty." At first shunned by her family, and insecure about his own lack of pedigree, Lincoln broke off the engagement. But then he came around. He was thirty-three; she was twenty-three.

The marriage was an odd one, and in a number of ways the two couldn't have been more different. He grew up on dirt floors; she was waited on by enslaved people and attended finishing school. He was rumpled and disorganized, whether at home or at the office; she was neat and fastidious. He loved humor; she had none at all. She insisted upon servants; he would not keep a clerk. And if he were morose, she could be nasty and difficult.

Their marriage was sometimes filled with acrimony. More than once she drove him from the house in fury, brandishing a broomstick. Another time, she chased him down the street waving a knife. Meanwhile, he could sometimes be unforgiving with her, if not a little cruel. Yet as the years passed, the two became increasingly tender toward each other. She came to respect his righteousness, and, in turn, he came to rely on her moral support and political guidance. When he failed time and again in his quest for Congress, she propped him up, prodded him, and pushed him. Were it not for her, the distraught Lincoln might well have quit, and it's equally likely that the presidency would have eluded him. He learned to be decent toward her, affectionately calling her little names like "my Molly," or fussing over her as "my little woman" and my "child wife." She understood the prerequisites for the political Lincoln and, as no one else around him, understood the inner Lincoln. In her own right, she could be beset by her own deep and near debilitating moods and disappointments. Ironically, his familial empathy helped imbue him with empathy for the South, particularly as the crisis between the North and the South intensified.

By way of profession, Lincoln was a successful self-taught lawyer, earning up to $5,000 a year by the 1850s. But law per se never had much appeal for him. Politics did. Not the Jacksonian Democrats that his father was so fond of, which he rejected, but the new roads, central banking, and protective tariffs of the national Republicans and Whigs. "Republicans," Lincoln memorably said, "are both for the man and the dollar." Indeed, Lincoln always saw himself as a champion of the budding middle class. He gave his first stump speech at nineteen and never looked back. "Politics were his life, newspapers his food, and his great ambition his motive power," his final law partner, William H. Herndon, wrote. At twenty-three, only seven months after coming to the little Illinois community of New Salem, Lincoln was already running for office. He lost. But contrary to the tales he liked to tell, success soon came to him; two years later, in 1834, Sangamon County sent him to the lower Illinois House. From this time on to the end of his life—except for the years between 1849 and 1854, when his political prospects were at their lowest ebb—he was either campaigning, serving in office, or out on the stump for other office seekers.

But, ultimately, it was not within Lincoln's middle-class mantra or his fierce partisanship where he would make his lasting political mark. Nor his distaste for war. It was slavery: human bondage and human servitude. By a combination of design and fate, the slavery issue would not let Lincoln stray from public life, not let him fade into obscurity, and not let him rest.

———————

There is a legend about Lincoln on his second trip to New Orleans, at the age of twenty-one. There, he saw a handsome girl being sold on the block at the slave market. It was then that "the iron entered his soul," and he swore henceforth that if he ever got the chance, he would hit slavery and "hit it hard." The authenticity of this tale is suspect; but what is not suspect are the sentiments that haunted him: the image of the strutting enslaver, of the young woman, of the scorn in which slavery held freedom. To Lincoln, slavery was a dangerous, slippery slope. It was not solely an affront to freedom or to democracy; slavery was responsible for corrupting the South and human relations everywhere.

Lincoln's private hostility to slavery belied another significant record, that of public vacillation, even accommodation. And here lies one of the great questions about Lincoln the politician versus Lincoln the principled leader. In political life, Lincoln was careful never to step too far ahead of prevailing opinion; he frequently fudged and calculated. His explanations were often wry and not always convincing. And he was never above pandering and manipulating, both facts and opinions. Yet because he was always instinctively conservative, if not cautious, his public actions concerning slavery invariably stood in contrast to his proslavery arguments. Thus, despite his opposition to the peculiar institution, Lincoln frequently maintained that slavery was destined to disappear on its own, a victim of its own internal contradictions and of historical progress. In this sense, he was like a number of Southerners, including not just Robert E. Lee but his political and intellectual idol, Thomas Jefferson, who tolerated the institution while quietly holding his nose, and memorably once said, "We have the wolf by the ears, and can neither hold him or let him go."

As a lame-duck congressman in 1849, Lincoln was provided his first opportunity to weaken the institution he so despised, drafting a "Bill to Abolish Slavery in the District Of Columbia." It was to be enacted by local referendum, but Lincoln watered it down, adding a section that required municipal authorities of Washington and Georgetown to provide all "active and efficient means" of arresting and restoring to the enslavers all fugitive slaves escaping into the district. In essence, the bill split the difference between the two extremes of slavery haters and enslavers, but in seeking to offend nobody, Lincoln only ended up offending everyone. Once he made his bill public, all support for the measure evaporated. The bill went nowhere, and when the House debated the morality of slavery, Lincoln sat by, silent. He spent the next five years in much the same state, back in Illinois, practicing law and unhappily watching events pass him by.

Of course, it was the pugnacious Douglas who in 1854 opened the door to let Lincoln back into public life. It was in that year that Douglas unveiled the Kansas-Nebraska Act, which put the question of extending bondage in the new territories to majority vote. This was Lincoln's chance to make a name for himself on the national stage, a way to rehabilitate his political fortunes. At the outset, his moral zeal was tempered by his political pragmatism. Lincoln took great pains to emphasize that he was not an abolitionist, nor was he advocating political or social equality; he merely opposed extending slavery into the new territories. He knew all too well that most of his supporters were not only not abolitionists but outright Negrophobes who did not want to live or work alongside Black men, free or enslaved. But this equivocation would not last for long.

His breakthrough moment came on May 29, 1856. Called upon to deliver the adjournment speech at the convention inaugurating the new Illinois Republican Party, Lincoln staked everything in kind. Gone was his usual timidity. Now he made good on his promise to hit slavery and "hit it hard." It was the best speech of his life, a stunning oration so mesmerizing that reporters ceased transcribing it. Even Lincoln's close friend and legal partner, William H. Herndon, normally a prodigious notetaker, threw "pen and paper away," and got caught up in the inspiration of the hour.

Lincoln's gambit paid off. Within months, he became a champion of the fledgling Republican Party and soon was being pitted against Stephen A. Douglas, whom he had taunted and connived into a series of public debates whose sole topic was slavery. Lincoln, once the most obscure of figures, won the prize he coveted so deeply, having been transfigured from a minor state politician into a budding national figure.

It was heady stuff, and Lincoln kept pushing. Denied the Senate seat, he still sniffed the opportunity for the presidency. His ultimate goal was not intellectual consistency on slavery, but strategy, namely, the challenge of how to meld old-line Whigs with antislavery men into one potent political party. In a series of well-attended and highly regarded lectures over the following months across the Northeast and the Midwest, Lincoln hammered again and again at the ostensible Democratic plan to extend slavery and the dangers it would inflict upon the nation. Thus he was able to create a historically unique amalgam of political forces under the same tent: abolitionists and Negrophobes, high-tariff men and low-tariff men, former Whigs and embittered Democrats, immigrants and Know-Nothings, German tipplers and Maine law prohibitionists. It was nothing short of masterful politically, for here was a coalition that could one day boldly sweep him into power.

Before the national convention Lincoln was still sufficiently obscure in certain circles that a number of pundits did not even include his name on the list of a dozen or even twenty-one potential candidates. A former one-term congressman, a small-town lawyer, a failed senatorial candidate (twice), a man beset by recurrent depression and lacking a formal education, he was so unsophisticated that he said "kin" for "can" and "git" for "get" and was widely regarded as a "baboon" and "a village hick." Several newspapers mistakenly spelled his first name "Abram." The most improbable of candidates, he was no one's first choice. By contrast, his challengers were national figures, men of stature and erudition, on the glide path to becoming the icons of their day: William H. Seward of New York, Salmon P. Chase of Ohio, Simon Cameron of Pennsylvania, and Edward Bates of Missouri.

At the Chicago Republican Convention, Seward led on the first ballot, as everybody predicted. Yet, in rumbles and whispers, it became apparent that each of his foes had their own set of weaknesses. Chase, a former Ohio governor, was a radical and did not even enjoy full support from his home state. Cameron had been a renegade Democrat and a Know-Nothing and was regarded as little more than a spoiler. Bates was colorless and old—he was sixty-seven—and had alternately been an enslaver and a Know-Nothing. Which left Lincoln, who had many qualities of an optimal candidate and few of its glaring weaknesses. And despite his "House Divided" speech, and his assiduousness as an antislavery proponent, he had still cultivated the aura of a Midwestern moderate. He was humble "Abe" of the common people, a homespun hero brimming with prairie wit and folk wisdom. Meanwhile, the selection of Chicago as the convention site considerably strengthened Lincoln's candidacy. For it was here that massive, ecstatic crowds of Illinoisans packed the convention hall (famously nicknamed the "Wigwam") as well as the galleries and streets outside.

The first ballot had Seward ahead by a healthy lead. However, it also demonstrated Seward's surprising weaknesses—in truth, Seward had been hoping for a first-ballot nomination—and Lincoln's surprising strengths. A total of 233 votes was needed to nominate, and Seward fell 60 short at 173½ while Lincoln polled 102. So it went to a second ballot, and this time Seward gained fewer than a dozen votes as Vermont, Pennsylvania, and a smattering of other states, including Ohio, switched to Lincoln, bringing him almost even with Seward at 181 votes. During this time, the crowd in the Wigwam was ecstatic, stomping its feet with a fervor rarely seen in American politics. Ten thousand spectators, the majority of whom were for Lincoln, made so much noise that a reporter exhausted his treasure chest of descriptions to describe it: "Imagine all the hogs ever slaughtered in Cincinnati giving their death squeals together…A herd of buffaloes or Lions could not have made a more tremendous roaring."

Now, suddenly, there appeared to be an irresistible momentum behind Lincoln. Could it actually happen?

The third ballot began, and virtually everyone was on edge. The votes began trickling over to Lincoln, and soon the trickle became a flood. New England switched six of its votes to Lincoln. New Jersey switched eight to him. Maryland switched four, as did Lincoln's native Kentucky. Then another fifteen Chase votes from Ohio were switched to Lincoln. The rafters literally shook with enthusiasm, as people clapped and hooted at the top of their lungs. While dozens of partisans were tallying the vote, the clerk soon declared it: Lincoln had 231½ votes. There was a pause, and for the slightest of moments, a quiet. The Ohio chairman then leaped onto his chair and announced the change of yet four more votes to Lincoln. Thousands of people began cheering insanely.

Not one of those four thousand people in the Wigwam ever forgot that moment. An unknown named Abraham Lincoln was the nominee of a political party barely six years old. The convention sought to balance the ticket by nominating Hannibal Hamlin of Maine for vice president; Hamlin was a former Democrat but also one of Lincoln's earliest supporters, as well as a friend of Seward's. That mattered. In the meantime, the Republicans toned down their platform, including the plank denouncing John Brown's raid as "the gravest of crimes." At the same time, their forward-looking platform embraced a future Homestead Act, river and harbor improvements, and federal aid for the construction of a transcontinental railroad. It also eschewed nativism—this mattered to Lincoln—and then spoke directly to Southern disunionists by promulgating a stern warning against "contemplated treason."

Lincoln, the most improbable of candidates, was back home sitting on the edge of his seat in Springfield when a telegram arrived informing him that he had been nominated for president at the Republican National Convention in Chicago: "TO LINCOLN YOU ARE NOMINATED."

"Well," Lincoln said, "we've got it." Outside, cannons began to boom and church bells began to toll hysterically. In the streets, Republicans were dancing and singing and hurrahed deliriously when Lincoln walked outside, illuminated by the effervescent glare of torches. Overhead, fireworks were exploding.

Speaking to his supporters, Lincoln joked that he would invite the entire crowd into his house if it were large enough to hold them. Someone shouted back from the crowd, "We will give you a larger house on the fourth of next March!"

16

The Election

A week before the Republican Convention, another party had held its convention as well. Formerly the Whig Party, which was Lincoln's original party, these conservatives now branded themselves the Constitutional Union Party. They nominated a wealthy enslaver, John Bell of Tennessee, for president, and the irrepressible New England Whig Edward Everett (later of Gettysburg fame) of Massachusetts, for vice president. The Constitutional Unionists rejected putting together a platform and were remarkably silent on the pressing question of slavery. Instead, they adopted the sole principles of "The Constitution... The Union... And the Enforcement of the Laws." In sharp contrast to the youthful Republican Party, most of the delegates were over sixty years old, leaving this "Old Gentlemen's Party" as an object of ridicule by the youthful Republicans, who described the Bell-Everett ticket as aging and hopelessly feeble, "laid away in a box of musk, and kept there." Meanwhile, Southern Democrats insisted that the Constitutional Unionists were "insulting" the intelligence of the American people by trying to organize a party that ignored the slavery question.

The Constitutional Unionists did not believe they had a chance to win the election outright. Their strategy was more complicated. To start, they hoped they could weaken Lincoln in the lower North and deny him an electoral majority. The election of a president would then be thrown into the House instead; here, each state had one vote, but no party controlled the majority of states. One route to victory was a coalition of Democrats with the Whig American Unionists to elect John Cabell Breckinridge, the vice president, detaching him from his extremist Southern rights backers. There remained also the possibility that Bell could be elected by the Constitutional Unionists. Alternatively, if the House were unable to name a president by March 4, 1861, the vice president elected by the Democratic Senate would become acting president. That meant Breckinridge's running mate, Joseph Lane of Oregon—a proslavery native of North Carolina—or New England's Edward Everett of the Constitutional Unionists.

Then there were the Democrats, many of whom were Southern and a number of whom came from the North. Their passions ran high, and they were deeply skeptical of Douglas. One Alabamian writer dismissed him as the "demagogue of Illinois" and insisted he deserved to perish and have his "loathsome carcass to be cast at the gate of the federal city." In fact, the Alabama Democratic Convention took the first step in January by instructing its delegates to walk out of the national convention if the party would not embed the federal slave code for the territories in its platform.

Indeed, the Senate Democratic caucus endorsed a series of resolutions on slavery, which ultimately defined the Democrats' convention in Charleston, South Carolina.

In the pitched environment of 1860, Charleston was arguably the most inflammatory place possible for the convention. Fire-eaters were everywhere, and the Douglas delegates felt as if they had dropped into a hostile alternate galaxy. Inside the convention hall itself, because delegates were apportioned the same way as electoral votes, Northerners commanded a three-fifths majority. If Southerners were determined to adopt a slave code plank, Douglas's supporters were equally determined to block one. As a talented young journalist from Cincinnati, Murat Halstead, reported, here then was an "irrepressible conflict" in the party. The South would not yield; nor would the North, seeing slavery as a form of political "suicide."

The tug came with the report of the platform committee. With the connivance of Oregon and California, the Democrats adopted a slave code plank similar to what Jefferson Davis had endorsed in February. Meanwhile, the minority report affirmed the 1856 platform sanctioning popular sovereignty—each state got to decide on whether to have servitude. This, however, was not good enough for Democrats. The committee chairman, a North Carolinian, insisted that slave property needed federal protection, which meant that if the United States acquired Central America, or Cuba, or Mexico, any enslaver could bring his property there. William Lowndes Yancey, among the great orators for Southern rights, stood and delivered a rousing speech in favor of the majority report. "We are in a position to ask you to yield," he said to Northern delegates. "What right of yours, gentlemen of the north, have we of the South ever invaded?" The galleries were filled with stomping boots, broad grins, and a cascade of cheers. Yancey continued, "OURS are the institutions which are at stake; OURS is the property that is to be destroyed!; Ours is the honor at STAKE!"

Finally, Douglas's men were able to push the platform through by a vote of 165 to 138. At that point, 50 Southern delegates walked out, and Douglas was unable to secure the two-thirds majority required for his nomination. But the convention couldn't agree on anything else, even after 57 acrimonious ballots. Disgusted and at wit's end, the convention organizers adjourned; six weeks later they would try again in Baltimore, which they hoped would be more hospitable. Yancey gave them an acrimonious farewell, then made his way through a bustling crowd in Charleston's courthouse square. It was a moonlit evening, and Yancey roused a massive crowd to give three deafening cheers "for an independent Southern Republic!"

Could the Democrats be reunited like the Republicans? This hope now seemed more elusive than ever. Northwest Democrats were furious at their Southern brethren, who in turn were furious at them. "I never heard abolitionists talk more uncharitably and rancorously of the people of the South than the Douglas men," observed one reporter. But the prominent congressman Alexander H. Stephens, a Douglas supporter, observed that the strategy of the Southerners was "to rule or ruin." There now was the possibility that the delegates of the upper South would bolt from the Democrats and join their Cotton State compatriots to form a new party.

Yet in Baltimore, meeting at the Front Street Theatre, the Northern Democrats had a change of heart and were now willing to compromise

with the discontented Southerners. However, the anti-Douglas Southerners stiffened, wanting all or nothing. Once more they walked out, this time
followed by delegates from the upper South and a handful of proslavery
Northerners as well, amounting to more than one-third of the total. These
"bolters," amid a storm of confusion, quickly organized their own convention, nominating the current vice president, John Cabell Breckinridge of
Kentucky, for president. He was chosen based on a slave code platform
for the inauspiciously named Whig American Union Party. Meanwhile,
the dispirited loyalists nominated Douglas and returned home, fearful
that a divided Democratic Party would end up ensuring the election of a
Republican.

But who were these Republicans by comparison? On the whole, they
all stood together on the Republican platform: They opposed the *Dred
Scott* decision, opposed popular sovereignty, and opposed the slave power.
They ardently supported the Northern free labor system and the principles
of self-help and personal liberty. While they hated slavery and wanted it
to die out, they sought no fundamental transformation of the American
system, nor did they seek a fundamental break from basic American ideals
and traditions. They wanted to repeal the fugitive slave law, and refused to
surrender another inch of territory to Southern enslavers. That said, they
were, as they repeated over and over, not abolitionists. And as Lincoln
himself put it, the Republicans were a "conservative" party, in the sense
that they carried on the ideals of the founders.

As the campaign went into full swing, Republican speakers heralded their party as the spirit of a new age, an age of free soil, free labor,
and free men. When they were at barbecues or rallies or parades, young
Republicans—and the lion's share were young—extolled the virtues of
Abraham Lincoln, a man of the people who personified the "distinctive
genius of our country and its people."

The Democrats thought otherwise, heaping scorn upon Lincoln. He
was a "chimpanzee," a "John Brown," "a bastard," "a vulgar southern
hater," and "illiterate and coarse." He was a "bloodthirsty tyrant" and
"a horrid looking wretch" who was seeking to goad enslaved people to

rebellion. He was, as the Democrats put it, the greatest "ass" in the United States, a scoundrel and abolitionist who would free four million enslaved people and wipe out untold millions of slave investments; his running mate was a "mulatto" and his victory would sound the bells of doom for the white man in the South. Lincoln would urge Negroes to copulate with and marry white women, not surprising coming from the "free love, free n***er" party.

Meanwhile, a great debate raged in the South, and among the Democrats. There were those who insisted the South would never submit to such mortification as the inauguration of Abraham Lincoln; they would rather see the United States smothered in blood than capitulate to Lincoln as president. Lincoln shrugged off such warnings, having heard these pro-secession editorials before. "The people of the South," he noted, "have too much of good sense, and good temper, to attempt the ruin of the government." Huddling with his advisers, Lincoln believed that the tug of Southern Unionism—of the United States—was much too powerful for secession to triumph. All the talk about disunion, he believed, was little more than an "empty threat."

———————

Thanks to John Brown, the election of 1860 was not one election but actually two: in the North, Lincoln versus Douglas; in the South, Breckinridge versus Bell. Remarkably, Lincoln did not even appear on the ticket in ten Southern states, and in the remaining five slave states—all in the upper South—as it happened, Lincoln would receive only 4 percent of the popular vote. Breckinridge would fare little better in the North, where he would win 5 percent of the popular vote.

It was a hard-fought contest from the outset. Even if he were dismissed by the South, and treated little better by the Buchanan administration, the charismatic Douglas was a formidable opponent. For one thing, he eschewed tradition, and rather than observe the customary silence of presidential candidates, he vigorously campaigned for himself. From July to November, he stumped throughout the country, despite ill health, a chronically hoarse voice, and mounting exhaustion. Douglas's message was the same both to the North and to the South: He was the only national candidate who could save the country "from disunion." The Southern Democrats thought otherwise and regarded Douglas as nearly as fanatical about slavery as Lincoln.

Lincoln, meanwhile, was as restless as ever. His campaign was virtually unprecedented in enthusiasm and vigor; young people streamed out to work for him, while Republican Party elders stumped across the country delivering approximately fifty thousand speeches, a staggering figure. Tactically, they were shrewd, playing down the moral issue of slavery while highlighting other matters of national concern. Thus, they were the party of tariffs to the voters of Pennsylvania and New Jersey; to the voters from Ohio to California they were the homestead party, the Pacific Railroad party, and the party of internal improvements. But the Republicans also tactically overstepped, especially in New York, where they placed a constitutional amendment to enfranchise Black men on the ballot. This prompted howls of protest from the Democrats. If you want to vote "cheek by jowl with a large 'buck n***er,' if you want to support a party that says 'a n***er is better than an Irishman,' if you are ready to divide your patrimony with the Negro...Vote for the Republican candidate." One Democratic banner summed up its sentiments this way: "Free love and free n***ers will certainly elect Old Abe." The largest Democratic newspaper in the country, the *New York Herald*, insisted that "hundreds of thousands" of fugitive slaves would "emigrate to their friends—the Republicans—North."

As the election neared, the possibility that Lincoln would become president generated in the South a witches' brew of hysteria, gloom, and paradoxical enthusiasm. Democrats were terrified, while at the same time, growing numbers of secessionists now toyed with the possibility of Southern independence. It didn't help that national figures like Frederick Douglass fed their fears, maintaining that a Lincoln victory would be "an anti-slavery triumph." Driven to the point of frenzy, and repeatedly trafficking in hysteria and gross misrepresentations, Southerners agreed.

With increasing fervor, this mushrooming mass frenzy prompted even Southern Unionists to warn the Yankees that a Republican victory could only result in disunion. As one Mississippian pointed out, "The minds of the people are aroused to a pitch of excitement probably unparalleled in the history of our country." Listening to the Democrats in the South, it was hard to disagree. One paper in Georgia sputtered indignantly, "Let the consequences be what they may—whether the Potomac is crimsoned in human gore, and Pennsylvania Avenue is paved ten fathoms deep with mangled bodies. The South will never submit to such humiliation... as the inauguration of Abraham Lincoln!"

Yet Republicans, Lincoln foremost, refused to take these warnings to heart. They had heard them from Democrats in 1856. They read them in their history books about the nullification crisis with Andrew Jackson. It was, they believed, "the old game of scaring and bullying the north into submission to southern demands," as the Republican mayor of Chicago said. Seward himself mocked the Southern effort "to terrify or alarm" the North. Conservatives pleaded with Lincoln to make a statement, to mollify the South, to quell their concerns. He refused. "What is it I could say which would quiet the alarm?" he asked in October. "I have said this so often already that a repetition of it is but a mockery, bearing an appearance of weakness." The inexperienced candidate believed that speaking out, far from soothing disunionists, would be an act of political "timidity and cowardice."

By contrast, Douglas did speak out, loudly and often. In North Carolina he said he would hang every man "who would attempt to break up the Union by resistance to its laws." Even as his health grew poor, Douglas repeated his alarms against secession. He firmly believed that the election of any man on earth was "no justification for breaking up this government."

Southern Democrats listened carefully to Douglas, but they did not hear.

––––––––––

On Election Day, November 6, Lincoln awoke early, walked over to the Springfield telegraph office, and stretched across an old sofa as the superintendent read off the initial tallies. Everything pointed to a Republican triumph, but Lincoln knew he couldn't take it for granted. In an inauspicious sign, by day's end, a massive 81 percent of registered voters had gone to the polls.

An enthusiastic senator named Lyman Trumbull joined Lincoln and they listened to the tabulations together. The telegraph brought the news from the Northwest and New England and suggested a sizable Republican triumph in the upper North. Then more good news; they began to receive private messages as well. Pennsylvania, as it happened, was certain to go Republican; Indiana, too. By contrast, Virginia, Georgia, Florida, Alabama, South Carolina, and North Carolina, among others, were bound to go Democratic. Yet if Lincoln were to get New York, with its massive treasure trove of thirty-five electoral votes, Seward would have been prophetic when he said, "It now really looks as if the government is about to fall in our hands."

But would it?

As the day wore on, so did the results. Yet at 10:00 p.m. there was still no word from New York. Meanwhile, votes for the Democrats were piling up in New York City. Lincoln grew "fretful." How many times, he wondered, had his dreams been shattered at the last moment? Could this be his Senate race all over again? He began to anguish. Without New York, Lincoln would fall seven electoral votes short of a majority. Finally, at 11:30 p.m., came the news that Lincoln had indeed won the massive prize of New York, which virtually guaranteed victory. Outside, a large, delirious Republican crowd had begun to assemble, and upon hearing about New York, they screamed "like demons" while other supporters rolled on the ground "in ecstasy." Then the returns from the South started to trickle in, in earnest. "Now," Lincoln boasted, "we shall get a few licks back." A crowd of Republican women, jumping the gun, beamed at Lincoln. "How do you do, Mr. President?" Then they fetched him sandwiches.

He wanted to make sure that he had been elected before turning in. In a telling sign, in popular votes his opponents defeated him by a healthy margin of more than one million votes, 2,815,577 to 1,866,452, with Douglas earning 1,376,957, while Breckinridge came in third with

849,741 and Bell fourth with 588,879. Though Lincoln did not have a majority of the popular vote—he won only a paltry 39.8 percent—he defeated his combined opponents in the Electoral College, racking up a total of 180 votes while Breckinridge garnered 72, Bell 39, and Douglas just 12. For the Southern Democrats, the most distressing feature of the vote was the fact that Lincoln and the Republicans won handily with more than 60 percent of the vote north of the forty-first parallel.

It was a split country.

To the *New Orleans Crescent*, the election was "full of portentous significance," and as the *Richmond Examiner* put it, "The idle canvas prattle about northern conservativism may now be dismissed." It continued that at this stage, "a party founded on the single sentiment of hatred of African slavery...is now the controlling power." With antislavery men in control, as Charles Francis Adams Sr. approvingly put it, "the great revolution has actually taken place...The country has once and for all thrown off the domination of the slaveholders."

At 1:30 a.m. a tired Lincoln ambled the streets, then climbed into bed at two o'clock, too keyed up to sleep. After all his defeats over the last six years, after all the bitterness, the hurt and depression, he had finally won. Beneath the blackened sky, celebrations outside continued on into the waning hours, and Republicans sang in the statehouse throughout the morning. At 4:00 a.m. Republicans rolled out a huge cannon and fired a furiously explosive shot. Back at home, Lincoln's own windows were rattling. He was still tossing and turning.

The next morning, the president-elect rose early, wanting to waste no time. Giddy but sleep-deprived, he made his way to the governor's office to start the process of selecting a possible list of cabinet members.

It was a different story in the Deep South, where telegraph dispatches shouted out news about Lincoln's election, and people everywhere thronged the streets of Southern cities with once unthinkable talk of war and secession.

17

Secession and Buchanan

In Charleston, South Carolina, on that Election Day, an extraordinary event took place. In opposition to the election of Lincoln, the US flag was taken down and the state flag was defiantly raised. Then a federal officer sought to transfer supplies from the Charleston Arsenal to Fort Moultrie; he was arrested by the city's authorities. Already this was shaping up to be a crisis of the highest order. Were state authorities in charge? Or federal? In Charleston, the *Mercury* editorialized, "The tea has been thrown overboard, the revolution of 1860 has been initiated!"

The next two days, Wednesday, November 7, and Thursday, November 8, bore that out. The lion's share of business in the city was largely suspended, while people flowed into the streets to read bulletin boards bearing the latest updates. Upon Lincoln's election, three cheers went up for a Southern confederacy, a refrain that was heard over and over again. One judge went as far as resigning, informing his court, "So far as I am concerned, the Temple of justice raised under the Constitution of the United States is now closed. It shall never again be opened. I thank God that its doors have been closed before its altars have been desecrated with sacrifices to tyranny," a clear reference to the newly elected president. While joyous victory meetings sprang up across Northern communities all across the Union, and in Springfield waves of congratulations poured into Lincoln's statehouse office, countless Southern communities held what they deemed "indignation meetings."

In Washington, DC, President James Buchanan was torn. He strongly opposed secession, but as a lame duck, he felt helpless to do anything to prevent it. And his cabinet, not unlike the nation at large, was split between pro- and anti-secessionists, pro– and anti–United States. On Friday, November 9, the president assembled his cabinet to discuss the State of the Union message. He polled them on their views toward secession; just as he feared, they were badly split. Lewis Cass, the secretary of state, strongly opposed it and advocated the use of force. Attorney General Jeremiah Sullivan Black favored marching a force to Charleston as Andrew Jackson once threatened. The secretary of the Treasury, Howell Cobb, by contrast, thought disunion necessary, and not just necessary but "desirable and legal." Equally ominously, the secretary of the Interior, Jacob Thompson, who came from Mississippi, warned that any show of force by the government would move Mississippi to disunion.

If Buchanan and his cabinet were indecisive, South Carolina was distinctly not. On Saturday, the legislature passed a law calling for a convention to meet at Columbia on December 17 to consider seceding from the Union. Lest anyone doubt the seriousness of their purpose, the two South Carolina senators in Washington resigned their seats and prepared to leave the capital. South Carolina was now the tip of the spear for the secession movement, with other Deep South states watching carefully; meanwhile, the border states and the middle South were quietly waiting. There were those in the North who sighed to the South, "Good riddance." But others spoke of secession as the greatest of calamities. For its part, Wall Street thought so. The market didn't like that instability and on Monday, November 12, experienced heavy selling with a sharp drop in prices.

Back in Springfield, the president-elect was still reluctant to speak out. He wrote, "I could say nothing which I have not already said, and which is in print, and open for the inspection of all. To press a repetition of this upon those who *have* listened, is useless; to press upon those who have *refused* to listen, and still refuse . . . would have the appearance of sycophancy and timidity, which would excite the contempt of good men, and encourage bad ones to clamor more loudly." To one Missouri editor, Lincoln added this: "I am not at liberty to shift my ground—that is out of the question." Maybe he was not at liberty, but Buchanan was, and the president struggled mightily to navigate a course of action for the final three months of his presidency. He consulted with his cabinet frequently, conferred often with his general-in-chief, Winfield Scott, and prepared his message to Congress.

What to do? Buchanan's attorney general informed Buchanan that the states remained subject to the laws of the United States while they were still in the Union. Thus, the president could collect duties and he could protect public property despite resistance; in fact, it was his duty to do so. However, he could not employ troops against elements that opposed the government only with talk, and law enforcement needed to proceed through the courts. The government could repel aggression but could not wage an offensive war against individual states; it could act only on the defensive.

At this stage, the major subjects of the day were not slavery and its expansion, but the right of secession and the use of federal coercion. In Buchanan's formulation, the right of secession was denied, but the federal government could do little in advance to stop it. The South, by comparison, believed in the right of secession and viewed as outright coercion any federal efforts to oppose it. And some Northerners felt that any secession movement could be legally put down by force. Lincoln quietly stepped into the breach, affirming that the Republicans would leave the states alone to control their own affairs. That wasn't enough, for few in the South believed it. So there was repeated discussion of the laws, repeated arguments over technicalities, and endless quarrels about constitutional points, but little was being done to halt the steady and accelerating drift toward disunion.

On December 8, in a bitter blow to the Union cause, the secretary of the Treasury, Howell Cobb of Georgia, resigned. Previously, he had been a strong Unionist, but he had come to believe that the election of a Republican justified secession; he also dissented with Buchanan's message to Congress. Cobb wrote to Buchanan: "The evil has now passed beyond control, and must be met by each in all of us." This was the first real break in Buchanan's cabinet. Then a delegation of South Carolina congressmen called upon the president and said that if reinforcements were going to

Charleston, it would be a sure way to bring about precisely what he wanted to avoid: war. They asked for negotiations with South Carolina commissioners to consider the turning over of federal property to the states, namely the US forts in Charleston Harbor. Biding his time, the president asked for a memorandum.

Two days later the South Carolina delegation in Washington spoke again with the president. This time they presented to him a memorandum saying the state would not attack or molest the United States forts in Charleston Harbor prior to the act of secession and, they hoped, not before an offer had been made to negotiate for an amicable arrangement between the state and the United States, providing no reinforcements were sent to the forts. The delegation had the impression that no change would be made by federal authorities in the military situation in Charleston. For their part, state authorities would try to prevent any premature collision. This interview later became the subject of serious dispute.

The president also moved to prepare the limited military resources of the nation for possible action. By this stage, Major Robert Anderson was frantically reporting every day or two from Charleston to Lincoln, who memorably wrote to Senator Lyman Trumbull, "Let there be no compromise in the question of extending slavery. If there be, all our labor is lost and, ere long, must be done again. The tug has to come, and better now than any time hereafter."

From all directions, while Buchanan waffled, President-elect Lincoln was exhorted to do something about the South. But to do what? Again it was asked: Make a public statement? Give a speech? Announce a program? Institute a grand gesture? Sitting in his office back in Illinois with his legs crossed, stroking his chin, Lincoln repeated in his correspondence and in interviews that he still didn't take secession seriously; "Southern Unionism" was too strong to let it take place. At the same time, he emphasized that his views on slavery were well-known. As he saw it, the frenzied state of current affairs was the work of politicians in the South who were stirring up a crisis just to scare the Republicans into making concessions.

In truth, he was concerned. One New York reporter found him reading a history of the South Carolina nullification crisis of 1832, studying how President Jackson had handled the dilemma. Jackson had issued a proclamation to the people of South Carolina, as well as threatened to hang John C. Calhoun and send an army into the belligerent state to enforce federal laws. Did Lincoln agree with Jackson? Was this a template for how to handle the South in the current crisis? He said nothing one way or the other.

Lincoln ran up a trial balloon, extending his hand to the South. He inserted a couple of conciliatory passages in a speech given by Trumbull in Springfield, affirming that the Republicans would not lay a hand on Southern slavery. The extended hand failed. The opposition press in the South declared this "an open declaration of war" against the slave states. For Lincoln, this was just as he feared; as he quipped, the South "has eyes but does not see, and ears but does not hear." He now resolved that he would say little, if anything, about the secession threat until his inauguration. Meanwhile, back in Springfield, Lincoln sat down with a Philadelphia journalist to talk about the sectional tensions. He remained optimistic. "I think, from all I can learn," he said, "that things have reached their worst point in the South, and they are likely to mend in the future." He kept telling himself that secession simply wasn't going to happen; the majority of Southerners loved the United States too much to wreck them.

On Tuesday, December 4, Buchanan reported on the state of the union, a curious message that ended up satisfying no one. He insisted that the slave states should be left alone, while laying the blame for the crisis on the Northern people and their "long continued and intemperate interference" on the question of slavery in the Southern states. At the same time, he lectured the South that the election of "one of our fellow citizens to the office of president" does not provide just cause for dissolving the Union. He pointed out rightly that the president-elect had committed no "overt or dangerous act."

Like Lincoln, the president said that he believed slavery was on the way out. Concerning the forts in South Carolina, most notably Fort

Sumter, Buchanan was strangely passive, arguing that the executive branch had little authority to decide relations of the federal government with South Carolina. In spite of that, he insisted that if there were any attempt to take the forts by force, he would defend them. Despite the fact that he was politically powerless, or at least felt that he was, he proposed a constitutional amendment recognizing the right of property in enslaved people where it existed and protecting the right in the territories until they should be admitted (with or without slavery) as their state might prescribe. In effect, however, the president was suggesting remedies nobody could live with. The North was unhappy because the president opposed secession but proposed no way to meet it; and the South was unhappy because he condemned secession.

Meanwhile, it was not just South Carolina that was agitating for change. In Georgia, the legislature issued its own call to South Carolina, Alabama, Florida, and Mississippi for delegates to be appointed to a convention "to consider a Southern Confederacy."

On December 17 the people of South Carolina gathered in the Baptist Church of Columbia, South Carolina, the state capital. South Carolinian president (Governor) David Flavel Jamison stated, "If anything has been decided by the elections which sent us here, it is that South Carolina must dissolve her connection with the federal Confederacy as speedily as possible." Then, in the spirit of the Declaration of Independence, Jamison proceeded to list grievances: "Let us be no longer duped by paper securities. Written constitutions are worthless, unless they are written at the same time, in the hearts, and founded on the interests of the people; and as there is no common bond of sympathy or interest between the North and South, all efforts to preserve this Union will only be fruitless."

That evening the South Carolinians promulgated a new resolution: "That it is the opinion of this convention that the state of South Carolina shall forthwith secede from the federal union, known as the United States of America." The question of secession passed 159 to nothing, and with that, South Carolina effectively withdrew from the Union.

In Washington, Buchanan was facing another dissolution, that of his cabinet: Lewis Cass, the secretary of state, resigned in protest at Buchanan's failure to reinforce the Charleston forts. The cabinet itself, increasingly divided, was rapidly becoming a microcosm of the nation at large.

Events now moved with breathtaking speed. On Tuesday, December 18, the South Carolina convention reconvened in Charleston. Mobs cheered and there was a fifteen-gun salute, a number corresponding to the number of slave states. The delegates gathered in a newly renovated eighteenth-century building, Institute Hall, where committee work was being hurriedly carried out for the brunt of the day. At the same time, commissioners from Alabama and Mississippi rode into town to discuss the situation.

It was on this day, as old age crept over him in the nation's capital, that Senator John J. Crittenden of Kentucky presented his "Crittenden Compromise" for the nation. It was rebuffed.

Then, on Thursday, December 20, it was done. At precisely 1:00 p.m. South Carolina, as if Crittenden didn't exist, brazenly acted on its own, dissolving the Union: "We, the people of the state of South Carolina, in convention assembled, do declare and ordain, and it is hereby declared and ordained, that the ordinance adopted by us in convention on the 23rd day of May…And that the Union now subsisting between South Carolina and other states, under the name of 'the United States of America' is hereby dissolved." A great roar went up among the waiting crowds, and the bells of St. Michael's Church tolled furiously. By a vote of 169 to 0, the convention severed the ties of the Union, and with that fateful act a joint in the arc of history was ripped apart, with consequences every bit as profound as when the colonists promulgated the Declaration of Independence. On that momentous day Benjamin Franklin had explained: "We shall now all hang together, otherwise we shall hang separately."

But in contrast to the founders' original union, secession was not achieved by collective action, but rather on a state-by-state basis. A huge sign was hung: THE WORLD WANTS IT.

Having acted first, Charleston was wild with joy and expectation. It was a warm, bright, cloudless day, and the streets were filled with immense, excited crowds sporting blue cockades, the symbol of secession. From afternoon on, cannons roared, placards announced the news, and church bells rang. Consumed with revolutionary fervor in this titanic drama, people literally danced in the streets. Public officials, giddy with Robespierrean zeal, sang "The Southern Marseillaise" and urged the formation of dreaded Committees on Public Safety, as if they were modeling themselves after the bloody French Revolution. Was this excessive? The correspondent of the *London Times* observed this: "There is nothing in all the dark caves of human passion so cruel and deadly as the hatred the South Carolinians profess for the Yankees." The enmity of Greek for Turk was child's play "compared to the animosity evinced by the 'gentry' of South Carolina for the 'rabble of the north.'"

There was not uniformity of opinion, however. Even in South Carolina, public opinion was split. Judge James Louis Petigru, a highly respected pro-Union citizen of Charleston, struggled on with the day's events. Petigru sputtered indignantly, "I tell you there is a fire; they have this day set a blazing torch to the Temple of constitutional liberty, and, please God, we shall have no more peace forever." He added that "South Carolina was too small to be a Republic but too large to be an insane asylum."

Meanwhile, in the streets the popular demonstrations of joy buzzed with exuberance and continued from early morning into the night. Military companies paraded, salutes were fired, and as evening came, bonfires were lit throughout the streets. In the distance rockets were discharged and innumerable crackers were fired off by enthusiastic boys. According to one observer, "The whole heart of the people had spoken."

It had indeed. Swiftly, the news spread elsewhere. And the rest of the South, indeed, the world, could hear the full-throated cry of South Carolina: "Free!" "Free of Yankee Invasion and abolitionists!" "Free at last!"

Meantime, back in Washington it was, as George Washington once said, "a period big with events." The news from South Carolina was deeply upsetting to Lincoln, as well as to his good friend Thurlow Weed. Upon hearing the news, Lincoln was pale and furious. Weed melodramatically mumbled to the president-elect that unless he compromised on slavery in the territories, he would have war on his hands. Lincoln, much like James Chesnut Jr., saw it differently. Weed's views, he insisted, were not those of most Republicans and certainly not his. "While there are some loud threats and much muttering in the cotton states," Lincoln defiantly said, he was ineluctably opposed to concessions that "would lose us everything we gained by the election." The best way to avoid disaster, he maintained, was through forbearance and wisdom, not to mention, as he had said repeatedly, relying on Southern Unionists like Judge Petigru in South Carolina, whom he still believed would be the saviors of peace in the end.

On December 22, a despairing Lincoln sought to nudge events in his direction. Demonstrating clearly that he was no blinkered despot, he cloistered himself away from the crowds and sat in his study to pen an urgent letter to Alexander H. Stephens of Georgia. Lincoln had served in Congress with the thoughtful man, who had made a vivid impression on him; he had long admired Stephens's eloquence and his ingrained Unionism. Moreover, Lincoln, though unable to captivate or overawe all those around him, was heartened by the fact that in November, Stephens had risen in the Georgia legislature to deliver an impassioned speech against secession, imploring Southerners to do nothing unless and until the Republicans committed an explicit act against them.

After reading Stephens's speech in the newspapers, Lincoln wrote to Stephens and asked for a revised copy. In truth, he was feeling Stephens out. Stephens explained that he "hadn't made any revisions," but took the opportunity to then warn Lincoln of the "terrible responsibilities on him" in the present crisis. Lincoln understood. Three days before Christmas, he gravely fired back with his own letter, intended "*for your eyes only.*"

"Do the people of the South really entertain fears that a Republican administration would, *directly* or *indirectly*, interfere with their slaves?" If so, Lincoln answered, delivering a heartfelt plea: "I wish to assure you, at once a friend, and still, I hope, not an enemy, that there is no cause for such fears." Indeed, the South was in no more danger than it was in the days of George Washington. "I suppose, however, this does not meet the case. You think slavery is *right* and ought to be extended; while we think it is *wrong* and ought to be restricted. That I suppose is the rub." He concluded, "It is certainly the only substantial difference between us."

"In addressing you thus," Stephens warmly replied, "I would have you understand me as being not a personal enemy, but as one who would have you do what you can to save our common country."

Common country. Those words must have rung like a bell in Lincoln's ears. Yet Stephens also resented any political party that continued to make slavery the primary issue in the country. In the end, Lincoln had undoubtably misinterpreted a dejected Stephens's understanding of the Union, for the Georgian felt that a United States upheld by force was "nothing short of a consolidated despotism." In concluding, Stephens appealed to wisdom from Proverbs 25:11 to encourage Lincoln to speak publicly on behalf of reconciliation—before it was too late. "A word fitfully spoken by you now would be like 'apples of gold in pictures of silver.'"

This baleful drama never played out, for Lincoln never replied.

On the same day that Lincoln wrote to Stephens, there were wild rumors that President Buchanan was about to surrender the three Union forts in Charleston Harbor. For a brooding Lincoln, this was a nightmare. He angrily snapped, "If that is true, they ought to hang him." Upon reflection, however, Lincoln could scarcely believe that Buchanan would actually hand over the forts to South Carolina secessionists. It would be an insult to the Union, and an insult to the national government. And Lincoln resolved that if it happened, he would make a public announcement that upon assuming the presidency, he would retake the forts in March.

"There can be no doubt," he told his good friend Billy Herndon, "that in *any* event that is good ground to live and to die by."

But this was still bluster.

As a matter of course, Buchanan didn't "surrender" anything. Two of the forts were not even garrisoned, and South Carolina seized them and ringed the harbor with guns. But a small Union force dug in at Fort Sumter, whose Union flag was the last symbol of federal authority in South Carolina. In vain, Buchanan sought to provision Sumter, but without success. Meantime, by this stage Lincoln's Republicans were convinced that Buchanan's government was brimming with secessionist sympathizers and traitors.

———————

Was war on their mind? With a blitheness of spirit, Southerners believed that Yankees were cowards and would not fight, and if they did fight, women and children alone could repel them "with pop guns." "We have no fear," an Atlanta editor brashly declared, sounding as overconfident as the near delusional kaiser Wilhelm II at the beginning of World War I when he boasted, "Lunch in Paris, dinner in St. Petersburg." Speaking for many Southerners, Senator James Chesnut of South Carolina offered to drink all the blood that resulted from secession; indeed, it became a common refrain during that secession winter that "a lady's thimble will hold all the blood that will be shed." Stephens, with his characteristic candor, believed otherwise, predicting, "War I look for as almost certain." He added, "Revolutions are much easier started than controlled, and the men who begin them [often] themselves become the victims." It happened to the once invincible French revolutionaries Jean-Paul Marat, Georges Danton, and Maximilien Robespierre, and it could happen to the Americans.

Part IV

THE TUG
TOWARD
PEACE

18

Crittenden 1:
The Hope

As both sides grew ever more entrenched, members of the US Senate increasingly waded into the debate and made their voices known in search of a solution. They pleaded not so much with Lincoln but with Kentucky's senator John J. Crittenden to be the agent of compromise and salvation—in short, to be the nation's hope for peace. "The best services of your best day will be needed as pacificator," one colleague told him. Too often forgotten is that before the Civil War, the legislative branch was every bit as powerful as the executive branch; in nearly all past crises, the Congress had forged the necessary compromises to preserve the Union. So it could happen again.

Now, as the crisis mounted, Crittenden, one of history's unsung figures, was grim-faced but calm. Recent months had not been easy. Watching the rapidly unfurling events, he was horrified; to him, this was the Union bleeding and dying. With this jolting news of South Carolina, he felt an anxiety for the nation's future that he had never felt before. A breakup of the country was threatened, and for him it was a calamity too horrible to contemplate. As he saw it, disunion would shock the civilized world, and he refused to believe that "God in his providence" would permit it. Whatever may have transpired, his heart was still full with affection for the United States and disgust for the "aggressive talk" in and out of Congress that had led to measures against the Union. Agitators, he believed, were found in all states, but in these fateful days he felt that if leaders would only retain their reason, "delusions fed by fanatics" would melt away. There were, he noted, "traitors in both North and South," but much like Lincoln, he did not think their numbers were great. Their influence, he believed, could be blunted.

So the eyes of the nation were upon him, every bit as much as on President-elect Lincoln and President Buchanan. Crittenden, now seventy-four years old, had but one ambition left: to save the United States. And to do that, he believed he had to rise above the petty spats, the endless rivalries, and the unceasing partisan politics. Indeed, he was disillusioned with party politics, disillusioned with politics as a general matter, and disillusioned with the posturing that threatened to engulf the nation. "I'm tired of public life," he wrote an old friend, "disgusted with the low party politics of the day, and the miserable scramble for place and plunder."

It was not as though he had an exalted belief in his own destiny. He did not. But there was no doubting his inexhaustible patriotism and his ability to captivate those around him. For weeks now, he had been suffering from a lethal combination of too little sleep and too much stress. True, after four decades of service, he had seen it all. His first term had begun the day of James Monroe's inaugural, remarkably enough before Daniel Webster, John C. Calhoun, or Thomas Hart Benton had set foot in the chamber, and long before any other of the present members. Yet in recent months he had aged considerably. Gaunt and self-deprecating, he was not a handsome man. In fact, he was routinely disheveled, equally sloppy in grooming, and invariably seen chewing tobacco. But, nearing the end of his final term, he was considered one of the nation's preeminent lawyers and a master of the Senate. And he spoke with such eloquence and evident sincerity that even his adversaries respected him.

To his friends and foes alike, John Jordan Crittenden's reputation as the nation's potential savior had become the stuff of folklore, and he himself had become almost a living myth. It was widely believed that his legislative mind was like a chest of drawers that could be opened and closed at will. But who was the man behind this mounting reputation? That was a good question.

Crittenden, born in 1787, was raised on the frontier of Kentucky in the fabled Bluegrass region, which was then a part of Virginia. In a curious irony, the two regions embodied the Union at large; they were separated by a mountain barrier, making their eventual split seem almost inevitable. The second-youngest child, John had eight siblings. At the age of seventeen, he enrolled in Washington Academy in Lexington, Virginia, today's Washington and Lee University. There he was exposed to a classical education: the Latin and Greek classics, Hebrew, rhetoric, mathematics, and the "reformed philosophy" of Aristotle. The idea of his education was to make him a member of "a community of the educated." But times were changing, largely spurred on by the progressivism of Thomas Jefferson. The school revamped its curriculum to one that pointed boldly to the future. Now an aura of intense Republicanism pervaded his education. More so than Aristophanes and Plato, Crittenden was suddenly exposed to Molière, René Descartes, Jean-Jacques Rousseau, and the other Encyclopedists. He read Shakespeare's plays, Edward Gibbon's *The History of the Decline and Fall of the Roman Empire*, Adam Smith's *The Wealth of Nations*, Emer de Vattel's *The Law of Nations*, William Blackstone's *Commentaries on the Laws of England*, and the *Federalist Papers*, a series of essays written by Alexander Hamilton, John Jay, and James Madison. It was a formative time for him, not just intellectually but also socially, and he frequently was a guest at private dinner parties or outdoor barbecues, as well as balls. In 1811 he married his first wife, who was from another aristocratic Kentuckian family, settling in the western part of the state on a plantation where he enslaved a number of people. That same year, he was elected to the Kentucky House of Representatives, launching a long and heralded political career. Crittenden served as a US senator on four separate occasions, was US attorney general under both William Henry Harrison and Millard Fillmore, and, from 1848 to 1850, was the governor of Kentucky.

While he never lost his sense of fealty to his home state, Crittenden was also a consummate Washingtonian. He knew seemingly everyone and was a regular at balls and social functions, living on upscale H Street and then in a pleasant neighborhood near Lafayette Square. William

H. Seward once reported seeing Crittenden, "a Washington fixture," at three galas in the same week. At Crittenden's own dinners, he served fish, venison, and oysters along with good bourbon. There was political talk. Whether the subjects were natural history or geography, matters of state or the human condition, the nature of man or the nature of government, Crittenden was always an engaging host, and his guests reciprocated in kind.

In matters of state, unlike many Southerners, he was not militant. When war was threatened with Britain over Oregon in 1846—this is too often forgotten in history—Crittenden warned against the spirit of "rash and reckless men" and the dangers of lumbering into "needless war." Later, when President James K. Polk and the Democrats declared war on Mexico, Crittenden opposed it even as he acknowledged that "American blood had been spilt, and all must now stand by the country while hostilities existed." And in 1846 he told the Senate, "War is a positive evil, even when stripped of all of its horrors."

The following year, a young congressman from Illinois, Abraham Lincoln, vociferously denounced both Polk and his penchant for war. Another Whig politician suggested Lincoln model his behavior more after the tactful Crittenden. The young rail-splitter hotly objected, insisting that he had been doing precisely that. Crittenden's conduct in the Senate, Lincoln added, had in fact been his model. "Wherein," he asked rhetorically, "is my position different from his?" What, then, was the difference between their courses, he wondered aloud in frustration, "except that he is a great man and I am a small one?"

A man of his time, who enslaved nine people yet called slavery itself "evil," Crittenden had watched with a combination of dismay and anticipation as slavery in the lower South became so deeply woven into the social fiber that people had come to regard the institution as their sole way of life and of more consequence than the Union itself. And Crittenden's Whig Party soon came to realize that however much it talked about issues like internal improvements, protection, and a national bank, the attention of the nation was increasingly riveted on the matter of slavery. Crittenden came to believe that conservative factions of the Whig and Democratic Parties could be united into a powerful new Union party, casting off the extremes of both abolitionists and secessionists. Then came Stephen A. Douglas's Kansas-Nebraska bill in the winter of 1853–54. This bill expressly repealed the Missouri Compromise, which for a third of a century had prohibited slavery in the Louisiana Purchase north of latitude 36° 30' N. The new bill provided that the decision for or against slavery would be left to future settlers, or to Douglas's "popular sovereignty," as it was called.

Few well-intended acts of Congress had inadvertently started such a tragic chain of events as did this one. Northern Democrats and Northern Whigs denounced popular sovereignty as a betrayal of a sacred agreement. Despite being shaken to its foundations, the Democratic Party managed to hold itself together, partly because its control of national patronage was a unifying influence. However, it soon became clear that the Whigs, lacking any such common bond, could not long survive. Northern Whigs, like Lincoln, could join the newly formed Republican Party, which was dedicated to the repeal of the Kansas-Nebraska Act and to the prevention of the spread of "the peculiar institution." But border Whigs like Crittenden, located in states where slavery was an accepted tradition even though it was not nearly so vital to the social and economic order as it was farther south, could unite with neither. They needed a new party, and that party came in the form of one devoted to nativism. Dubbed the Know-Nothing Party, its goal was to halt immigration, "suppress Catholics," and save America from the menace of "Popery." Lincoln detested the Know-Nothing Party because of its anti-Catholic bigotry. Fortunately for Crittenden, he had come to the party rather late and with obvious reluctance, emphasizing the Union-preserving principles of the American party's platform instead of its bigotry toward Catholics and foreigners.

Meanwhile, Crittenden, resolving to be "more of a patriot and less of a politician," was increasingly becoming absorbed in the titanic struggle to save the Union. The struggle was being waged on all fronts, from Kansas to Georgia, from New York to New England. Its focal point, however, was Washington, DC. And, as always, Crittenden was dismayed at the sharp divisions developing in the Senate: the scathing denunciations of parties and of the sections, the bitter personal insults, and the rigid, unyielding, and uncompromising partisanship. Still, more than ever, Crittenden could summon the magic in his speeches. Indeed, on the Lecompton bill, he closed with an eloquent plea for a return to the spirit of tolerance and moderation that had been demonstrated by the Founding Fathers of the republic. As Crittenden sat down, there was a deafening burst of applause that could not be quieted until John Cabell Breckinridge threatened to clear the galleries.

Crittenden hammered home the theme of unity time and time again. He insisted, "Evil generates nothing but evil. Injustice generates nothing but injustice." When he wasn't discussing morality, he was discussing practicality. He told the senators from the West that they "of all people" had no interest in a "separation," which would cut them off from markets of the world through tolls and taxes charged in New York and New Orleans. In other words, they were bound by "an everlasting and perpetual bond" to stand by the Union. If loftier motives did not demand it, then commerce did. And if commerce did not demand it, then trade did. He eloquently told the guardians of the nation "to swell the heart of the nation, to give it a dignity and consequence . . . to raise it above all the little mists and fretful policies of the day."

He had his detractors. Reviled as an abolitionist both in the South and by James Buchanan supporters in the North, Crittenden was branded by the Louisville *Courier* as "John Judas Crittenden"; even his good friend Robert Toombs denounced him as a "traitor." More than ever, he was a man without a party, even as he was determined not to be a man without a country. Ironically, as it happened, he was one of Mary Lincoln's father's dearest friends and his groomsman at his second marriage.

It was in this environment of profound agitation that the last session of the 36th Congress convened on December 3, 1860. Too often overlooked by modern lights is the fact that the majority of Washington residents were intensely pro-Southern. Government clerks and officers openly paraded in the streets with anti-Union cockades on their hats, waving their arms and hollering for secession. President Buchanan's organ, the *Constitution*, was now openly calling for the forceful prevention of Lincoln's inauguration, the first time this had ever happened.

Buchanan, "cold and calculating" (ex-president John Tyler's words), was trapped between Scylla and Charybdis. He was the retiring head of the minority wing of a divided party that had just been repudiated at the polls. And he was tugged in all directions by his cabinet. How to preserve the peace in a divided country? With South Carolina having started the machinery for secession, and with other states preparing to follow, even men who during the recent election had led the fight for Unionism in Southern states were now joining the secessionists. How, then, to present a more forceful image of his government?

In the meantime, Southern senators and representatives began pouring into Washington and started holding secret meetings in an effort to create a concerted disunion plan. What was more troubling for Buchanan, and Lincoln, too, was the fact that Southern Unionists were specially invited to these caucuses; the squeeze was being put on them to join the disunionist movement. On December 6, the senators from Mississippi, Texas, and Georgia openly said that attempts at reconciliation were now useless. On December 13, thirty Southern members of Congress agreed, wiring their constituents: "The argument is exhausted. All hope of relief in the Union...is extinguished. We are satisfied the honor, safety, and independence of the southern people are to be found only in a Southern Confederacy."

Honor. Safety. Independence. These words echoed loudly, but it was unclear what, if any, practical advantage Southern extremists gained from secession. Actually, fire-eaters were at their wit's end to explain how "Southern rights" would ensure slavery further than the federal and local laws already did. This was the rub. The matter of slavery was complicated and complex, yet at the heart of the issue was the right to expand into the territories.

But it remained a fact that this right had been guaranteed by the *Dred Scott* decision, not to mention favorable territorial legislation in New

Mexico, Utah, and Kansas. The expansionist talk, in reality, was just that: talk. Indeed, the census of 1860 showed that only 2 enslaved people were in Kansas, 15 in Nebraska, 29 in Utah, and 24 in New Mexico, 70 in all, and about half of them were enslaved by government officials on temporary duty.

Yet, fire-eaters asked, beyond numbers, wasn't the other great source of the controversy the question of fugitive slaves? In truth, it was like *Alice in Wonderland*, and here again the facts told the tale. In 1860 only 803 enslaved people escaped from the South, which amounted to approximately one-fiftieth of 1 percent of the slave population. The lion's share of this group fled from the border states, the very region where secession had least support. As a reality, it was unlikely that more than a handful of enslavers from the Deep South had ever lost an enslaved person into the Northern territories. Yet secessionists from the Deep South cited violation of the fugitive slave law most often as the grievance that had to be addressed if they were to remain in the Union. Left unsaid was the fact that as long as slave states remained in the Union, a harsh federal law made it possible for claimants to recover fugitives when they were apprehended, in addition to even kidnapping free Black Northerners.

Whatever their motives, then, it was a fair question to ask if the specter of secession was not ill-considered or impetuous or downright disingenuous. The Southerners had a rich political tradition, and a vaunted political heritage, yet (as Crittenden believed) they acted by most indices irresponsibly. In the meantime, the Republicans were guilty of their own irresponsibility.

In November 1860, the Republican Party found itself in a position to lead the country when it was not yet in control of the presidency and was a minority in the Congress. And that minority had no clearly defined program, and no real organizational leadership. As Lincoln quickly came to find, in December 1860 he had three options upon assuming the presidency. One was to compromise and preserve the Union. The second was to let the seceding states go in peace and enjoy their self-determination. And the third was to crush them by force, much as the British had sought to do with the colonists.

The Republican Party itself comprised two separate factions: One was conservative; the other was radical. Where the secretive Lincoln sat, nobody was quite sure. As Senator John Sherman said, "We are powerless here because we don't know what Lincoln wants. He communicates nothing even to his friends here and so we drift along." Seward echoed that sentiment. "I am without schemes, or plans," he wrote. "Hopes, desires, or fears for the future." Mired in the muck, the Republicans simply procrastinated. Then, on December 3, 1860, the Republicans met in their caucus and agreed on a position of what they deemed "masterly inactivity." For their part, the conservatives continued to debate the merits of compromise versus accepting secession. As for the radicals, they would have none of it. They regarded both as weakness and timidity and they came to Washington fiercely unwilling to compromise. They were animated by the words of some of their constituents, one of whom bellowed, "I think the country is ready for war," while another stubbornly asserted, "The Republican pulse speaks high for war."

As a grim reality, the truth was that Lincoln as well as his Republican leaders misjudged the secession crisis, chalking it up to bluster and bluff. Charles Francis Adams Jr. confessed, "We all dwelt in a fool's Paradise," to which he added, "We knew nothing of the South, had no realizing sense of the intensity of feeling which there prevailed; we fully believed it would all end in gasconade." And in any case, there were those like Adams Jr. who further believed (as did Lincoln; as did Lee) that the natural laws of economics would bring an end to slave labor, and that the "peaceful loss of trade may do the work which agitation has attempted in vain."

A number of Republicans vehemently opposed the spread of slavery for reasons of morality. Others were not so ethically minded. As one Illinois Republican blithely asserted, "Let them keep their n***ers if they will, but they must not bring them in contact with us."

Whatever the case, there were those like Crittenden who pointed out that compromise was in the American political tradition. Beyond the slavery issue, they noted that all the great issues of the republic, starting with the creation of the Constitution, itself a profound compromise, had been settled by give-and-take. The makeup of the Union, the location of the nation's capital, the Kentucky and Virginia resolutions, the Hartford Convention: Had not all these issues followed a regular pattern of proposal, heated resistance, and vigorous debate, followed by hard-won compromise? Had not compromise quelled the longer-term effects of the Whiskey Rebellion and then settled the gnawing Missouri question in 1819–20? Or the nullification controversy that threatened war in 1833? Or all the issues following the Mexican-American War in the years before the secession crisis?

Likewise, there were the votes for the election. True, they were cast at a time of rancor, but they were also rendered at a time of peace. And secession, if heard about at all, seemed remote indeed to most of the people of the North. It is a great what-if of history to ask whether a Northern plurality would have chosen the same platform of the Republicans if they knew it meant breaking up the Union and precipitating a bloody four-year war. In fact, it is likely that 60 percent of the people who voted against Lincoln favored compromise; it is equally likely that a sizable number of the 40 percent who voted for him also favored compromise. It is a fact, then, that an overwhelming majority of the Northern and the Southern people preferred compromise rather than either a dissolution of the Union or a protracted civil war.

What did this mean? Stripping away the angry rhetoric, the country was open to reconciliation. And so, as Congress reconvened, all eyes of the nation turned away from Lincoln, the president-elect, and Buchanan, the president, and toward Crittenden, an elder statesman, to work out the details of a compromise that would stitch the country indelibly together.

Could it work? Would it work? These were now the questions that haunted the nation.

A few days after the election, Republican papers were predicting that Lincoln would offer not Seward but Crittenden the plum position of secretary of state. In the same breath, it was also rumored that Lincoln had rushed to South Carolina to plead for delay of any hasty action toward secession. Yet another report spoke of Southern leaders preparing a statement for Crittenden that announced their minimum demands, which he in turn would discuss with the demands of Northern leaders, if not with Lincoln himself.

As this happened, Crittenden was working quietly and patiently to fashion some sort of agreement, all the while keeping himself from being identified with any sectional or partisan faction.

At stake was the future of the United States.

19

Crittenden 2:
The Great Compromise

Fully aware of the awesome responsibilities standing on his shoulders, old friends rallied around John J. Crittenden, believing he could overcome the old wounds that were opened and ritualistically nursed. One colleague urged him to "preserve yourself for that." From all across the country, people submitted proposals of compromise. One suggestion that landed on his desk spoke of dividing the Union into two equal parts. Others recommended improving the fugitive slave law. Still another suggested emancipating all the enslaved people in thirty years, while yet another suggested holding a plebiscite to address various compromise suggestions.

They all had one theme in common: They were relying upon Crittenden to "save the country." And Crittenden never lost sight of the fact that the two sides, the North and the South, shared one language, one culture, and one common identity.

During the first two weeks of the congressional session, matters began to heat up. Upon reading Buchanan's message, a North Carolina fire-eater, Thomas L. Clingman, lambasted Lincoln's election, insisting that it justified secession in the South. Crittenden rushed to the floor to refute this inflammatory message and called upon all senators to "restrain their passions" during the trying period ahead. Crittenden also took heated issue with Buchanan's contention that the federal government had no right to coerce a seceding state. In private, he was harsher, angrily bellowing to colleagues that he saw Buchanan's message as "a base surrender of the Union." Then, in a carefully coordinated measure, Lazarus Powell, the other senator from Kentucky, "moved" for the appointment of a special "Committee of 13" to consider the president's message relating to sectional issues, namely, the "protection of property and rights of citizens and equality among the states."

During the next two weeks, the Senate heatedly debated Powell's resolution. Delay was the objective. Crittenden made his way to the floor once again, this time to make a second, briefer speech, one urging that the resolution be speedily adopted. Once more, Crittenden called for restraint. Once more, Crittenden called for calm. But not everyone heeded Crittenden's call. Senator Louis T. Wigfall of Texas made an incendiary speech on December 13, praising South Carolina's efforts to secede. Stunned and angered, the radical Republican Benjamin F. Wade, of Ohio, responded with his own biting speech. He mocked the significance of South Carolina and, in what to later times would seem prescient, denied the right of secession while predicting that Lincoln would use force against any seceding states. As to the fate of the secessionists, he said they would eventually be dealt with as nothing but "traitors." Ignoring Crittenden, he renounced talk of compromise as "humiliating to Republicans."

In the meantime, Crittenden stubbornly refused to concede defeat. He searched for considerably more enduring answers to the slavery issue, consulting with colleagues of all political stripes, including liberals and conservatives, Northerners and Southerners, and enslavers and abolitionists. It occurred to him that all the compromises in the past, dating back as far as 1787, were legislative measures. As such, they were subject to change or repeal by subsequent congressional actions. Thus, the Kansas-Nebraska Act repealed the Missouri Compromise, thereby eviscerating the peace so painstakingly earned in 1850. Crittenden decided that rather than enact yet another legislative measure, the time had come to find something more permanent.

Events were moving too swiftly to prevent South Carolina from withdrawing from the country. Yet as Crittenden mentioned to his friend Orlando Brown, decisive measures might hinder other states "from following her bad example."

In an exalted mood, he came upon the idea of attaching a slew of "unamendable amendments" to the Constitution itself. There was something for everyone. Among the proposed amendments were: to guarantee slavery in the states against future interference by the national government; to prohibit slavery in territories north of latitude 36° 30' and protect it south of that line in all territories "now held, or hereafter acquired"; to forbid Congress to abolish slavery on any federal property within slave states (forts, arsenals, naval bases, etc.); to forbid Congress to abolish slavery in the District of Columbia without the consent of its inhabitants and unless it had first been abolished by both Virginia and Maryland; to deny Congress any power to interfere with the interstate slave trade; and to compensate enslavers who were prevented from recovering fugitives in Northern states. These constitutional amendments were to be valid for all time, and no future amendment could override them. These amendments, then, and not wrath or retribution, were the enduring thread that would bind them together.

On Wednesday, December 18—just as the South Carolina convention was meeting in Charleston to plan for secession—Crittenden rose to his feet in the Senate to present his proposals. There was a visible hush as he spoke, as if nobody wanted to miss a single syllable. Everyone understood that at the end of the session Crittenden would retire from public life. Everyone understood this was the climactic effort of his long, illustrious career. And everyone understood this would be the last issue on which he would be heard—whether the United States would survive or not. His five Senate terms were marked not by partisanship but by moderation. His political genius—and it was genius—was that he was as comfortable with a radical Republican or a former Whig as he was with a Southern extremist. One young Democratic congressman elbowed his way into the chamber to listen as Crittenden spoke. He described it this way: It was "as if the muse of history were listening" to Crittenden.

Crittenden explained how he prepared his proposals, how he impartially consulted with those from one section of the nation to the next, how he tried to get at the heart of the causes of discontent and the ways to remedy them. And what was at stake? "The life of this great people," he growled. So while he understood that Northerners would find it grossly unpalatable to legitimize the legality of slavery south of the 36° 30' line, that would be a pittance if it averted the crack-up of the United States, which would be, he insisted, "the greatest shock that civilization and free government have received." Without a hint of overstatement, he added that it would be greater than even the French Revolution—a revolution that upended all of civilized Europe—and even "more fatal to mankind."

He wanted everyone to give a little and everyone to get a little. And in that spirit he made it clear that his proposals were working documents that would be open to amendments, which might make them more acceptable to the nation at large. Yet with that caveat came a strict warning: If the North were to refuse a version that the South could live with, an unremitting struggle would commence and, just as likely, a cataclysmic war. Therefore, he wondered, wouldn't it be far better to settle the question peaceably on the Missouri line, which the nation had done, in effect, for some thirty years? He reminded the Senate, and the entire country, that the founding of the Republican Party was premised on the principal aim of the restoration of the Missouri line. If this proposal, or some variation of it, was not accepted, Crittenden predicted a divided country within six months. Consequently, wasn't compromise infinitely preferable? Was it not the "cheapest price at which such a blessing as this Union was ever purchased"?

At no point did Crittenden label one side right or wrong, except to note that "right and wrong, in this world, and in all such controversies, are mingled together." Once again, he called for an end to partisanship, adding that in such a crisis, party "ceases to deserve consideration." Only one thing mattered, which was the preservation of the United States, a goal that "demands our highest and our greatest exertions."

After a pause, Crittenden's exhortations began to make an impact. Both senators from Rhode Island stepped forward to make conciliatory speeches. So did James Dixon of Connecticut. For his part, John Sherman made a fascinating proposal that all the western territories be admitted to the Union as a single state, with the provision that later it could be subdivided into a number of states. In each case, they would be governed by popular sovereignty. Meanwhile, Charles Francis Adams Sr. worried that Crittenden and like-minded members of Congress from the border states would be spurned by their constituents unless the North demonstrated a willingness and spirit of concession. And if these moderates were rejected, Adams believed secession in the upper South and border states would then inexorably commence. What to do? Adams suggested a constitutional prohibition against congressional interference with slavery in the states, as well as admitting New Mexico as a slave state.

Crittenden pushed and prodded. So great was the desire for compromise at this juncture that there was not one campaign for peace launched, but two. Exhausted and heartsick at the threat to the nation, virtually all the titans of American life were now involved, including Southerners and Northerners, enslavers and abolitionists, Democrats and Republicans, and Constitutional Unionists and former Whigs, too. The House had created its own special "Committee of 33," a committee of one member from each state that would consider proposals for adjustment. The Senate quickly followed suit. A gathering of "old friends," it now formally formed the "Committee of 13," appointed by the vice president, John Cabell Breckinridge of Kentucky. All in all, this distinguished committee included four Southern Democrats, three Northern Democrats, five Republicans, and, of course, Crittenden, who at this stage belonged to no party. It included such powerful voices as Jefferson Davis and Robert Toombs representing the Deep South; Robert M. T. Hunter of Virginia; such Northern Democrats as the "Little Giant" Stephen A. Douglas; and such heralded Republicans as William H. Seward.

Even President Buchanan acknowledged that never before had a committee of such significance been created. And propelled by John J. Crittenden, on their shoulders rested the success or failure of the entire enterprise: the preservation of the United States.

———

To be sure, much was expected of the two intellectual giants on the committee, Douglas and Seward. But much was also expected of their Southern counterparts, Toombs and Hunter. With his imperious ways and his overbearing manner, Hunter was one of the most influential men in American politics. Once known as "Run Mad Tom," he was no great political philosopher. But courageous and haughty, he could rightly be considered the Danton of the Southern revolution. Many thought that where Hunter went, the South would go. If he were the Danton, then Toombs, with his broad shoulders and expressive eyes, was the Comte de Mirabeau of the South, at once ideological and at the same time practical. His words and gestures were sharp and clear-cut, and he spoke in ringing tones.

Day and night, the revolutionary tempest toward civil war raged. But so did the tug for peace. On Saturday, two days after South Carolina seceded on December 20, the Committee of Thirteen met, surrounded by the huge marbled halls and endless corridors of the Senate. From the windows of his Senate office, Crittenden could look out and see wild celebrations mingled with incipient outbursts of mob fury about the developments in Charleston, South Carolina. But he could also see that the tide of sentiment favoring compromise was now mushrooming among influential Republicans outside of the Senate and, he hoped, inside as well.

Increasingly, even radical Republicans began to waver because "anything," as one man urgently wrote to Lincoln's good friend Lyman Trumbull, "is better than Civil War."

The most significant part of Crittenden's proposal was acceptance of the line of 36° 30'.

Seward's good friend and influential mentor Thurlow Weed had already urged acceptance of this part of Crittenden's proposal. Now, with Seward's approval, Weed, his closest ally, once more floated his proposal to the Albany *Evening Journal*, where it was quickly endorsed. The influential *New York Times* followed suit, as well as the New York *Courier and*

Enquirer. Then, on a Tuesday night, a group of thirty influential New York representing a vast cross section of political outlooks, including such men as Hamilton Fish and William B. Astor, met in New York City and unanimously urged the North to adopt a "spirit of conciliation." Amid all this, Seward, now Lincoln's influential pick for secretary of state, was the most important voice of the lot. He, too, favored Crittenden's measure. One day he coolly explained to James Barbour, a Virginia Unionist, that nothing short of Crittenden's plan would "calm the South" and that he himself supported it. On December 20, while South Carolina was withdrawing from the United States, Seward stepped forward again and told a New York Democrat that Republicans were willing for the sake of peace to have the territorial question "settled by the Missouri compromise" bill running the line to the Pacific.

Seward now waited in New York for the return of Weed, who had gone to Springfield to cement the president-elect's support for the Crittenden plan.

That was now the question for the nation. Where was Lincoln?

And would he, like Seward, like Weed, like the *New York Times,* accept the Crittenden plan?

Despite all the events swirling around him, Lincoln was the picture of serenity. Back in Springfield, Illinois, he continued to radiate optimism about the South. He told a Philadelphia journalist, "I think, from all I can learn, the things have reached their worst point in the South, and they are likely to mend in the future." He kept telling himself that secession was largely talk on the part of a few loudmouthed hotheads, and simply wasn't going to happen. He also kept telling himself that any secession would be stamped out by the overwhelming Unionist sentiment in the South. When all was said, for Lincoln, the majority of his Southern compatriots loved the Union too much to take a wrecking ball to it.

Did Lincoln egregiously misjudge the temper of the Southern people? It is a telling fact that he seemed to believe the average Southerner could somehow distinguish between the niceties of Lincoln's own nuanced philosophy on the slavery question and that of sweeping abolitionists like William Lloyd Garrison or the late John Brown.

For the time, while he kept himself informed about the various congressional machinations, Lincoln began assembling his cabinet, a process that had begun with his invitation on December 8 to Seward to become secretary of state. Seward, always cagey, hemmed and hawed, replying that he would "think it over." After Christmas, with snow settling on the ground, he officially accepted. Meantime, Seward carefully studied the Crittenden plan, while over the course of a frenetic week the work of the Crittenden Committee of Thirteen continued.

In truth, Lincoln, recoiling at some of the conciliatory trends he spotted in Washington, had already taken an inflexible position against the core of the Crittenden plan, restoration of the Missouri line. Moderate Republicans such as John Sherman and Charles Francis Adams Sr. didn't know this. Thurlow Weed, on his mission to Springfield to win Lincoln's support for Crittenden's plan, didn't know this. And at the time, even Seward didn't know this. Lincoln was being cagey. When Seward left for his rendezvous with Weed, Lincoln had already informed other trusted lieutenants in the capital of his views to relay to their colleagues.

Lincoln was now unequivocal: "Let there be no compromise in the question of *extending* slavery," he wrote to Trumbull on December 10. And then in words that left little room for misinterpretation, he barked, "Have none of it. Stand firm. The tug has to come, & better now, than any time hereafter." The next day he composed essentially the same note to William Kellogg: "Entertain no proposition for a compromise in regard to the extension of *slavery*," he said. "The instant you do, they have us under again; all our labor is lost, and sooner or later must be done over."

In the same vein, he fired off a message to Elihu Washburne two days later. "Prevent," he warned, "as far as possible, any of our friends from demoralizing themselves, and our cause, by entertaining propositions for compromise of any sort, on '*slavery extension*.' There is no possible compromise upon it...Whether it be the Missouri line, or Eli Thayer's [popular sovereignty] it is all the same...Have none of it." "We are not," he said, going to let the Republican Party "become a mere sucked egg, all shell and no meat,—the principle all sucked out."

And then in words that would resonate for decades, this peroration: "Hold firm as with a chain of steel."

The president-elect and Crittenden were now talking past each other. In Lincoln's interpretation, all of Crittenden's compromise measures were ultimately designed to bring about the spread of slavery and put the country once again on the high road to a slave empire. Therefore, he was "utterly opposed" to the Crittenden plan and to any concessions on slavery in the territories, even at the price of losing the peace.

Congressional Republicans rallied to Lincoln's side. Seven plans were presented to the Committee of Thirteen, but all were resoundingly voted down, most of them getting little or no support. Only Crittenden's measure received serious consideration in Senate deliberations. Not knowing about Lincoln's communiqués, the eight non-Republicans on the committee were shocked at the rigidly irreconcilable position taken by their Republican colleagues. Tragically for them, the leadership of Seward, who was in New York receiving Weed's report, was, for the time being, missing. So for Crittenden, confronted with such immutable partisanship, it was a near impossible task. At the outset of its deliberations, the committee agreed that unless a majority of Republicans in addition to a majority of Democrats on the committee supported any proposal, then it should be considered "rejected." Put differently, in effect, three Republicans or four Democrats could veto any proposal even though all other members of the Committee of Thirteen approved.

The numerous parts of Crittenden's proposal were voted on separately. Each one got at least six votes; most got eight. Playing it safe, Davis and Toombs announced they would accept Crittenden's plan only if the Republicans did, but the four Republicans voted against most parts, including the main one, restoration of the Missouri line. At that point, Jefferson Davis also voted against it. So did Toombs. The machinations got even more curious when Toombs offered that his state would rally behind the proposal, yet he chose to vote against it himself. For his part, perhaps puzzling to future generations because he would soon become the president of the Confederacy, Davis pronounced his "entire satisfaction" with the proposal.

In truth, this exemplified how difficult it ultimately was for these statesmen to give up on the United States.

For this reason, Crittenden had been confident that his plan would receive sympathetic Republican consideration. But then the rug was pulled out from under him.

One by one, Republican members of the committee refused to support Crittenden. The measure lost by a hair, 7–6. By this stage, he was in despair. Crittenden lectured his Republican colleagues for refusing "to lower their party standard a single hair's breath," and to present their hard-line Chicago platform as their "ultimatum." Crittenden believed that the North was laboring in delusion. By spurning compromise, and believing that the South was only "bluffing," the North's best policy turned Lincoln's logic on its head and had become "to stand firm and to do nothing." This had the side effect of leaving Unionist moderates in the South alone to quell the winds of secessionist movements sweeping through the cotton states.

Yet even now, Weed, after much soul-searching, agreed with Crittenden. He flatly warned Lincoln that unless he wanted "a war on [his] hands," he must compromise on slavery in the territories. But Lincoln took his own advice to stand firm and shook his head in disagreement. Weed's views, he insisted, were not those of most Republicans and certainly "not mine," he told Seward's close ally. "While there are some loud threats and much grumbling in the cotton states," Lincoln maintained, he was still unalterably opposed to concessions that "would lose us everything we gained by the election." The best way to avoid disaster, he resolved, was through wisdom and forbearance.

Of course, wisdom was in the eye of the beholder, as was forbearance. Political genius, Otto von Bismarck once instructed, entails hearing the far-off hoofbeat of the horses of history and rising to catch the galloping horseman by the coattails. The difficulty, of course, is that one may hear the wrong horse or leap after the wrong horseman. Was this to be Lincoln's fate? Or Crittenden's?

———————

While Lincoln was peddling his message in Springfield, Seward was in New York City, where he gave a major speech at the Astor House before the New England Society. Sounding as much like Crittenden as Lincoln now, he assured his audience that the threat of secession would wane in the face of a conciliatory North. Then, once back in DC, he joined the discussions among the Committee of Thirteen. The Republicans had drawn a line in the sand, he explained; they could not and would not accept the principle of slavery expansion implied in Crittenden's first resolution. However, they were prepared to accept other measures proposed by Crittenden, including the resolutions guaranteeing slavery in the states where it already existed, as well as those seeking the repeal of the personal liberty laws. Was this enough? Not for a now-wavering Toombs and Davis, both of whom voted it down. Could they be swayed by a change in the Republicans? In hindsight, everyone agreed that adoption of the Crittenden measure would likely have prevented the secession of the cotton states other than South Carolina, which would then be isolated, staving off the beginning of a civil war in the cold winter of 1861. It remained a fact that it was the Republicans in December, every bit as much as the Southerners blithely urging South Carolina's withdrawal, who defeated the Crittenden Compromise. Patch up that problem, and the possibilities for peace were numerous. And, too, Crittenden thought, there remained the possibility of a national plebiscite to stem the tide if the Committee of Thirteen couldn't produce resolution in the legislature.

The debate was at once complicated and at the same time simple. Arguably, it was asking a lot for the Republicans to accept an enduring division of the territories into slave and free-soil sections. By later lights, and by their founding, asking that of the Republicans was a heinous moral affront. But as Crittenden knew, there was another way of looking at it.

Heated rhetoric aside, it had long been conceded that slavery would never prosper in the western territories, as there were few if any enslaved people anyway in New Mexico, Utah, Nebraska, and Washington. Already, popular sovereignty, despite all the Republican denunciations of it, was working to exclude slavery in the territories as effectively as any congressional prohibition could. However, many Republicans had taken their positions at a time when the prospect for the spread of slavery seemed an imminent problem in Kansas. Yet, in the face of a cataclysmic war and national dissolution, was it not the case that such policies were shortsighted and unstatesmanlike, every bit as much as the rash conduct of Southern extremists who were urging secession?

———————

There were anomalies and inconsistencies on both sides. By signaling that they would accept some of the restrictions embodied in Crittenden's measures, the South was actually demonstrating a willingness to countenance a restriction of the lawful limits of slavery as determined by the *Dred Scott* decision. As for the Republicans, there was a curious hollowness to their own alarums. Before Lincoln was even inaugurated, the Republican-controlled Congress swiftly passed bills for territorial governments in Colorado, Nevada, and Dakota Territory. In each case, there was no prohibition on slavery. Without a single howl of protest, the Republicans were disregarding their very own raison d'être. At the precise moment that such radicals as Thaddeus Stevens, Washburne, Ben Wade, and Sumner were howling about how Crittenden's proposal was a betrayal of their core principle—freedom—on which the nation was founded, not a single Republican uttered a word about the omission of any antislavery provisions in these bills.

A stunned Daniel E. Sickles pointed out this glaring omission and asked that the Colorado bill be read again before a vote was taken. Upon its reading, Sickles noted that the Wilmot Proviso of the Republicans had been all but abandoned. He asked for an explanation from the Republicans.

They offered not a single word.

Once these bills passed, Seward himself acknowledged that the territorial question "was settled" and that it had "ceased to be a practical question." With little hint of irony, Stephen Douglas pointedly noted, "The whole doctrine for which the Republican Party contended as . . . to the territories is abandoned. Noninterference is substituted in its place." Nor was it lost on these members that Lincoln maintained he had voted for the Wilmot Proviso forty-two times in his one congressional term.

Was Lincoln leading the Republicans, or were the Republicans leading Lincoln? We think of Lincoln as a consummate statesman, a humanitarian, a cosmic thinker, but at this stage of his career, he wasn't. In the run-up to his inauguration, he was often unable to lead some of his own subordinates. He did not routinely dwarf his own aides or offer a compelling vision, as strong presidents must. At this point, Lincoln was still seen as a plain country lawyer, or in Jeremiah S. Black's words—Black was once Buchanan's secretary of state—"small potatoes." He had not a single shred of executive experience, and he had never served in actual combat. Nor was he cosmopolitan or worldly, or, like Seward, schooled in the fineries of diplomatic arts. Nor did he have the experience of having apprenticed as secretary of state or vice president, as was the case with a number of his more distinguished predecessors, like Thomas Jefferson or John Adams or Andrew Jackson.

As to Lincoln's hesitancy to embrace Seward's desire for compromise, Charles Francis Adams said flatly that Lincoln was "ruining everything."

No doubt Crittenden would agree. With the United States on the precipice, many continued to widely dismiss Lincoln as a "guerrilla," regard him as a "third rate lawyer," and consider him a "nullity." And, too, many continued to mock him as a "duffer," a "rough farmer," and a man in the habit of "making course [sic] and clumsy jokes." Even as he meticulously assembled his cabinet, its own members derided him behind his back: Stanton called him "the original baboon," "a Western hick," and that "giraffe"; his first attorney general said he was "unexceptional"; his Treasury secretary was "openly discourteous" to him. Lincoln's high-pitched twang was an oddity in the genteel salons and artful councils of official

Washington. The real Lincoln, a curious amalgam of candor and obfuscation, country boy and learned lawyer, was alien to the city's elite. Yet here he was, in a face-off with the elder statesman Crittenden, learning his way on the job. And unknown to most of his critics, there was an even more troubling question about Lincoln: the simmering matter of his temperament, the fact that he was so prone to depression and a fathomless gloom that he once mourned, "I laugh because I cannot weep." Too often one could see Lincoln uneasily treading his way through depressed moods, hoping for a reprieve.

In the cold winter of 1861, was this the man to guide the country through its greatest crisis? The haunting question now confronting him, and the country, was ultimately no longer slavery per se or freedom in the territories, but the very United States itself. Somehow, at the hour of fate and the crack of doom, and in the sobering days ahead, both Lincoln and Crittenden would need to find themselves—and each other.

———

Weed wasn't the only one who traveled to Springfield to persuade Lincoln to accept Crittenden's compromise. A week later President Buchanan's envoy, Duff Green, carrying a copy of Crittenden's resolutions, arrived in Springfield with a similar mission. Lincoln did acknowledge to Green that adoption of the Missouri line could quell secessionist fever, although he worried the agitation would be renewed by attempts to annex Mexico. But then Lincoln made an extraordinary concession. While underscoring that he and his fellow Republicans were committed to resisting the expansion of slavery into the territories, he would acquiesce and "give full force and effect" to any decision by the people to adopt Crittenden's (and the Committee of Thirty-Three's) proposal as the Thirteenth Amendment to the Constitution. Moreover, it was to be unamendable. Lincoln wrote a letter to Green affirming all this, but instead of sending it to him directly, he sent it to Trumbull in Washington to deliver to Green, if Trumbull and "our discreet friends" thought it would do no harm.

But Trumbull did think it would do harm, and he never delivered this extraordinary concession to Green. At that point, Green gave a statement to the *New York Herald*, reiterating what he thought Lincoln's position to be, which created great consternation among the radical Republicans in Washington. They were overreacting. Lincoln met with Orville Hickman Browning and stood firmer on the territorial question than Browning had expected. The president-elect said firmly, "No concession by the free states short of a surrender of everything worth preserving, and contending for what would satisfy the South, and that Crittenden's proposed amendment ought not to be made." Ward Lehman, another Lincoln intimate, said the president-elect hoped for a peaceful reconstruction, "even after the formation of the southern Confederacy." Meanwhile, Horace Greeley later wrote that Lincoln was "the victim of a grave delusion," adding that the president-elect fully believed "that there would be no Civil War."

For that reason Lincoln saw no basis to agitate the radicals in his own party by making unnecessary concessions. They, like Lincoln, believed secession was merely a bluff. With each pronouncement, these radicals pushed Lincoln increasingly further into the war camp and away from compromise. Thus it swayed him when the radical senator from Michigan, Zachariah Chandler, insisted, "Without a little bloodletting the Union will not be worth a rush." The same when Governor Oliver Mark P. Morton of Indiana urged coercion of South Carolina. "If it was worth a bloody struggle to establish this nation," he said, "it is worth one to preserve it."

―――――――

Watching all this, President Buchanan—he was affectionately called "Old Buck"—was exhausted. It wasn't supposed to be this way. One of the most qualified men to win the presidency, he had served the nation as a tireless representative to Congress, as a gifted US senator for his state, and as an influential secretary of state. Ahead of his time, he was the first to suggest that the United States acquire Alaska from Russia. Tall and ruddy-faced, he had also been the US envoy to the courts of Czar Nicholas II and Queen Victoria. And a creature of his era, his interpretation of the

Constitution, not to mention of the presidency, was that Congress, not the White House, was responsible for forging domestic policy.

There seemed to be no easy answer for him in the matter of South Carolina: Should he act with delicacy and tact, or audacity and firmness? Should he coerce South Carolina, or compromise with her? He had appointed a cabinet carefully balanced between Northerners and Southerners, and was himself moderate in tone as well as in fact. He was careful not to disparage constitutionally sanctioned slavery and had no love for abolitionists, whom he considered rabble-rousers stirring the pot. But he was devoted to the United States. However, in his own capital, many of his own government clerks flirted with treason, wearing blue cockades on their coats, the very symbol of secession that people were sporting in Charleston. A hard worker, he was fastidious and a virtuoso with details, but, arguably, when he should have been leading he was instead burying himself in the minutiae of the office, sixteen hours a day, enough so that some have called him the "hardest working president in history." Hardworking, yes, but visionary? That was another matter. He thought the route out of this miasma was by expressing judgments that all factions would equally concede were wise and fair. However, he only got misery. In truth, he lacked the necessary art of persuasion and he ended up satisfying no one. Millions of Northerners detested him as a paralyzed appeaser of the slave power, while Southerners saw him as little more than a weak and vacillating ally. The *Cincinnati Enquirer* called him "lame and impotent," while the *Atlantic* lampooned his annual message as nothing more than "the last juice of the squeeze of the orange."

It took a toll. His hair, which had once been silky and glistening, turned all white. Increasingly feeling unwell as events swirled around him, he ceased going into his office, instead cloistering himself in his private library. There, dressed in a silk robe, he chewed nervously on an unlit cigar. Some worried that he was cracking under the strain. Lewis Cass, the secretary of state, observed that "the president is pale with fear. He divides his time between praying and crying."

20

The Forts

The original purpose of the forts in Charleston Harbor was to be part of a regional defense system, guarding the American coastline from foreign invasion. Each morning, in solitude and quiet, the sergeant on duty would raise the American flag; each evening, it would be lowered. Fort Sumter, named after Thomas Sumter, the famous Revolutionary War general from South Carolina, was designed to be one of the world's greatest fortifications. Employing all the latest military ideas, its cannon—the fort could mount 146 big guns—would be able to shoot farther and hit harder. Its walls were to be thicker and higher. And the fort itself, a brick pentagon hewn by slave labor and created from 2,423,250 blocks, was to have a foundation made entirely of rock specifically imported from quarries in New York and New England. There were two large barracks for the men, and a three-story building with offices for the commanders. The fort was designed to look out toward the harbor's mouth, to face the sea, so it would be ready to fight invading fleets out in the ocean. Simultaneously, the water itself around Fort Sumter was quite shallow, meaning deep-sea vessels could not approach the fort or its walls.

However, Fort Sumter was, in 1860, not yet complete—nor were the other forts. Major Robert Anderson, a Kentucky native and a distinguished graduate of West Point, was now in command at Fort Moultrie, located on the edge of Charleston Harbor. In November 1860, Anderson reported to Washington that once the fort was appropriately garrisoned, it would be capable of "making a very handsome defense." That was wishful thinking. The same went for Fort Sumter, which was set on a rocky shoal in the harbor and was woefully incomplete, even as work was proceeding on the mounting of guns. In truth, the two forts had been left in a state of general stagnation. Sand dunes had piled up around Fort Moultrie so that little children or even cows could walk right in, while Fort Sumter, begun thirty-one years before, languished perilously unfinished. The truth was, if beleaguered or attacked by South Carolina, which was now being "openly and publicly threatened," these US forts could not hold out for long. And they were the strategic key to the "entrance of this harbor."

With quickened tempers pushing matters over the brink, Anderson reported, "The clouds are threatening, and the storm may break upon us at any moment." He begged Washington for reinforcements, again and again, to no avail. Meanwhile, South Carolina continued to gather state troops, beginning to arm and build its own defenses.

On Saturday, December 8, a delegation of South Carolina congressmen called upon Buchanan and said that if reinforcements were going to Charleston, it would bring about the very war that Buchanan wanted to avoid. They asked for negotiations with South Carolina commissioners to consider turning over federal property to the state; Buchanan asked for a memorandum.

Two days later the South Carolina delegation came to the White House, again to speak with Buchanan. They had stated that South Carolina would not attack or molest the United States forts in Charleston Harbor prior to the act of secession. The delegation received the impression from Buchanan that no change would be made by the federal government in the military situation in Charleston.

Then, on Tuesday, on a secret mission at the behest of the War Department, Major Don Carlos Buell arrived at Fort Moultrie. He was bearing a message from Secretary of War John B. Floyd that was so delicate he had committed it to memory as opposed to putting it in writing. An ardent Southerner himself, Floyd pointed out that he had refrained from sending reinforcements in order to avoid a collision with the South, and that he felt South Carolina would not yet attempt to seize the forts. So the instructions for Anderson were straightforward: that he should not take up any position that could be construed as hostile, but that if he were attacked, he should "defend his position." However, a tour of the forts convinced Buell that Fort Moultrie was much too vulnerable and would be overrun by the South Carolinians sooner rather than later, if not by military action then by mobs. Moreover, he felt that Moultrie was of dubious military value anyway.

Instead, he concluded that Sumter was a significantly more inviting target, but that it could be reinforced to the point of being "almost invulnerable." Thus began the fateful talk of transferring Anderson's command from Fort Moultrie to what the United States hoped could become its Rorke's Drift: Fort Sumter.

In the meantime, across the South the disunionists were increasingly raising their voices. Theirs was a culture in crisis. Beyond South Carolina—the fever for the infection that coursed through the bloodstream—the Georgia legislature sought to entice Alabama, Florida, and Mississippi to send delegates to a convention to consider "a Southern Confederacy." Suddenly, talk of broader secession was no longer just talk.

For the Buchanan administration watching and waiting in Washington, there were signs of additional growing peril, notably around the three disputed forts in South Carolina. Meanwhile, the four congressmen from South Carolina formally withdrew from the House of Representatives, but in a parliamentary maneuver, their names were retained on the roll; thus, the secession of the state was not recognized. The South Carolina convention in Charleston shot back that the Constitution had been "overthrown" and that the Union was "no longer a free government, but a despotism."

Actually, in a matter of days the War Department itself was going to be in turmoil. Floyd, embroiled in scandal and politically out of step with Buchanan, was on the cusp of being forced to resign.

Meantime, touring Charleston, Don Carlos Buell knew about none of this. Instead, he would long recall the harrowing mood after the Carolinian secession ballot, the streets filled with agitators, the bonfires roaring on the corners, and the waves of patriotism sweeping through the South. On one level it was hard to imagine that this picturesque city was the epicenter of the revolution. Here was an attractive town of some fifty thousand inhabitants, where the homes were densely packed, and where three-story mansions filled with French antiques and fine European art lived next to backyard slave cottages. The American telegraph office on Broad Street downtown hummed incessantly, now working overtime, while ladies dressed in the latest fashions from New York or Paris floated along the promenade and gentlemen rode by in their horse-drawn carriages.

The porches of the homes were a portrait of seeming serenity. It was an illusion. "The very moment I passed the borders of South Carolina," Buell recalled, "I realized that I was among a people who were insane about their political rights and wrongs and were determined to fight."

Rarely had truer words been spoken. The governor of South Carolina, Francis Wilkinson Pickens, mistakenly believed that the guns of the federal forts were no longer pointing seaward, but were now ominously trained on Charleston. He cabled Buchanan, demanding that Sumter be turned over to him; otherwise, he threatened, he was not responsible "for the consequences." Hearing about this, Buchanan was outraged. So was Jefferson Davis.

In a rousing thunderclap, Seward sought to stem the downward spiral and continued his own personal quest as a peacemaker: He supported Crittenden and the Southern Unionists by proposing an amendment to the Constitution stating that Congress should never interfere with enslaved people in the states, and that in turn jury trials would be given to fugitive slaves. For his part, Anderson, who had seen too much of war, was, like Seward, trying to prevent a national Armageddon.

He cabled back to Washington, "Anything that can be done which will cause delay in their attack will give time for further deliberation and negotiation, and may, by God's blessing, save the shedding of blood."

———

In Charleston, Edwin Pearce Christy's minstrels were in town. They were singing at "Secession Hall" for the Christmas season. The minstrels, who were from New England, asked the city council to permit "colored persons" to attend their shows; in reply, this prompted angry signs by some citizens threatening "DEATH TO YANKEES." Still, the Christmas season was filled with happy tidings—readings of Charles Dickens, stores festooned with decorations, and a brisk local business along King Street selling turkeys for Christmas dinner.

Yet on December 25, Christmas Day was eerily quiet. One diarist from Arkansas wrote, "Another Christmas has come around in the circle of time but it is not a day of rejoicing. Some of the usual ceremonies are going on, but there is a gloom on the thoughts and countenance of all the better portion of our people."

That gloom continued to be shared by Major Anderson. Like Buell, he was convinced that Fort Moultrie would shortly be overrun by the South Carolinian militia, and probably in a matter of days. Sumter could soon follow. He likened his position at Moultrie to being "a sheep tied watching the butcher sharpening a knife to cut his throat." And feeling surrounded by land and by sea, he couldn't tell whether his fort was the object of surveillance or imminent attack. So with Buell's implicit support ("You are to exercise a sound military discretion"), but not President Buchanan's, Anderson made the weighty decision to secretly spirit his men from Moultrie to the unoccupied Sumter. The move, in retrospect one of the odd vagaries of history, was fraught with peril. It would take place under a full moon, giving him just enough light to make the journey across the harbor using several small boats. If discovered by the Carolinians standing watch, his cover story would be that he was taking the women and provisions to Fort Johnson. In truth, it was a dangerous gamble. To complete the ruse, he told this to his own men as well.

––––––––––

That Christmas day, without any explanation, Anderson strongly urged his officers to go to church. He knew his men were pawns in a great political chess match. He thought prayer was needed.

He was concerned that his garrison would be helpless while rowing across the harbor—the Carolinian patrol boats were still there, spying on the forts. Yet he had no choice but to take the risk anyway. Even after his men arrived at Sumter, he knew they would remain dangerously exposed for hours while they unloaded the boats in darkness, an operation that could easily take all night. To prevent them from being used against his own men, Anderson spiked the guns at Moultrie and destroyed the cartridges.

However, Anderson was foiled. The weather turned nasty. He deferred the exodus for twenty-four hours.

Throughout the morning of December 26, a misty rain fell and a cold fog hung over the beach, obscuring Sumter in the distance. It was a chill forty degrees. Meanwhile, Anderson's men steadily packed provisions—four months' worth of food and supplies, as well as medical equipment—onto boats tied up at Moultrie's wharf in preparation for moving over to Sumter. But this was risky business. For one thing, the suspicious governor had already heard rumors about twenty of Anderson's men being transferred from Moultrie to Sumter. For another, the boats the governor detailed to steam back and forth between the two forts were still keeping careful watch to prevent any attempt to garrison Sumter. Finally, Anderson received intelligence that militia units outside Charleston had begun arriving in town with scaling ladders.

Anderson was anxious, and well he should have been. He knew that in the cause of peace, a single mishap might precipitate war.

As a table in the officers' quarters was set for tea, Anderson finally revealed the mission to his officers. "I have determined to evacuate this post immediately," he gravely explained. He gave his men only "twenty minutes" to get started. Aware of the risks, one of Anderson's men, Captain Abner Doubleday, explained that "[my wife and I] took a sad and hasty leave of each other, for neither knew when or where we would meet again." The seaborne soldiers, carrying guns and knapsacks, were clad in the regulation uniform—greatcoats with brass buttons, big black hats with upturned brims, and plumes for the officers.

Company E went first, followed by Company H.

They dipped their oars into the water and began to row. Inside Moultrie, a hot beef dinner was laid out on a table. It was left untouched.

Suddenly a South Carolinian ship, the *General Clinch*, appeared. Here was peril: They were in sight of the Charleston patrol duty. The men were ordered to take off their coats and lay them over their guns to prevent any telltale reflection in the darkness. It was estimated that it would take fifteen minutes to row from Moultrie to Sumter. Anderson was clutching the American flag. Oars rhythmically dipped into the water; they continued to row.

A few minutes later, Anderson and his men could take a deep breath, as they bumped against the Sumter wharf. It was seven o'clock.

A great deal had to be done to make Sumter habitable. A barracks was promptly prepared for the women and children, but there was no bedding. They improvised, using wood shavings left by laborers. The worst seemed to be over. One man produced a bottle of brandy, and Anderson and his men toasted their fortune. Perhaps now, with enough time, Anderson hoped, cooler heads in Washington could solve this matter without bloodshed.

Anderson's men were exhilarated. One man boasted, "Tomorrow morning, the stars and stripes will be hoisted over our new position, although the sight will sting South Carolina to the quick."

And then this, as the men spontaneously shouted: "Hurrah for Major Anderson! Huzzah! Huzzah!"

––––––––––

The Charleston governor sent a representative, J. Johnston Pettigrew (who would one day cover himself with glory at Gettysburg), to speak with Anderson about his move, which he characterized as a "violation" of an agreement between Buchanan and the previous South Carolina governor, William Henry Gist. According to this prior understanding, South Carolina would make no attempt against public property in the state, while the Washington government would not "alter" the military status in the harbor. So Pettigrew asked Anderson to withdraw back to Moultrie.

His blood up, Anderson refused.

At the same time Anderson explained that his personal sympathies were entirely with the South, but stressed his greatest duty was with his role as the "United States Commander" in the harbor. The two men were at an impasse. Having resolved nothing, Pettigrew left. Then the celebration began on Sumter. The garrison was brought to parade rest, and Anderson marched out in military stride carrying the folded flag he personally brought from Moultrie. The chaplain said a prayer of Thanksgiving; having proved his unflinching courage the night before in Charleston Harbor, Anderson knelt and bowed his head, then pulled the flag upward until it cleared the walls and was caught by a stiff breeze. With the flag flapping in the wind, ten stories high, the band played "Hail, Columbia," and the men broke out into more spontaneous cheers "repeated again and again."

It was a different picture in Charleston. Irate, swayed by angry advisers, Governor Pickens resolved to take action against federal property. He sent three companies of men to take Castle Pinckney, another possession of the United States. At the governor's command the military move on Pinckney was armed aggression; it was also arguably the first overt act of a war to come. Answering Anderson's ceremony with their own, Pickens's men lifted the palmetto flag up over the first Union fortress lost in the brewing conflagration. In a poignant moment, a South Carolina officer found a sergeant's fifteen-year-old daughter weeping bitterly. The Carolinian assured her she "would not be harmed." He then dutifully patted her head. She assured him she was not afraid.

He asked why she was then crying.

She wept, then said, "Because you put that miserable rag up there."

She pointed to the palmetto ensign.

––––––––––

Fort Moultrie was the next target. It was soon seized by approximately two hundred South Carolinians slowly scaling a wall of the fort. A white flag with a palmetto on it was raised overlooking the harbor, then three rockets were fired off, signaling that Moultrie, too, was now theirs. The Charleston *Courier* wrote, "Major Robert Anderson, USA, has achieved the unenviable distinction of opening civil war between American citizens by an act of gross breach of faith."

In New York, the *Herald* said this:

IMPORTANT FOREIGN INTELLIGENCE
  Major Anderson Abandons Fort
  Moultrie and Spikes the Guns
MAJOR ANDERSON DISOBEYS HIS ORDERS

The day after, it drizzled.

The day after that, a hard rain began to fall. With almost biblical proportions, it lasted a week. The madness rousing passions on both sides was becoming an epidemic.

On Wednesday, December 26, three commissioners from South Carolina arrived in the capital by train, including James Lawrence Orr, the former Speaker of the House and an old Washington hand. In a sign of the new times, friends said they regretted to see Orr as "a foreigner." Presaging Lincoln's policy, Buchanan agreed to meet with them at one o'clock on December 27, but only as "gentlemen" rather than ministers. The talk rehashed all the familiar grievances. They got nowhere. So another South Carolinian, William Henry Trescot, who had just resigned from the War Department, then rounded up a livid Jefferson Davis and Robert M. T. Hunter to talk further with Buchanan.

They marched into Buchanan's upstairs office of the Executive Mansion. Here, Davis repeated the facts and then snapped, "And now, Mr. President, you are surrounded with blood and dishonor on all sides!"

"My God," a haggard, sleep-deprived Buchanan exclaimed, having never dreamed that Anderson would move against Sumter of his own accord. Anderson's actions, he bellowed, were "against *my* policy." Davis, the distinguished chairman of the Senate's Committee on Military Affairs and a good friend of Anderson's, had no doubt, however, that either way, the US had violated the "implied pledge" to maintain the status quo.

And he had no doubt that there would be dire consequences.

In occupying Sumter, Anderson had little idea what whirlwind of forces he had unleashed. He was now the most renowned man in the country, praised and damned in equal measure. He had unwittingly prostrated an already enervated president, convulsed the already fractious cabinet, effectively forced out the secretaries of war and interior, and fostered disgust among the South Carolina commissioners. A former enslaver himself—this was often overlooked—he created hysteria mixed with exuberance in the nation's newsrooms, inspired songwriters to lionize him, and sent a warm shudder into the hearts of millions of Northern supporters. From Maine to the distant frontiers, he fostered a wave of jubilation and provided hope to Americans who had hungered day after day for a hero to tame the renegade Southerners. Was he a hero? Peel back his shy, composed demeanor and you found a core unchastened by the events swirling around him. And in truth, he *was* a hero for a Northern government crumbling in the face of secessionism, and for spirited citizens who thumbed their noses at the "arrogant" South Carolinians and agonized over Buchanan as if he were an itchy patch of psoriasis to be somehow tolerated stoically. "You are today the most popular man in the nation," insisted one Chicagoan to Anderson. Meantime, a Boston Democrat named Leverett A. Saltonstall praised Anderson as the "*one true man*" in the country. "While you hold Fort Sumter, I shall not despair of our noble, our glorious Union."

Or as the *New York Times* cheered in Anderson's wake, "We have a government at last."

By his own lights he was simply a good Southerner who would have been embarrassed at the now ubiquitous 100-gun salutes for him, not to mention the toasts in the pubs of Boston (with beer) and the salons of Manhattan (with the finest champagne), and cheers in the capital with incessant urgings by Republicans to promote him in rank; he was to be made brigadier general. Listening to Anderson, though, he was merely a humble Army major doing his solemn duty, giving hope to the cause of peace and precious time to the peacemakers on both sides to hammer out a nonviolent solution. And standing in isolation behind fifty-foot-high brick walls at the entrance to the bay—Governor Pickens forbade all communication of the Sumter garrison with Charleston except by mail—he was unaware of all the adulation surrounding him, including the multitude of thirty-three-star flags now lovingly hoisted across the states. He was, however, not unaware of the criticisms, and he chafed at the slander and calumny hurled his way in the South Carolina convention. What stung the most was when he was called "a traitor to the South" and "a villain" to the North's angry Democrats.

Was he fated for destiny? This had to be asked. Old enough to remember the nation as a loose hodgepodge of eighteen states, Anderson was born in Kentucky in 1805 into a remarkably connected family. In an uncanny quirk of history, his father, Virginia-born major Richard Clough Anderson Sr., had fought for George Washington and against the British, from, of all places, the old Fort Moultrie in 1779. He was captured when the city fell to the Redcoats and languished nine months there in prison. Then, beyond the Revolutionary War, he seemed to be everywhere and with everyone across the growing republic. Not only had he served the Marquis de Lafayette as an aide-de-camp, but he knew the irrepressible Andrew Jackson, dined with the great orator Henry Clay, and befriended President James Monroe as well. Moreover, Anderson's stepmother was related to Justice Thurgood Marshall and Thomas Jefferson's famed explorer, William Clark.

Discreet, restrained, and modest, Robert Anderson admired "courage" and despised boasting. He had a poetic side, too, once listening to a mockingbird and telling it, "Sing on, sweet bird." Academically, he was a lackluster student at West Point, standing fifteenth in a class of thirty-seven, known less for his intelligence or wit than his sense of duty.

However, duty was the word. Upon graduation, he became a secretary to his half brother, the minister to Colombia. From there he married the young daughter of a wealthy Georgia planter, Eliza Bayard Clinch. He affectionately called her Eba. They wed on March 26, 1842, when he was thirty-six and she was just twenty. She was a Southern belle who chronically suffered from headaches, hypochondria, insomnia, dizziness, and debilitating weakness in her legs and feet. They inherited, sold, and enslaved slaves, and shared a fortune worth $7 million in today's dollars. Concluding that her condition worsened in warm climates, Eliza settled in New York City, living comfortably in a suite at the Brevoort House, a posh hotel on Fifth Avenue.

Meanwhile, for years a protégé of the venerated general Winfield Scott, Anderson launched a brilliant thirty-five-year Army record, making his mark as a distinguished war hero and a respected military scholar. He became an artillery instructor at West Point and wrote a wildly popular textbook, *Instruction for Field Artillery*, which became the bible on the subject for America's artillerists. Moreover, as a West Point field instructor, he taught such promising cadets as legendary future generals on both sides, William Tecumseh Sherman, George G. Meade, Joseph Hooker, Jubal A. Early, Braxton Bragg, and P. G. T. Beauregard. As a frontier officer he fought bravely and well; he survived cholera in the Black Hawk War, was brevetted for gallantry in the Second Seminole War, and was brevetted again in the carnage of the Mexican-American War. And with Jefferson Davis he personally transported the captured Indian warrior Black Hawk. Watching this, his fellow officer and good friend Davis called him "a true soldier and man in the finest sense of honor." Still, Anderson's health suffered, too: Wounded five times at the Battle of Molino del Rey, he had lain in a pool of blood for a time and almost died. He survived, but with a musket ball that was permanently lodged in his right shoulder, which left him in discomfort for the rest of his life. This was not the only way he suffered. He had recurring dysentery, malaria, neuralgia, fevers, chills, "boredom," and depression.

Buchanan was a furnace of emotions, unable to differentiate between passing political glances and fatal blows; Anderson, too, lacked the necessary art of political dealing. But in a thousand little ways he inspired his men. Believing that a soldier had no place in politics, his patriotism was absolute. And he eschewed voting: As one friend of Anderson's observed, "The Ten Commandments, the Constitution of the United States, and the Army regulations were his guides in life." In yet another of history's little ironies, he had sworn into the Army a lanky young Illinois recruit who served for eighty days: Abraham Lincoln. Actually, Anderson himself was a confused creature of historical circumstance, and it almost strains credulity that he entered West Point as opposed to the ministry: He hated war, insisting during the Mexican conflict, "I think that no more absurd scheme could be invented for settling national difficulties than the one we are engaged in—killing each other to find out who is right."

Anderson's hair was a dull gray, his deep-set eyes were a soft hazel, and his smile was genuine; five foot nine (he seemed taller) and handsome, he had a sweet Southern voice. And he was ruled by Southern courtesy that more than matched Jefferson Davis's and equaled Robert E. Lee's. What Anderson was not ruled by was an unwavering devotion to the spread of slavery or as a stout defender of the racist theories undergirding the "peculiar institution." It was the United States he most cared about. Curiously, he also thought he was destined for obscurity, that he would end up a simple man of "peace" or just another nameless military bureaucrat. Or perhaps one day be living in morbid seclusion as a farmer. He once noted to his wife that when future history was written, "I fancy we shall not have much ink wasted on us."

Yet as the North and the South increasingly lurched into battle, as Anderson was haunted by a tragic vision of war dividing his family, his state, and his nation, he could not have been more painfully wrong.

———

One day, while Buchanan was in one of his endless cabinet meetings on the brewing conflagration, Senator Robert Toombs of Georgia called on the president and asked what he planned to do about Sumter. Piqued, Buchanan told him the matter was still under discussion, then inquired why the question "of a fort" at Charleston should have any interest for Georgia.

"Sir," Toombs rumbled, "the cause of Charleston is the cause of the South."

"Good God, Mr. Toombs," the president exclaimed. "Do you say that I am in the midst of a revolution?"

"Yes, sir," the senator growled, adding: "More than that!"

It was a turning point for the president, made more pronounced by the reshuffling in his cabinet: The Southern members, notably War Secretary John B. Floyd, the former governor of Virginia, had resigned in December; and in January, his fifty-year-old secretary of state, Judge Jeremiah Sullivan Black; his attorney general, Edwin M. Stanton; and his postmaster general, Joseph Holt, emerged as Buchanan's most powerful advisers. Their advice was that the president was making too many concessions to the Palmetto State. Black, a longtime friend of Buchanan's, was now the foremost voice in the cabinet. Slouching and unkempt, he was a brilliant lawyer and classical scholar. Black had loyally supported the president's hands-off treatment of the South Carolinians—until now. Where he had before opposed the coercion of South Carolina, by this stage he came to resent South Carolina's mounting demands and incessant belligerence. He boldly insisted that "the Union is necessarily perpetual." And he rejected the South Carolinian commissioner's demands to give up Sumter, pressing Buchanan not only to allow Anderson to stay at Sumter but to "reinforce" him. Confronted with this pressure from within, Buchanan wavered.

Still not satisfied, on Sunday, December 30, an increasingly disenchanted Black was on the verge of quitting, with Stanton and Holt not far behind. This would leave the administration in disarray, and even raise the specter of Buchanan's impeachment.

Backed into a corner, the president confronted his secretary of state: "Is it true?" he asked. "You are going to desert me?" Black nodded: "Your action [has] driven me away."

His voice dripping emotion, Buchanan defended himself with practical considerations, arguing that with the North divided, the Army woefully small, and Congress hostile to military engagement, there was a need to avoid war. He also admitted his tacit agreement with the previous South Carolinian governor. Black was unrelenting: He had heard it all before and it didn't wash. This time, Buchanan capitulated. Now, at the president's urging, it fell to Black, with help from Stanton, to compose the administration's policy. About Sumter he wrote, "It is a thing of the last importance [and] should be maintained, if all the power of this nation can do it." He argued that Anderson "saved the country when its day was darkest and its peril most extreme." And he entreated the president to order reinforcements. Moreover, he argued, Buchanan should let Anderson know "his government will not desert him."

General Winfield Scott was on the same page, asking the roused president to send 250 recruits, extra muskets, more ammunition, and subsistence stores from New York Harbor to shore up Sumter "as secretly as possible." At this crucial juncture, the peace-loving president said yes. With Lincoln in the wings, and war looming large, there was at this stage seemingly no walking away from Sumter. Anderson would not only stay but would be reinforced, setting a precedent for the incoming president-elect. Confronted with the reality of this "massive revolution," Buchanan gazed at the crossroads tilting south and rejected it. He instead decidedly turned north.

In Charleston, however, the powder keg was lit. South Carolinians were arming themselves to the teeth. Every day and every hour and every minute counted. Catching wind of these developments—they would soon leak to the press—the commissioners promptly wired home: "We believe reinforcements are on their way. Prevent their entrance into the harbor at every hazard." So much for Scott's cherished secrecy or tamping down the emotional temperature.

The next day was January 1, 1861, New Year's Day. An Episcopal minister summed up the national mood, saying, "The year begins with feelings of enmity & apprehensions." Meanwhile, in New York hundreds of citizens poured into the Brevoort House hotel to shower praise upon Anderson, whose young son stood proudly while wearing a uniform that was an "exact facsimile" of Anderson's.

By contrast, 225 miles south, in Washington, it was gloomy and tense. All official business was suspended while the president held his traditional reception at the White House. On the surface it was a celebratory affair, but that was an illusion. A number of guests, emotionally aligned with the disunionists and believing "the sovereign state of South Carolina" had been "deceived and cheated" by a lying president, flaunted secession cockades, while others purposely insulted the president "by refusing to shake his hand." For Buchanan and his men, being in Washington was like residing in an alien universe. No wonder its most important figures were being upended by rancor and uncertainty and immobilized by lack of leadership.

South Carolina, having set itself up as a sovereign republic complete with a cabinet, frenetically continued preparations for war. The state was a whirlwind of activity with the organization of troops, incessant night patrols, guards at wharves and vessels, and sharpshooters positioned in the seaside house windows.

On Sunday, the unarmed *Star of the West* sailed from New York with some two hundred government troops and ample provisions. It couldn't arrive one day too soon, for Sumter, though four times the size of Moultrie and potentially the strongest citadel on the South Atlantic, was still in shambles. Building materials were strewn about the esplanade and littered across the wharf. The big parade was choked with piles of sand, masonry, and temporary wooden shacks to house equipment and shells scattered about. Built for 146 guns, so far Sumter had only three guns on the upper tier. By most estimates, it could be taken by a few hundred men. Meantime, as the Sumter troops furiously worked like stevedores to mount guns and plug holes, newspapers and letters brought by mail revealed to Anderson that he was indeed increasingly hailed as a national hero. A trickle of personal letters began reaching Anderson as well, growing into a river, then a flood.

Fervor was swelling in Charleston as well, but so was panic. The town was suddenly in chaos. Banks suspended payment. The surgeon general called on women to make bandages. The mail to Sumter was cut off. So was all other communication. So were even the lights. Workshops in the city frantically made new gun carriages for those Anderson had burned, and the state militia, when not busy molding its rough, untrained recruits into deadly soldiers, marched from block to block making an immediate survey of the harbor defenses.

Remarkably, the United States troops at Sumter, once the closest of friends, were referred to as "the enemy." Equally remarkable was the sight the men at Sumter saw in the distance: a bustle of activity as South Carolinian ships ferried soldiers, workmen, and armament back and forth to harbor posts.

The South Carolinians were slowly surrounding Sumter, isolating it from help.

Fatefully, the newspapers reported that Anderson had resolved to "die at his post" if necessary.

And lest there were doubters, the *Star of the West* was on its way.

21

War at Sumter?

At Sumter it was so frigid that as they walked, Robert Anderson's men could see their breath. They had only a paltry supply of coal, and fuel was strictly rationed for cooking and hospital use. The men consoled themselves with the knowledge that help from the federal government was soon to arrive.

Yet then, almost unfathomably, the *Star of the West* enterprise was badly bungled. Not only did the Southern commissioners suspect imminent reinforcement, but the operation details leaked to the press. And then Jacob Thompson of Mississippi, the secretary of the Interior, flirted with sedition, telegraphing Charleston that the *Star* was coming. In the end, just about everyone knew about the reinforcement ship's arrival at the harbor entrance on January 9 except for Anderson himself; the US War Department had inexplicably failed to get notice of it to him. After some despair and chaos, the administration sent a telegram to New York to stop the *Star* and avoid a tragic mishap. It was too late. Hastily, Buchanan and Scott agreed they must do what they could to protect the defenseless ship. So on January 7 the secretary of the Navy ordered the USS *Brooklyn*, under the command of William S. Walker, to find the *Star* and give whatever aid it could without provoking war—it had twenty-two nine-inch guns and was capable of outshooting the South Carolina batteries.

Confrontation now loomed large, and near midnight on January 8, the *Star* arrived with darkened lights. The ship waited till dawn to move into the harbor, her rustling, anxious troops concealed below the decks.

Daylight began to brighten the sky.

The officers of the *Star* were unaware that the South Carolinians were waiting for them. And the USS *Brooklyn*, the victim of the same sort of bureaucratic bungling that would later bedevil Lincoln, was nowhere to be found. As it happened, it still had not left Fort Monroe in Hampton, Virginia.

The *Star* kept going, drawing perilously within two miles of Sumter.

———

Captain Abner Doubleday was on the Sumter parapet looking through his spyglass. It was not yet 7:00 a.m. Then there was a loud boom, which came from a battery on Morris Island. Doubleday looked up as a cannon-ball arced above the *Star*. Then another, from just a thousand yards away. Here, then, were the first shots of a burgeoning conflagration between the states. Doubleday raced downstairs to the officers' quarters, where he found Anderson, not yet dressed, and reported the news.

South Carolina artillery had scored two hits and continued to fire at the *Star*. Meanwhile, Anderson ordered the roll to be called and his men to be posted at their guns. Most of them were already awaiting the signal to fire back. Normally, any firing on the United States flag would bring instant retaliation, but this situation was anything but normal, and every-one knew that.

Then another seeming surprise: The *Star*'s civilian captain turned his ship around while still taking fire. He headed out to sea and soon dis-appeared on the horizon, heading back to New York. This could have been the opening salvo of a civil war or violent revolution, but discretion eclipsed valor, and Anderson saved the day. He shouted, "Hold on; do not fire!" Even though Union men like Captain Doubleday thought it "shame-ful," and a chagrined Anderson had to swallow his pride, if not manage his rage, he did not fire back.

So the guns of Sumter remained silent. An uneasy lull prevailed.

Despite mutual charges of aggression, neither side had an appetite for war. Yet.

The ultimate fate of nations is often measured and swayed not by large events but by tiny ones—small, symbolic gestures that shape men's passions, assuage or incite their fears, and quell or inflame hostilities for years to come. On its own, John Brown's raid did not cause all the North-South tensions over slavery, just as Lincoln's election was principally a proximate as opposed to the sole cause. But such events are catalysts, sparks, or symbols that ignite a series of chain reactions on the much longer, rutted road to war or peace. More than anything else, Sumter was a catalyst, sending the nation either over the abyss or to salvation.

The more Anderson thought about his predicament, the more he believed some decisive action was needed. At a minimum, he regarded South Carolina as "a spoiled child that needed correction." He considered closing the harbor with his guns and firing at any South Carolinian vessel that came within range, which, in itself, would be an act of war. Yet, in the end, he thought twice about that, too. In a civil war, or bloody revolution, he could barely stomach the notion of kinsman killing kinsman, American killing American. Nor could he stomach the fact that his home state of Kentucky would be a side casualty, becoming a killing field with neighbors holding guns to one another's heads. He was also horrified that his move to Sumter had hastened other states into secession. When he first arrived in Charleston, the hope was that the secessionist contagion could be isolated to South Carolina, but now Mississippi and Florida had joined her, with Alabama and Georgia and then Louisiana not far behind. So instead, he collected himself and hoped to seal off the hostilities. He wrote to the South Carolina governor, expressing his view that this naked aggression was carried out without South Carolina's "sanction or authority." But the one hand was clearly not talking to the other. Speaking the language of war, four South Carolina artillery experts drew up a report for preventing Union reinforcements from reaching Sumter as well as "reducing" the fortress.

Even as the administration was divided and uncertain, Anderson found it difficult to believe the North would take up arms against such a powerful segment of the South, just as for many it seemed incomprehensible that a portion of the South would challenge the full might of the federal government.

Governor Pickens once again sought to negotiate with Anderson and, after deftly bluffing the North, worked out an uneasy truce, giving him precious time to get Southern batteries in place. In Abner Doubleday's opinion, things were going from bad to worse. By his reckoning, negotiation had become war by other means, and Anderson was allowing the South Carolinians to surround the fort without lifting a finger against them.

The Charleston *Mercury* added to the bellicosity, writing, "Yesterday the 9th of January will be memorable in history. [Charleston] has spoken from the mouth of her cannon...she has not hesitated to strike the first blow, full in the face of her insults...We would not exchange or recall that blow for millions! It has wiped out a half century of scorn and outrage."

––––––––––

The garrison at Sumter was now suspended in an indefinable netherworld, neither peace nor war. No one could yet estimate its duration or determine its significance. What they knew was this: January was cold. There was a constant chill rain and a floating fog, and the fort was often enshrouded in a gray mist. The men shivered violently, and they were hungry, too. Day after day, they stared at their breath and scavenged for warm clothes. The quartermaster made an inventory and found alarming shortages. There was barely any salt or sugar or coffee. Soap and candles were almost gone; the same with beans, hard bread, tobacco, and whiskey. So the men, as if under siege, endured half rations of coffee and a paucity of coal, not to mention sunlight; the walls were so high that on the days when the sun shined, it peeped in for just a few hours. If ever anyone had a reason to complain, these men had it.

But they did nothing of the kind. Almost jauntily, Anderson described his command as in "excellent health" and "in fine spirits."

His men were becoming as famous as the 300 Spartans: Not a day went by when speeches weren't made about them in the halls of Congress, or when they weren't mentioned in church sermons and college lectures, or in arguments on street corners. These men couldn't be expected to divine the machinations of politicians in Washington, but Anderson was acutely aware of this: His men were a palpable symbol, seventy troops representing the entirety of the United States in a hostile South Carolina harbor.

Yet, as a sign of the ambiguity of the situation, on January 20, moved by the plight of Anderson's semi-starving men of Sumter, Governor Pickens sent a boat from Charleston carrying precious provisions from what was now referred to as the sovereign Republic of South Carolina. Here were two hundred pounds of red beef, bags of turnips and potatoes, and other staples these hungry men had been dreaming about since they fled Moultrie a month earlier.

A detail of troops began hauling the provender into the kitchen, only to have Anderson hotly send it back, insisting that he was not about to "take charity."

"Charity?" Many wondered, how long could this hostile truce last? Amid the long winter nights, Anderson had the simmering suspicion that he would have to be withdrawn, or there would be no escaping eventual war on *his* watch. Yet, back in Washington, Secretary Joseph Holt instructed Anderson: "You will continue, as heretofore, to act strictly on the defensive." Meanwhile, the work of war continued. Sweating and swearing, South Carolinian slaves now labored by torchlight night and day to build merlons between the guns at Moultrie for protection from Sumter's fire. Another group was building a huge new battery for eight guns at the northern tip of Morris Island, just thirteen hundred yards from Sumter's weakest point, its unarmed gorge wall. This was the equivalent of the doomed picket fence manned by the Tennesseans at the Alamo.

This was where the Union could fall in the blink of an eye.

Anderson was changing his thinking as well. Now that a whole bloc of Southern states had seceded, he had come to believe that war would be not only monstrous but hopeless—that instead of reuniting the states, it would fatally divide them. Better, he reasoned, to let the seceding states go in peace, and hope that wiser, more careful minds would eventually bring them back. Otherwise, the nation would be washed in blood and cleaved in eternal hatred. War, he was convinced, would be national suicide. It was better to accept the inevitable, he thought, and evacuate Sumter after all. But as long as he was ordered to hold Sumter, he resolved to do his duty: He would defend it to the last, despite his belief that there would be fateful consequences if strife were forced upon him. In such a scenario, he was convinced that his detail would be overcome by the sheer numbers, and "not a soul will...be found alive in the ruins" of Sumter.

And all this would be wrought by Charleston, the Rome of the South, which, with a population of less than fifty thousand, still acted as if it were a powerhouse like New York, Philadelphia, or Baltimore. War preparations continued. Charleston's aristocrats began raising money for volunteer companies to fight. The women began dutifully scraping lint for bandages and sewing soldiers' uniforms. To them, there was no doubt as to what the result would be. After the *Star of the West*, South Carolinians were in agreement that the Yankees were afraid to fight. And even if they did fight, their numbers were paltry, as was, they believed, their courage; the Carolinians knew that Anderson had only some seventy men, while the state forces now numbered in the thousands. Wealthy planters were also loaning the people they enslaved by the hundreds to work on the Charleston batteries. Headstrong and cocksure, the planters now asked themselves: Didn't Anderson know what was in store for him? Didn't he know he was surrounded by an overwhelming arsenal?

And at home in the South, they wondered why the governor hesitated. Why not attack without delay?

With equal audacity, some felt that now was the time for Virginia and Maryland to abandon neutrality and capture the capital of Washington, taking over the reins of government.

22

Washington and Dissolution

Back in a perturbed Washington, others were nervously asking this question as well. It was a breathtaking sight: Signs of disintegration were everywhere. Washington had become, according to one observer, a "frightened city," dreary and anarchic. Many up north now predicted the South would seize the capital, a city that seemed to be falling apart anyway. Terrified husbands began sending their wives and children away to escape violence. Some carried household items with them: bedding, cooking utensils, heirlooms, china, rugs, family furniture, and tintype photographs. Others stayed but retreated behind shutters and drawn blinds. Increasing numbers of Southern congressmen were making their farewells; leaving by train, they carried heavy trunks and suitcases and crowded the railway station. While the mansions of the old Southern aristocracy were closed, their Southern plantations awaited them. In Washington their trains pulled away, jerking and clacking; their whistles blew, then they vanished in a puff of smoke. And there was the ominous sight of Southern officers of the Army and Navy who followed them, masking their emotions with exquisite politeness while handing in their resignations and taking leave. Washington seemed less like George Washington's hallowed republic than a bewildered ancient Roman outpost being assaulted by Huns.

While Anderson's men languished in Sumter in a state of not quite yet war but not quite peace any longer, John J. Crittenden also continued to be a rallying cry for people across the country. Not a day went by that Crittenden didn't receive bundles of mail in the Capitol post office exhorting him to stand up for peace. They were letters or parcels, packages or envelopes, some wrapped in twine, others with brown paper, coming from all over the nation. The residents of Harrisburg and Carlisle, Pennsylvania, both conservative towns, were the first to send mass petitions urging Crittenden to stand firm. And the petitions kept coming. Now they came from Illinois and from Philadelphia, and then from all across New England. Two petitions arrived from New York City, bearing some sixty-three thousand names. Not to be outdone, the people of St. Louis sent a petition filling ninety-five pages of "foolscap paper," which was wrapped in the American flag. With equal ardor, Massachusetts sent a scroll so massive that it had to be rolled like a cartwheel onto the floor of the House. Crittenden was particularly proud of the petition he received that was signed by a staggering fourteen thousand women—even though they couldn't vote—in states from Vermont to North Carolina. Crittenden told the Senate, "I hope their interposition may have some influence upon the sterner nature of man."

Despite the January cold, massive outdoor rallies were also held on Crittenden's behalf. In Philadelphia, on a snowy night, six thousand "workingmen" gathered outside Independence Hall and unanimously endorsed Crittenden's plan with a rolling cascade of cheers.

The burdens of pending war were becoming more palpable. In the days after Lincoln's election, the stock market at first sputtered, then halted; then it plunged outright. Wealthy bankers watched their investments dive as much as 30 percent. If the market were in a free fall, so was the morale of textile manufacturers and their shareholders. Terrified at the prospect of watching the South's cotton shipments dissipate, they saw their stocks fall almost 50 percent. The economic picture was equally bleak for steamboat lines and western merchants. It remained a real likelihood that commercial shipping would be barred from the entire lower Mississippi. How long? For a month? Six months? A year? Longer? No one could say. If that weren't distressing enough, would the debts of Southern planters become uncollectible, or waived altogether?

Factories up north quickly felt the economic sting as demand for new goods evaporated. Predictably, they did their best to retain workers, but the burdens were too great, and they began cutting them loose. Soon, tens of thousands of workers were laid off, grumbling and unhappy. The *Boston Courier* grimly reported: "Boston streets to-day are full of discharged workmen. Our laboring population have a dreary winter before them."

Reinforcing these sentiments, an ad by E. Williams & Company in a New York newspaper was anything but subtle. It stated:

In consequences of the
PANIC! PANIC! PANIC!
We are determined to offer our very large stock of fall importations for the balance of the season at such prices as will command an immediate sale.

W. J. F. Dailey & Co. was equally pointed in its fears:

Owing to the troublesome times into which our country has
Fallen we have made a
FURTHER REDUCTION
In our prices, in order to convert our goods into cash before the
UNION GOES TO PIECES!

Wall Street and Crittenden now seemed joined at the hip. On a cool January day, a rumor reached Wall Street that Crittenden's compromise measures "had been agreed to unanimously." The market promptly soared, only to plummet when the news proved inaccurate.

Yet, in the days that ensued, Crittenden kept plugging away, and as a groundswell of support for his efforts mounted, so did stocks. Then a high-powered group of Wall Street financiers and businessmen, headed by Hamilton Fish and others, journeyed to Washington to urge Republican leaders to compromise on the question of war. There they gave a dinner at the Willard for some eighty Republican members of Congress.

———

It was a tug-of-war. In Washington, there was the ultimate horror: talk of an impending coup d'état against the federal government, a generalized popular uprising against the "official imbecility" that was allowing the nation's inexorable slide into disaster. Meanwhile, footsteps in the streets were heard. They were of militia units forming, hastily at first and, to be sure, improvised; they donned uniforms by night and drilled in the remote corners of the district, swearing that they would rather see the capital "reduced to ashes" than to allow Lincoln—"a black Republican"—to be inaugurated as president.

As the days passed, Crittenden was confronting not just secession fever in the South and anarchy in the capital, but now in the North as well. New York's mayor, Fernando Wood, announced his support for secession, both in the South and in New York City itself, which would become an "independent trading republic" composed of Manhattan, Staten Island, and Long Island. To the astonishment of Lincoln and the Republicans, Wood's idea was endorsed by the New York City council, as well as by leading businessmen. Said one: "I would have New York a free city," to which he added, "not a free city with respect to the liberty of the negro, but a free city in commerce and trade."

Alliances were found in the unlikeliest of places. At a packed meeting in Boston, noted abolitionist Wendell Phillips now celebrated not the integrity of the Union but the withdrawal of the slave states. "The Covenant with Death is annulled," he declared. "The agreement with Hell is broken to pieces. The chain which has held the slave system since 1787 is parted."

Phillips paused, then added with a flourish, "All hail, then, Disunion."

Controversy stalked Phillips for this speech. Love for the Union still ran strong. The *New York Times* lamented "THE UNHOLY

ALLIANCE" in which the abolitionists gave the "Right Hand of Fellowship" to the disunionists. Phillips's next appearance was a few days later at the annual meeting of the Massachusetts Anti-Slavery Society. Every seat was taken. The balconies were packed. The minute Phillips opened his mouth, he was drowned out with cheers for Crittenden and songs for the Union. The audience began stomping its feet, making barnyard noises, jeering, and hissing at the top of their lungs. They even played several stanzas of "Dixie." Not appreciating the storm to come, Ralph Waldo Emerson was the next speaker. Carrying a stack of notes, he stepped up to the stage, where he was mocked and booed off the platform. The pandemonium soon got out of hand, and it fell to the Boston mayor to clear the hall before it became a full riot.

That didn't stop crowds from flooding the streets, or several hundred incensed rioters from chasing Phillips back to his house on Essex Street. Policemen did their best to hold the mob back. They failed. The crowd, in a rapturous mood, shouted at Phillips, "Carve him out!" They brandished brickbats and waved their fists in the air. Boston toughs were suddenly everywhere, and just as suddenly the mob was the master of events. And to his chagrin, Phillips became a prisoner in his own home, notwithstanding the bodyguards standing permanent watch outside his front door.

Back in Washington, a sense of mounting alarm began to speed through the city. Rumors were rampant. The real Crittenden, humble, patriotic, dignified, was carefully monitoring the pulse of the American public in the North as well as the South. He worried that the situation was becoming ever more dire, and in a profound sense, it was. His was a warning about the destruction of the system, the United States, the victim of an infant revolution poised to go awry. Like Saturn—like so many revolutions—it seemed destined to devour its own. Increasingly desperate and worried, Crittenden never missed an opportunity to take to the Senate floor brandishing his latest petitions or his most recent words in support of the Union. One evening, he bravely hosted an elegant dinner party for thirty luminaries at the National Hotel, a headstrong, fractious mix that included an illustrious set of guests—distinguished senators and congressmen from both parties, justices of the Supreme Court, and even General Scott. Still, Crittenden failed to make the necessary headway. So he then made an unprecedented proposal: He suggested that rather than address the compromise package in its entirety, Congress should instead submit it to a nationwide popular referendum.

The people, Crittenden said, were the source of government power and "should be heard from." Although such a procedure was unprecedented, he said preservation of the Union was cause enough "to depart from tradition." He tried to sweeten the deal with two new constitutional amendments, which had originally been suggested by Stephen A. Douglas. One would bar free Black men from voting in elections or holding public office, while the other would guarantee that if any state wished to eliminate its free Black population entirely, the federal government would pay to have them shipped off to Africa or South America. (However outlandish this may seem to modern sensibilities, President Lincoln would embrace a comparable policy in 1862.)

For those who questioned the cost of such a policy, Crittenden dismissed it as merely "a little atom which is to be sacrificed," or nothing more than "barley corn." To his dissenters, he shot back with a wry post about the whims of war: "Peace and harmony and Union in a great nation were never purchased at so cheap a rate." And to the partisans, he said that while the nation was being destroyed, "we are spellbound in our party politics, and in opinions which they've generated and fastened upon us against our will." As Crittenden sat down, Douglas jumped to his feet and offered his support of this unique proposal.

Increasingly, North and South, everyone was digging in. Every cartload of petitions supporting compromise—Crittenden also received the endorsement of President Buchanan—was weighed against the grassroots fervor of die-hard partisan Republicans seeking to contain slavery within its present bounds. While Lincoln had carried the nation as a whole with less than 40 percent of the vote, his partisans noted that all but three of the Northern states had provided him solid, if not overwhelming, majorities.

They dug their heels in deeper.

On January 7, Crittenden gave one of his strongest speeches to date. He conceded that South Carolina had indeed acted "irrationally," for there "is no right of secession." Her conduct had been nothing less than "revolution" and "a lawless violation of the Constitution." Laying a foundation for Lincoln's later actions, he said a constitutional right to destroy the Union would indeed be a "strange provision" for any government; after all, the Constitution was "a grand and inviolable instrument upon which no man should lay his unhallowed hand." Those who would do that were nothing more than "revolutionists," hiding behind the "little subtitles of law." Finally he explained, much as a father would to his children, that the Republicans' constant denunciations of slavery could not have any other effect than to make Southerners "fear for their very society."

There were moments when Crittenden hovered close to despair. To his dismay, radical slave state senators were drunk with their own success. Even as he had sought to explain their precarious dilemma, they coldly rebuffed the Kentucky statesman, and increasingly they indicated that the Crittenden plan would not satisfy them. Were they two-faced and double-dealing? Or were they ideologues? What is clear is that as an answer to Crittenden's plans, Senator Louis T. Wigfall of Texas proclaimed a "Southern Manifesto." Wigfall declared the debate "exhausted." He added, "All hope of relief in the Union...is extinguished, and we trust the South will not be deceived by appearances or the pretense of new guarantees...We are satisfied the honor, safety, and independence of the southern people require the organization of a Southern Confederacy."

More than ever, the nation was in convulsions.

Even moderate Northerners found themselves embracing secession and losing faith in the United States intact. A weary George Templeton Strong, who had long been hoping for a compromise, was fed up. He noted in his diary that all the slave states now seemed to be tilting toward secession. "But what can we do? What can I do?" he wondered. "What could I do if I were Webster and Clay combined? Concession to these conspirators and the ignorant herd they have stimulated to treason would but postpone the inevitable crisis a year or two longer."

Having maintained a strange silence for days now, Seward, outside of Lincoln the acknowledged spokesman of the Republican Party, announced he would take to the floor. By now it was common knowledge that while Seward refused to support Crittenden's proposals outright, he sympathized with them. The galleries were filled early. Seward, with his slouching figure, his casual manner, and his disorderly hair, was disarming from the start. Actually, few men in the Senate were as astute or agile in politics as this shrewd former governor turned senator, soon to be the first member of Lincoln's cabinet. Unlike Sumner, for example, he was ill at ease with pomposity or extreme oratorical flourishes; nonetheless, it was he who coined the ringing phrase "irreconcilable conflict." And today? With a cigar perpetually hanging from his mouth, his heavy brows furrowed, he sized up the crowd. He spoke for two hours, sounding much like Crittenden as he emphasized the horrors of disunion and civil war and vigorously urged "reconciliation." He made a dramatic offer to divide the territories into one part free and the other slave, which was more of a practical concession than even Crittenden's plan had called for.

As Crittenden heard this, the strain was too much. He was overcome with emotion. He bowed his white head and wept unashamedly. Then he sought to bring his resolution to a vote, but it was once more postponed by critics.

———————

Suddenly, however, it was clear that Crittenden's tireless efforts were making an impact. Thurlow Weed pronounced Crittenden's plan "fair and reasonable," and for weeks he commuted between Washington and Albany, urging Republicans to support it. The Albany *Atlas and Argus* agreed, demanding that both Northern and Southern extremists be "crushed out, by the patriotic, Union-loving sentiment of the country."

Then from Indiana came good news. It was reported that Crittenden's compromise would be endorsed there by a majority of fifty thousand votes. On January 7–8, conventions of both the Constitutional Union Party and the Democratic Union Party in Louisville also endorsed Crittenden's proposal as "a fair and honorable adjustment." Ten days later the Kentucky legislature urged Congress to also approve it. So did the Virginia legislature and the Delaware legislature. In Philadelphia, a week later, approximately six thousand workmen shivering in Independence Square at night during a violent snowstorm voted unanimously to endorse it. Much around the same time, in Mayfield, Kentucky, one of the largest meetings ever held there endorsed the compromise with "unparalleled unanimity." The same for a record-sized meeting in Van Buren, Arkansas. Even in Boston, the board of aldermen unanimously adopted resolutions thanking Crittenden "for his services" and inviting him to visit there as a guest of the city.

And originating everywhere from Kentucky to Maine, a flood of resolutions and petitions poured into Congress. On the week of January 21, Seward himself presented a petition from New York containing almost 40,000 names; this was in addition to a previous petition presenting 25,000 names.

Around this time, Crittenden and Douglas held a secret meeting with Seward. Playing it close to the vest, they never revealed the precise outcome of their get-together. But in his private correspondence, Seward was blunt. "Two thirds of the Republican senators are as reckless in action as the South," he wrote on January 13. In a Republican caucus he attended several nights later, he was disgusted that there was not one word said "to disarm prejudice and passion." In his view, Lincoln's closest associates were radicals who were telling him that compromise was not necessary to hold the Union together.

Distraction ruled the day, Seward averred passionately. Then, in one of his most memorable phrases, he spit out the encomium for the hour: "Mad men North, and mad men South," he said, "are working together to produce a dissolution of the Union by Civil War."

––––––––––

Monday, January 21, was a heartrending day, as five senators from Florida, Alabama, and Mississippi withdrew from the chamber. Their final speeches were filled with reluctance and determination, disappointment and sorrow. Stephen R. Mallory of Florida teared up as he called for "reason and justice" over "party and passion," and blasted abolition-ist Northerners for their "wickedness and folly." David Levy Yulee, with regret drawn across his face, stressed he had no choice but to follow his home state of Florida. Clement C. Clay Jr. of Alabama dwelled on the years of difficulty that had led to the present crisis. Benjamin Fitzpat-rick, like his Florida colleague, acknowledged his loyalty to his sovereign state. By this stage in the Capitol Building, there were effectively two rival assemblies embarking on a struggle for power and even survival.

Then came Jefferson Davis of Mississippi. Where Davis went, it was believed so would countless others from the South. The "hero of Buena Vista," a former member of the House and once secretary of war, Davis was tall, slim, dramatically handsome, and saturnine. It was not a fore-gone conclusion that he would leave the Union. By Southern standards, he was often liberal and astonishingly idealistic; much like Lincoln and Thomas Jefferson, he did not believe slavery was the permanent condition of Black people. "The slave," he said, must be made "unfit for slavery" and "must be made fit for his freedom by education and discipline." Saddled with an aloof and obstinate streak (Sam Houston, the Texas governor, thought Davis "cold as a lizard"), Davis could be warm and cordial in pri-vate. Yet deep within him also lurked a haughty vein that was uncomfort-able with the give-and-take of politics. Always a furnace of emotions, he got into unnecessary, even trivial quarrels, and had difficulty differentiat-ing between meaningless glances and fatal blows of politics.

In a number of ways, Davis was quite advanced for his time and place. He strongly supported the transcontinental railroad, free trade, and edu-cation, even helping to set up the Smithsonian. He took a progressive line on just about everything—that is, everything except the intertwined issues of Southern rights, states' rights, and slavery. He was a confused, even tragic creature of historical circumstance, flexible on just about everything except the greatest issue of his time: slavery. Yet, with his erudition and sonorous Southern voice, Davis was capable of delivering stem-winding, off-the-cuff speeches that quickly earned him the respect of his colleagues and the attention of the country.

By 1861 he was a sickly man, having suffered from malaria, pneumonia, habitual facial pains, chronic pain from a war wound, severe earaches, and eyesight that was permanently impaired by prolonged exposure to the blinding snows of the western frontier. All told, he was frail, gaunt, and agitated, with a recurring facial tic.

Many thought his ties to the North would outweigh his affection for the South; indeed, fire-eaters feared that Davis would succumb to "the dread spirit of reconstruction." It was a curious fact that in the days leading up to the speech, he had spent his time speaking on behalf of building a transcontinental railroad.

On January 20, Davis received notice that Mississippi had seceded. Now it was his turn to make his voice heard, but he was feeling unwell and frail. Moreover, he hadn't slept in days. He delayed his farewell speech to the Senate until the next morning. Yet he was so sick, not to mention "inexpressibly sad," that he could barely walk to the Senate chamber. Once there, he saw that every available space was taken. If people couldn't sit, they stood. If they couldn't find room to stand, they perched themselves on the floor. Finally, "in a state of mind bordering on despair," he started to speak. It was a moment that all the people there would never forget— the severing of the United States, right before their very eyes.

Dressed in black broadcloth appropriate for the occasion, the ailing statesman, "pale and evidently suffering," began, at first in low and deliberate tones, but as he continued, his voice gathered in force, becoming louder and clearer, "like a silver trumpet." A great hush fell over the chamber. Spellbound, everyone was hanging on each word. It was not his best speech. It was not his most inspiring speech. But it was at once historic and memorable.

Though he had long advocated "compromise" and "delay" as a way out of the crisis, today he planted his feet irrevocably with the Southern secessionists. His functions, he said, his hoarse but musical voice breaking with emotion, "were terminated here." And this: "I concur in the action of the people of Mississippi, believing it to be necessary and proper." His peroration continued, tearing at the hearts of virtually everyone who was there.

"I feel no hostility to you, senators from the north. I am sure there is not one of you, whatever sharp discussion there may have been between us, to whom I cannot now say, in the presence of my God, I wish you well."

He steadied himself for a moment and continued. "Mr. President, and senators, having made the announcement which the occasion seemed to me to require, it only remains for me to bid you a final adieu." With that, with a grave countenance, he gave his farewell to the Senate that he had served so ably for so long. Then his voice faltered and cracked. There were tears welling in his eyes. All was quiet in the chamber as everyone listened to him in "deep silence," periodically broken up with ringing applause. Davis appreciated it and then there was nothing left to do but leave. Surrounded by colleagues shaking hands with him, he made his way toward the exits. His wife, Varina, wrote that he was "inexpressibly sad" and "grief-stricken" as he left the chamber with but "faint hope."

And as for that hope? That night she heard voices coming from the drawing room.

She heard Davis praying for peace.

Varina Davis asked her good friend, Elizabeth Blair Lee, if she would be going down south "to fight her." Elizabeth advised her husband, "I told her no. I would kiss & hug her too tight to let her break any bonds between us."

It seemed no one was immune to the strain of the looming crisis. Charles Francis Adams Jr. was stunned when he saw the normally upbeat Seward. He hadn't seen him since the previous September, but he felt Seward looked "thin and worn," and "ten years older than when I had left him at Auburn." Indeed, when Davis and his four fellow Southerners slowly made their way up the aisle toward the exit doors, the whole chamber went silent. Legislators choked back tears and spectators sobbed in the gallery. Democrats and a few moderate Republicans lined up to shake the five men's hands and to wish them godspeed.

In the weeks that followed, Louisiana became the sixth state to secede, and in New Orleans business came to a standstill amid talk of war. On Tuesday, January 29, Kansas was admitted to the Union as the thirty-fourth state, while on February 1, Texas voted for secession.

Questions now stalked the nation. How long would the seceded states be gone? Was it in earnest, or like Lincoln still believed, a gamble or a bluff? What about the Southern convention that was now called for in Montgomery, Alabama? What about the peace convention that would soon gather in Washington? Could it roll things back? What about Buchanan, or his successor, Abraham Lincoln of Illinois? What would his policy be: Immediate action? Or wait? And what about the eight other slave states on the "border": What direction would they follow?

Four years earlier Lincoln had asserted bluntly, "All this talk about dissolution of the Union is humbug, nothing but folly." For those wanting compromise, Lincoln's insouciance was alarming. Actually, he had spoken with the Ohio journalist Donn Piatt, who later wrote: "He considered the movement South as a sort of political game of bluff, gotten up by politicians, and meant solely to frame the north. He believed that when the leaders saw their efforts…were unavailing, the tumult would subside." And this: "'They won't give up the offices,' I remember he said. 'Were it believed that vacant places could be had at the North Pole, the road there would be lined with dead Virginians.'" The total failure to perceive the Union on the brink of dissolution was, as one historian put it, "the cardinal error" of the Republicans.

Yet it remained a fact that once Texas seceded, the momentum of secession began to sputter, until it was seemingly spent. True, seven slave states had left the Union, but eight others had not. The slaveholding states were far indeed from forming a politically united South. However, while South Carolina was not stranded and alone, the Gulf Coast Confederacy lacked the population, resources, and wealth of the slave states that were still in the Union.

February 4, 1861, was an epic day. On the same day on which the incipient Confederate Congress assembled at Montgomery, and on which a Peace

Conference, with 21 of the 34 states in attendance, convened in Washington with the mandate to explore "every reasonable means" to avert a dissolution of the Union, Virginians went to the polls to vote in delegates for a state convention. Noticeably, only 46 of them were secessionists, and 106 were moderates. Seward had long maintained that secession was "a temporary fever" that had passed its climax, and events seemed to bear him out. On February 9, Tennessee voted against calling a secession convention, with Unionists getting more than three times as many votes. Nine days later Arkansas favored a convention but elected a majority of Unionists as delegates. In Missouri, Unionists vastly outpaced secessionists once again, and the same thing happened on February 28 when North Carolina rejected secession. Then secession lost out in three other slave states: Maryland, Texas (Sam Houston resisted pressures to call a special session of the legislature), and Delaware.

As exhilarating as the early winter of 1860–61 had been for secessionists—they had built a southern republic within a space of forty-two days—now it was depressing. Since February 4, secessionists had gained not a single success. While the month witnessed the birth of a seven-state Confederacy, it also saw the hopes of a larger Southern republic completely "demolished." Virginia, the "mother of all states," "the birthplace of presidents," was the key to everything, and it was unclear which way Virginia was going to go.

———————

The Second Continental Congress deliberated for fourteen months before declaring American independence in 1776. Devising the United States Constitution and establishing the new government required more time: two years. In stark contrast, the Confederate States of America organized itself, drafted a new constitution, and set itself up in Montgomery, Alabama, all within three months of Lincoln's election.

How was the South able to move so swiftly? Secession proceeded on a state-by-state basis rather than by collective action. Haunted by the lesson of 1850, when the Nashville convention dwindled into hesitancy and hindrance rather than secession, this time around fire-eaters were determined to see the secession of several states first, thereby establishing a fait accompli, and only then calling for a convention of states. After Lincoln's shocking election, the soil was ripe for disunion. Of course, it was South Carolina that acted first. In turn then, with "flushed faces," "wild eyes," "screaming mouths," and "jubilant demonstrations," it was followed by seven more: Mississippi on January 9, 1861; then Florida on January 10; Alabama on January 11; Georgia on January 19; Louisiana on January 26; and Texas on February 1. Even so, there remained a conservative group of "cooperationists" who were, in effect, "conditional Unionists" who were asking fellow Southerners to give Lincoln a chance to demonstrate his moderate inclinations. These Unionists included such distinguished men as Lincoln's friend Alexander H. Stephens. However, even they were swept along by the rush of events. As Judah P. Benjamin of Louisiana noted, it was a supreme challenge for "prudent" men of the South to "stem the wild torrent of passion which is carrying everything before it." Benjamin added, "It is a revolution...of the most intense character...And it can no more be checked by human effort...than a prairie fire by a gardener's watering pot."

But there still remained a silent majority of Southern Unionists. Was it a strong enough foundation to build a faith in Southern Unionism? That was the question for Lincoln, Seward, and Crittenden. The other questions: Was secession constitutional? Or was it an act of revolution?

23

The New Confederation

As Americans increasingly wrestled with the issue of secession, they quickly realized there was no clause in the Constitution that established the Union's perpetuity. Where the Articles of Confederation contended that "the Union shall be perpetual," the Constitution only spoke of "a more perfect Union"—actually, Charles Pinckney's draft resolution containing the provision "the Union shall be perpetual" was never even brought before the general body for consideration. Where the Constitution was framed in the name of "We the People," Article VII firmly declared that it would be ratified "between the states." In the end, to the degree that there was a discussion about the perpetuity of the Union, there was no clear consensus. No less staunch a Federalist than James Madison wrote, "Each state...is considered as a sovereign body independent of all others, and only to be bound by its own voluntary act. In this relation then the new Constitution will...Be a *federal* and not a *national* Constitution."

In truth, the wording of the Constitution gave neither the believers in the right of secession nor the early advocates of a perpetual Union a decisive case. As it happened, the founders, hoping for the best, had left the question of perpetuity to posterity, and the most common perception of the Union was that of George Washington: America was "worth a fair and full experiment."

But now the experiment was being torn asunder.

Moreover, each state had formed a state constitution *before* petitioning

Congress for admission to the Union. And putting the constitutionality of secession aside, many, including Unionist Southerners, believed in the rights of revolution established by the French when they violently toppled the Bourbon dynasty in the 1790s. Senator Alfred Iverson Sr. of Georgia actually conceded that states did not have a constitutional right to secede, but they did have "the right of revolution... The secession of the state is an act of revolution." For his part, the mayor of Vicksburg agreed, considering secession "a mighty political revolution which [will] result in placing the Confederate States among the Independent nations of the earth." Even Southern military officers insisted that they took up arms "upon a broader ground—the right of revolution. We were wronged. Our properties and liberties were about to be taken from us. It was a sacred duty to rebel."

On February 4, 1861, six hundred miles away from Washington, DC, in warm and sunny Montgomery, Alabama, Confederate delegates convened in the state capitol building to discuss the new republic. After a flurry of resolutions, amendments, and substitutions, their efforts seemed to be a model of accomplishment. In under a week they fashioned a temporary constitution and turned themselves into a provisional congress to oversee the new government. They elected a provisional president and vice president and then launched themselves into the effort to devise a permanent constitution as well as set up the machinery of government. In contrast to the United States, the constitution weakened its president and vice president by allowing them to serve only a single six-year term and to govern along with a bicameral congress. But even as it took away from the presidency with one hand, it gave with the other, conferring a line-item veto upon the presidency. And there were no political parties. Shrewdly, in these discussions, the radical fire-eaters hung back, thereby projecting a moderate image to Virginia and the upper South. Many from the South still believed, like Lincoln, that secession was merely a bluff and assumed that the Southerners had left the Union only temporarily in order to get better terms for themselves inside it.

For the most part, the opposite was true, as the delegates of Montgomery sought to outdo one another in their zeal for the permanency of the break from the North.

Most of the provisional constitution, as well as the permanent one adopted a month later, was copied almost verbatim from the original Constitution. There were departures, significant in style and also substance. They omitted the critical phrase calling for "a more perfect union" and added a clause after "We the People": "each state acting in its sovereign and independent character." Instead of the US Constitution's fudging about slavery—"the persons held to service or labor"—the Confederate version outright called an enslaved person a slave. It guaranteed the protection of bondage in any new territory the Confederacy might acquire. At the same time, it forbade the importation of enslaved people from abroad so as to avoid alienating Britain and especially Virginia and the upper South, whose economy was dependent upon a monopoly on the export of enslaved people to the lower South. It took a different tack on tariffs, permitting them for revenue but not for the protection of domestic industries. This new constitution also solidified states' rights by allowing legislatures to impeach Confederate officials whose duties lay completely within a state.

The largest share of interest in the convention focused on who would become the provisional president. There were many who craved the job, particularly fire-eaters. Interest, however, coalesced around three moderates, Toombs, Stephens, and Howell Cobb, all Georgians. But Toombs was not only a former Whig—Lincoln's original party—but also a drunkard. Stephens, a late convert to the cause, was suspect to most Georgians; and Cobb's candidacy just seemed to fade away. Then word was passed down from Virginia that its senators favored a West Point graduate who actually preferred to be the commander of the Confederacy's army: Jefferson Davis. Few delegates knew him well, but they knew him well enough, or at least felt they did. A secessionist but not a radical, Davis seemed to be the very picture of the ideal candidate. There was one problem, however.

He did not seek the job, nor did he want it. On February 9, the delegates elected him unanimously anyway.

Davis was pruning rosebushes with Varina at his plantation home back in Brierfield when he received the news from a messenger. He was stunned. Yet, however reluctant, he was driven by a sense of destiny and an unyielding fealty to duty. He accepted. The cry went up, "The man and the hour have met!" The vice presidential nod went to Alexander H. Stephens, who to most was a small, slight man whose stooped posture and gaunt facade made him appear unwell and much older than his forty-nine years. The next day Davis bade farewell to his family and enslaved people before hopping on a boat alone for Vicksburg and then eventually to Montgomery. Presaging later problems, and making twenty stops along the way, the trip was difficult due to lack of a direct railroad, poor traveling accommodations, and the haste with which the journey was made.

In Vicksburg, the Confederate president-elect made the first of many brief speeches, declaring he had "struggled earnestly to maintain the Union" and the "constitutional equality of all the states."

He added, "I hope that our separation may be peaceful. But whether it be so or not, I am ready, as I always have been, [to shed] every drop of my blood in your cause."

On February 16, it was official. A tired and worried Davis—actually, he was hesitant to rush into secession—was introduced to a large, cheering crowd in Montgomery while "Dixie" played. The radical's hour was now over; sensible men, not fire-eaters, would carry out the revolution made by others. Davis made a short, impromptu, and incendiary speech, fatefully declaring, "The time for compromise has now passed. The South is determined to maintain her position and make all who oppose her smell southern powder and feel southern steel." With this, cannon boomed and the crowds were delirious, while an actress named Maggie Smith danced on the United States flag.

Just as a great debate took place at the Philadelphia convention in 1787, so did one take place in Montgomery over the admission of new states to the Confederacy. When the delegates, ambitious men, completed their Southern constitution, they considered the Confederacy founded and themselves founding fathers.

Two days later Davis gave his inaugural address. This one was more peaceful, as he assured the North that the Confederacy wished to live in harmony and warmly outstretched its hand to those who "may seek to unite their fortunes to ours." Without a doubt, his task was an immense one. Born out of conflict, this fledgling Confederate nation was riven by rancorous factions, endless bitter disputes, and savage feuding. Also the striking lack of political parties meant that Davis had no organized structure with which to cultivate discipline or institutionalize loyalty. A martyr to its own ideology of states' rights, the Confederacy was saddled with a political system unsuited to the grim challenge of taking on the herculean industrial North. And it seemed as if the Confederacy was foolishly destined to repeat many of the mistakes of the early American republic, and that Davis would have to contend with struggles over men, money, and supplies that had nearly ruined George Washington in the 1770s.

Moreover, Davis insisted that secession was not a revolution, as asserted by many confederates: Such logic, he noted, was "an abuse of language." They had left the Union, he thundered later, "to save ourselves *from* a revolution." Davis's executive management was questionable, he lacked the necessary art of persuasion, and he was not only frequently ill, but short-tempered and autocratic. However, his expertise in military affairs was considerable, and the day was rapidly approaching, it seemed, when that would be needed. Moreover, and perhaps most importantly, Davis had guts—and a kind of religious, even mystical belief in his new country. The question was raised: Was he now acting like a dreamy madman? Or a crazy zealot? And did he not realize what was to come?

The point was moot. Having crossed the Rubicon, Davis got on with the business of governing and the weighty task of organizing a new nation—as well as enlarging its size and defending its borders.

24

To Washington

On the day that Davis departed Mississippi, February 11, 1861, Abraham Lincoln, the president-elect of the United States, was also boarding a train, going eastward. By all accounts, it was a moment freighted with emotion. Tears in their eyes, crowds assembled to see Lincoln off at the Great Western Depot in Springfield, Illinois. It was damp and biting cold. Then it began to drizzle. Like Davis, Lincoln was departing for a long trip to *his* capital, in this case, Washington, DC. More than one thousand citizens shuffled their feet and stood quietly in the rain. Lincoln himself was surrounded by his family and secretaries, by dignitaries and Army officers, and he shook hands with each of them. The murmuring crowd called for a speech, and despite his frequent awkwardness at improvising, Lincoln obliged them with some impromptu, poignant words. At times shaking with emotion—actually, he was "pale and quivering"—he spoke out in his reedy voice. "Here I have lived a quarter of a century, and passed from a young to an old man . . . I now leave, not knowing when, or whether ever, I may return, with the task before me greater than that which rested upon Washington. Without the assistance of that divine being, whoever attended him, I cannot succeed. With that assistance I cannot fail." Now there were tears in his eyes.

He continued, "Trusting in him, who can go with me, and remain with you, and be everywhere for good, let us competently hope that all will yet be well. To his care commending you, as I hope in your prayers you will commend me, I bid you an affectionate farewell." With that, under the rain-streaked sky, the train rolled slowly eastward across Illinois and Indiana, huge and enthusiastic crowds collecting at each stop.

Meanwhile, Lincoln, faced with the perilous situation, "sat alone and depressed" in his luxuriously decorated private car.

And the train ride was not without risk. Various authorities had warned Lincoln of plots to capture him or assassinate him en route. So it was determined that Lincoln's wife, Mary, and their sons should catch a later train, joining him in Indianapolis.

With flags and streamers snapping in the wind, the presidential train puffed across open country at thirty miles an hour. Lincoln would travel first across Ohio, then western Pennsylvania, back to Ohio again and across New York State, then down through New Jersey, Pennsylvania once more, and on to Washington, DC. Lincoln, fussed over by William Johnson, "a colored boy" who worked as Lincoln's hired servant, spent most of his time in the presidential coach, which was outfitted with heavy dark furniture, a rich red carpet, and tassels.

The train continued to chug its way through innumerable villages and towns, with crowds lining up all along the way waving Union flags as the coach of the president-elect swept by. For twelve exhausting days Lincoln stared out the train window, pondering the secession crisis. In the larger cities Lincoln attended receptions and gave speeches. Some were from the platform of his coach; some from a hotel balcony; some from the steps of a statehouse. Wherever he went, wherever he spoke, people wanted to know what he would do about the crisis. As always, Lincoln was hesitant to speak on this, concerned that any utterance might ignite the unsteady border states, Virginia most of all. Lincoln instead assured the audiences he would make an explicit statement of policy in his inaugural address. But the people were anxious. They pressed him time and time again to make a speech or at least a statement. So against his best wishes, he was forced to comment. But because he was actually a poor extemporaneous speaker—hard as that is to believe all these years later about the president who gave the world the beautiful words of the Gettysburg Address and the two inaugurals—he invariably needed a written script. So his remarks were often rambling, incoherent, or downright banal.

In truth, even at this late date he remained confused about the Southern problem. Exhausted and unsure of himself, he was still unable to comprehend the extent of what was happening in the Deep South.

In Indianapolis, thirty-four guns fired into the air before Lincoln emerged to face an ecstatic crowd of more than twenty thousand people. He delivered a meditation on "coercion," which provoked loud cheers and sustained applause. Meanwhile, in Washington, DC, itself, 480 Army soldiers and 240 Marines positioned themselves around the city to protect Congress, as the Electoral College vote was to be read aloud on February 13. General Winfield Scott warned would-be obstructionists or insurrectionists that there must be calm. "I have said," he bellowed, "that any man who attempted by force or on parliamentary disorder to obstruct or intervene with a lawful count of the electoral vote for president and vice president of the United States should be lashed to the muzzle of a twelve-pound cannon and fired out of a window of the capitol."

How dangerous were these conspiracies?

In Columbus, Ohio, Lincoln received a welcome telegram that the twelve-pounder was not needed; the electors had met peacefully in Washington and made his election official. Frederick W. Seward gaily reported, "The votes have been counted and the capitol is not attacked." The actual count itself—180 for Lincoln, 72 for Breckinridge, 39 for John Bell, and 12 for Stephen Douglas—was read by the forty-nine-year-old vice president, John Breckinridge, who in 1864 would be part of a Confederate army that attacked the federal Capitol. Meanwhile, the House Speaker had gaveled the chamber back to order, declaring that the "danger inside had passed." That was not quite true, as mobs, pounding their fists in the air, roamed the boulevards, as there was "much street-fighting," and countless "arrests by the police" were made. For many, a chaotic Washington resembled a "despotic European government" filled with "glittering swords and bayonets...and beribboned soldiers." But as Vermont's Lucius E. Chittenden noted, there was "no revolution."

And Lincoln himself, attending a lavish military ball, enthused: "There is nothing wrong...We entertain different views upon political questions but nobody is suffering anything. All we need to do to overcome the present difficulty is 'time, patience, and the reliance on...God.'"

In Pittsburgh, Lincoln addressed the crowd in a heavy downpour while the horde shielded itself with umbrellas. Lincoln's tune was the same: "There is really no crisis except an *artificial one*" whipped up by "designing politicians" in the South, a crisis that could never be justified from the Southern view. If people on both sides would only keep their "self possession," the crisis would clear up on its own.

In Cleveland, Ohio, people stood for hours in the snow, rain, and deep mud to hear him. Why, he asked, are Southerners so incensed? "Have they not all their rights now as they had ever had? Do they not have their fugitive slaves returned now as ever? Have they not the same Constitution that they have lived under for seventy-odd years?...What then is the matter with them? Why all this excitement? Why all these complaints?"

And that was how it unfolded as he lurched from one stop to the next. The crisis was artificial. If the South were simply left alone, matters would take care of themselves. Lincoln did not, in this formulation, have to save the country; the country would "save itself." Thus, it was not up to the president, but to the people to preserve the Union. However, if it were needed, he insisted that he would "put my foot down firmly."

On February 16 the presidential train hugged the shores of Lake Erie until it paused at Westfield, New York, just long enough for Lincoln to kiss a little girl named Grace Bedell, whose sole contribution to history is that she entreated Lincoln to grow a beard. The train then sped eastward toward Albany, where Lincoln was given the inauspicious news that back down in Montgomery, Jefferson Davis had been sworn in as president of the Confederacy, with none other than Lincoln's good friend Alexander H. Stephens as his vice president. Hearing this, Lincoln recoiled. He took this news hard, and in Albany, he admitted to the crowds that he was exhausted. "I have neither the voice nor the strength to address you at any great length," he muttered at the statehouse; meanwhile, the police and soldiers held back the restless crowd.

From there his train made its way to New York City, where sophisticates and opposition newspapers had a field day. They mocked the president-elect for being a "provincial hick." They mocked him for his "awkward gestures." They mocked him for being a "Western gauche." They mocked him for saying "inaugeration" and "sot" for "sit." And they mocked him for wearing black kid gloves to the opera and hanging his "huge ugly hands" over the rail of his box. How, they cried out in protest, could this "baboon" be our president? But it was here that Lincoln put his foot down, conceding that he would never "consent to the destruction of this Union."

The presidential train continued, this time across New Jersey, where it passed through neat little villages speckled with weathered whitewashed homes and handsome churches filled with worshippers. There, the engineer clanged the bells repeatedly, so that children and livestock would get out of the way. At Trenton, Lincoln spoke again, and from there it was on to Philadelphia, where the Founding Fathers had crafted the Constitution. There he checked into the Continental Hotel to attend yet another "packed and noisy reception." Then, invoking the founders, he spoke of the Declaration of Independence, which provided "hope to the world for all future time."

That evening, around eleven o'clock, Norman B. Judd summoned Lincoln to his room for "a secret meeting" with Allan Pinkerton, a Chicago private detective who also worked for the railroad. Pinkerton spoke with a slight Scottish accent enhanced by his trademark whiskers and darting eyes. Eschewing small talk, he informed Lincoln that his detectives had uncovered a well-organized plot in Baltimore. Why Baltimore? Because it was a rabid secessionist city bristling with pro-Confederates, assassins and spies, and dangerous "Plug Uglies." Lincoln's original plan was to change trains in Baltimore, but according to a beautiful female Union spy who went by the code name "Mrs. Cherry," the insurrection was intended to kill him when he took his carriage from one station to the other. Pinkerton and Judd were both firm in the belief that the conspiracy was real, and Lincoln had no choice but to take a train for Washington that night. Even Washington was a risk, they said, as secret societies were springing up throughout the region "geared for action"; there were whispered plans to blow up the Capitol, seize the arsenal and Navy Yard, and destroy telegraph wires and railroad tracks.

Lincoln adamantly opposed Pinkerton and Judd's plan. "Whatever his fate might be," Lincoln insisted, he would not "forgo his engagements for the next day," which was Washington's birthday. He was scheduled to speak at Independence Hall in the morning, where the founders had signed the Declaration of Independence; and Harrisburg in the afternoon, and he was loath to cancel either. Hoping to get some sleep, he returned to his room, where there was a knock on the door.

This time it was Seward's son, Frederick, who had just arrived from Washington, DC, bearing an urgent letter from the secretary of state and General Scott confirming that there was "definitely a plot to kill Lincoln in Baltimore" and that he must avoid the city "at all costs." He was chagrined at the fact that the nation was so torn asunder with such extreme emotions that its own president was the target of assassination "by his own people."

The next morning Lincoln woke up to celebrate Washington's birthday on February 22. Before an audience at historic Independence Hall, he spoke with considerable passion about the Declaration, pointing out that it was this key document that underpinned all his political ideals. His reading of history was that the founders did significantly more than achieve American independence from Britain. They also struggled mightily for the Declaration's abiding principle that gave "liberty, not alone to the people of this country, but hope to the world for all future time." It was for this purpose, these succeeding generations, the world at large, that Lincoln felt so strongly about saving the Union now—to preserve the noble promise of democracy. With great feeling, he added, "If this country cannot be saved without giving up that principle"—Lincoln then hesitated for a moment—"I was about to say I would rather be assassinated on this spot than to surrender it."

That afternoon, on the train to Harrisburg, politics surrendered to pragmatism. Judd cornered Lincoln and relayed to him a clandestine getaway plan that had been worked out with Army officers and railroad officials they could trust. It would work like this: At dusk, a special train would spirit Lincoln off to Philadelphia, where he would be ushered in disguise aboard a sleeping coach. A night train would then take it to Baltimore and another would take it to Washington "in secret." Meanwhile, on the next day, Judd and a carefully chosen military escort would protect Lincoln's family.

The president-elect was horrified at the idea of sneaking into Washington, but he capitulated to Judd's scheme, thereby, in his words, running the risk "where no risk was required." When a panicked Mary learned about these plans, she pitched a rage. She asked, what if Lincoln were murdered? What if she "lost him," whom she loved more than "life itself"? Mary at least insisted that Ward Hill Lamon travel with Lincoln and protect him with his own life. The faithful Lamon agreed. Heavily guarded, Lincoln would also be accompanied by Kate Warne, a Union spy who mingled easily among seditionist Southerners, and whose slogan was "We Never Sleep."

———

That night, Lincoln slipped on an overcoat and, disguised in a soft brown hat, slipped into a waiting carriage in West Philadelphia. He was accompanied by Lamon, who carried two large knives, two derringers, and two revolvers. Suddenly, they heard footsteps in the dark.

A Southerner? Plug-ugly?

No, it was Pinkerton himself, coming to help sneak the president-elect into the last sleeping car of the Baltimore train. There he climbed into a berth reserved for "the invalid brother" of Pinkerton's spy, Mrs. Cherry. But the berth was so short Lincoln had to draw his knees to his chest, and as the train raced forward, he was unable to sleep. Tossing and turning, he was haunted by ghastly images of mobs in Baltimore sacking the presidential coach bearing Mary and the boys. He could hear his name being screamed out in the night. He could see fights with soldiers and gunshots. He desperately tried to rest, but it was in vain. At 3:15 a.m., the train crawled into the empty streets of Baltimore and left Lincoln's car at Camden Station, where it would be picked up by the night train. Despite the hour, he heard a drunken voice singing "Dixie": *"I wish I was in Dixie. Hooray! Hooray! In Dixie Land I'll take my stand. To live and die in Dixie!"* It had been a difficult night for Lincoln; he hadn't slept at all.

Then there was a hiss and a squeal, and Lincoln's car lurched out of Camden Station, hooked to the Washington-bound train. On Pinkerton's order, all the telegraph wires were cut between Harrisburg and Washington until it was clear that Lincoln had arrived safely.

At dawn on February 23, the train glided slowly into Washington and the beautiful dome of the Capitol came into sight. Lincoln had finally reached DC. Accompanied by Congressman Elihu Washburne from Illinois, he immediately rode to the Willard Hotel, which stood at the corner of Fourteenth Street and Pennsylvania Avenue, within sight of the White House. Lincoln hadn't been in Washington in more than twelve years, but much remained the same. The Treasury Building was unfinished and there were stacks of building material piled all around the Capitol. On the bank of the Potomac, a white obelisk of marble punctuated the horizon: It was the unfinished monument to Washington. And Washington was a dirtier city than Lincoln remembered. Scrawny pigs still rooted in the dirt streets slanting off from Pennsylvania Avenue, and the city was also less attractive than he recalled. In every direction there were night saloons, hookers, and a plethora of livery stables. South of the presidential mansion lay sewage marshes and open drainage ditches, reeking with pestilential odors, not to mention dead cats and "all kinds of putridity."

Lincoln couldn't help but notice that some Black people were already up and hard at work, their patchwork of shanty huts, pitched tents, and run-down skeletons masquerading as homes clinging to the fine Southern-style mansions. Wherever he looked there were weed-choked ruins, vacant lots, and trash, not to mention squalor and excrement. Finally, having turned down lodging at the elegant Blair House on Pennsylvania Avenue, Lincoln arrived at the Willard, a massive cake-like structure that was known for its carved oak, running tap water in every room, and the key congressional deals brokered there while senators breakfasted on oysters, roast pigeons and robins on toast, and eggs. And it was here, in "Suite 6," his shadow Oval Office, that Lincoln would stay until the inauguration.

Lincoln was advised that he was now "public property" and ought to be where he could be reached "by the people until he is inaugurated." However, there was a downside to being where people had access to him. On the desk in his room, Lincoln found a threatening letter waiting for him. "If you don't resign we are going to put a spider in your dumpling," it read ominously, "and play the devil with you." More statements of intimidation followed, concluding with the chilling epithet: "You are nothing but a goddamn Black N***er."

The opposition press had a field day with Lincoln. It was New York all over again. They highlighted scathing cartoons about "the flight of Abraham" and relentlessly made fun of him. One story claimed that he snuck into Washington wearing a long military cloak and a scotch-plaid hat, and the Northern press simply repeated it. *Harper's Weekly* went as far as publishing a cartoon that showed Lincoln as a flimsy scarecrow, clad in a Scottish kilt, awkwardly dancing.

Spearheaded by the Democrats, the smear campaign about this "backwoods president" and his "boorish" wife was never-ending from the very start. Even one of Lincoln's cabinet members, Edwin M. Stanton, spoke maliciously about how Lincoln had "crept into Washington." Meanwhile, it was the same old story: Lincoln was derided as "illiterate." He was "crude." He was a "hick," unrefined and ill prepared for the subtleties of diplomacy. Lincoln took it all in stride, seeing it as part of the job description. Mary, stung by the criticisms, was a different story. She considered Lincoln brilliant and gifted, fated for greatness, so she absorbed the hurts.

Inaugural week was a circus for Lincoln. Suite 6 now became a bustling outpost. An unceasing flood of delegations came by to discuss

Southern policy as well as cabinet choices. So there was Buchanan and his cabinet (whom he met at the White House); there were senators, congressmen, and other statesmen. And there was none other than his great rival, Stephen A. Douglas himself—Douglas was, by now, dying—who came to Suite 6 with a dire request. Looking the president-elect straight in the eye, Douglas pointed out that they both had children, and pleaded with Lincoln "in God's name, to act the patriot, and to save our children a country to live in."

But how?

By endorsing the Washington Peace Conference.

Largely lost to history, the convention was now looming as the last best hope of averting war.

Part V

PEACE OR DISSOLUTION?

25

The Peace Conference

The Peace Conference opened on a chilly and wintry day, February 4, 1861, the very same day the Confederates met to draw up their constitution in Montgomery. With a blanket of snow on the ground, Lincoln would conduct business in one part of the Willard Hotel while the Peace Conference was held in another wing. For five days, hotel staff had prepared for the august meeting—polishing silver, cleaning crystal, dusting rooms. In the great conference room (formerly a church) known as Willard's Hall, three oil portraits of eminent Americans were hung: George Washington, Andrew Jackson, and Henry Clay. The conference was the brainchild of Virginia, the most important state in the South and among the most important states in the nation. All but a few Northern states answered the call. California and Oregon did not because of distance; and Michigan, Wisconsin, and Minnesota did not because of partisanship: Their Republican leaders distrusted the whole enterprise.

But the rest of the states came of their own volition, and for those sitting on the fence, Seward persuaded them to come as a gesture of "goodwill."

Amid much fanfare, delegates, eventually numbering 131 members from more than twenty states, assembled in the winter of 1861 with thoughts of the summer of 1787, the time of the Constitutional Convention, foremost on their minds. The delegates were an impressive array of leaders, a collection of deeply respected statesmen and national figures suffused with wisdom and perspective. In addition to former president

John Tyler of Virginia, who was there as a matter of duty—actually, he was feeling "very unwell" and was heavily medicated with "mercury and chalk"—there were a staggering sixty-four former senators and congressmen, nineteen ex-governors, twelve Supreme Court justices, a number of ambassadors and war heroes, no less than former senator Salmon P. Chase (soon to be Lincoln's Treasury secretary), and James Clay, son of the late, legendary Henry Clay, and even railroad owners. Former president Millard Fillmore would come, too, joining them midway through the conference.

The debates about to take place would be among the most momentous in the nation's lifespan. The delegates were meeting in what James Madison once celebrated as the "spirit of accommodation" that resulted in the great compromise of the Constitution. Yet it would speak to the intractable dilemmas of keeping the Union whole, and say much about what America was and what it would become. It would also speak to the widespread belief many held that America was a kind of miraculous Eden crafted by men. But lurking less and less quietly was a poisonous snake that increasingly was rearing its head.

Convening on the first day, the seventy-one-year-old Tyler, his voice dripping with emotion, evoked a shared history and purpose. "Our godlike fathers created, we have to preserve," he said. "They built up through their wisdom and patriotism, monuments which have eternized their names." He paused, then added, "You have before you, gentlemen, a task equally grand, equally sublime, quite as full of glory and immortality. If you reach the height of this great occasion, your children's children will rise up and call you blessed."

Speaking beneath chandeliers shimmering overhead, Tyler called for "a triumph of patriotism over party," and for rescuing the nation. He added, "The eyes of the whole country are turned to this assembly, in expectation and hope."

On Saturday, February 23, the evening an exhausted Lincoln arrived in town, he attended a 9:00 p.m. reception at the Willard with members of the Peace Conference. Lincoln was introduced to every delegate—he had an "apt observation" for each person he met—and then a lively discussion ensued. For many of the delegates meeting Lincoln for the first time, it was an eye-opener. As William Cabell Rives of Virginia, once a young protégé of an aging Thomas Jefferson, said, "They have looked upon him as an ignorant, self-willed man, incapable of independent judgment, full of prejudices, willing to be used as a tool by more able men. This is all wrong."

Beneath a fog of cigar smoke and surrounded by scattered papers, the search for peace continued. Writer Nathaniel Hawthorne, himself staying at the Willard, wrote that the building "may much more justly be called the center of Washington and the Union, than either the Capitol, the White House, or the State Department."

Was this, then, to be a moment of triumphalism and rejoicing? Of keeping the Union whole?

Of peace?

Yet peace proved to be elusive. Suddenly, public opinion was seesawing back and forth. Famed abolitionist William Lloyd Garrison warned portentously of the Peace Conference, "Trojans! Beware the wooden horse!" One Massachusetts newspaper insisted that the Peace Conference would "accomplish nothing," just as the House's Committee of Thirty-Three and the Senate's Committee of Thirteen had both failed. Newspapers that only weeks earlier had been frantic for compromise now mocked the Peace Conference as "the Old Gentleman's Convention." The *New York Tribune*, formerly a staunch advocate of an accord with the South, suddenly emblazoned the motto "NO COMPROMISE! NO CONCESSIONS TO TRAITORS!" on each of its morning editions.

But the Peace Conference was undeterred. This was to be politicking at its best. Everybody would give; everybody would get. When the conference had dispatched members to visit President Buchanan at the East Room of the White House, they were startled when he embraced each of the group "with uncontrollable emotion" and begged them to save the country from "bloodied, fratricidal war." The peace commissioners were struck by how Buchanan seemed "shaken," and "broken in mind and body." But the mandate was theirs. Former president John Tyler, his voice accented with robust timbre, agreed to continue to take up "the great work of conciliation." He assured Buchanan that Virginians were "almost universally inclined to peace and reconciliation."

Yet Buchanan was worn out, and to the Northern commissioners he seemed incapable of rising to the challenge of the national crisis. They were not far off the mark. For the most part, he mainly stayed upstairs in the White House, and by the day did less and less about the secession crisis. Instead, he busied himself with "diplomatic issues," like a disputed water boundary in the San Juan Islands, a treaty with the Delaware Indians, and settling differences with Venezuela and Paraguay.

For all its lofty goals, the Peace Conference had its detractors. Charles Francis Adams Sr., soon to be Lincoln's minister to Great Britain, sneeringly derided Tyler as an "ancient buffer" and Crittenden as "the other ancient buffer." He derided them for being mortals who spoke with the temerity of "thunder" emanating from "Olympus." And he derided them for acting as if they were "Solomon," somehow miraculously able to split the baby.

The debates in the Peace Conference, held over three weeks, were often acrimonious, while Republican Party participation was frequently perfunctory or even hostile. Partisanship was a factor. From the outset, the Republican peace commissioners agreed to act in unison under Salmon P. Chase's leadership. In a sign of how difficult agreement was, the conferees even voted against having an official stenographer. Still, a majority of the delegates believed they could offer "peace to the country."

Meanwhile, as some of the nation's most renowned statesmen toiled inside Willard's Hall to save their country, every day there was the loud thump, thump of federal troops ostentatiously marching outside the Willard. They were setting a backdrop of the Northern military's might. The Southern delegates found it intimidating, which perhaps was General Scott's idea in the first place. At the same time, sixty-eight-year-old former Connecticut governor Roger Sherman Baldwin, the grandson of a signer of the Declaration of Independence, Roger Sherman, as well as the lawyer for the African enslaved people on the famed *Amistad* case, insisted that what the conference came up with would reveal America's "national character in the eyes of the whole civilized world."

Despite official policies of secrecy, virtually every proposal was promptly leaked and telegraphed nationwide.

The work of the peace commissioners was punctuated by daily receptions, concerts, theater productions, and excursions to different parts of the city. But the great task was never far from the minds of the commissioners. As former Treasury secretary under President Franklin Pierce, James Guthrie, observed, "The storm is threatening, the horizon is covered with dark and portentous clouds…War! Civil War! Is impending over us. It must be averted!"

The resolutions committee toiled every day until 10:00 p.m., and many evenings often until midnight. They talked at great length about the stitches of nationhood: tariff issues, financial issues, agricultural issues, geographical boundaries, history, economics, constitutional precedents, and, of course, slavery and abolition. As a backdrop to the proceedings stood the immortal words of William Loughton Smith, who once said in a moment of candor, "We took each other with our mutual bad habits and respective evils for better or for worse. The northern states adopted us with our slaves and we adopted them with their Quakers."

Roused, the debate continued. Reverdy Johnson, though a Democrat, spoke for the Republicans when he referred to slavery as the "great affliction." Virginia's George William Summers, professing that his heart "was full," challenged his colleagues in Maine, saying they were there for one single purpose—"to save the Union." In a hopeful sign, he said that Virginia only asked that states "conferred together," and that they only expected "reasonable concessions, reasonable guarantees."

So how far apart were they?

James A. Seddon of Virginia, with a straight face, explained that the "colored barbarians" fared much better on Southern plantations than free Black men in the Caribbean. Former Massachusetts governor George S.

Boutwell bellowed that the doctrine of equality was the "fundamental doctrine of democracy." He added that by the will of God, "every man is born a free man, and enters into society with equal rights with every other man." Thomas C. Ruffin of North Carolina, with his mop of disheveled white hair, explained that he came to the conference "for Union and peace!" and appealed to his colleagues to "discard politics and party—let us be brethren and friends!"

Some of the most significant exchanges were between Lincoln and the peace commissioners themselves. The urbane William Rives boomed that he could "do little," but that Lincoln could "do much"—telling him firmly, "Everything now depends upon you." Lincoln said that the course was as plain as a turnpike road. "It is marked," he insisted, "by the Constitution." He asked Rives, "Suppose now we all stop discussing and try the experiment of obedience to the Constitution and the laws. Don't you think it would work?" Virginia's George William Summers jumped in: "Yes, it will work. If the Constitution is your light, I will follow it with you, and the people of the South will go with us."

Here, then, was progress. That is, until James A. Seddon interjected in a confrontational tone, chiding the North for failing to suppress its "John Browns" and its radical Garrisons who preached insurrection. A murmur could be heard in the background. An irritated Lincoln hit back hard: "I believe John Brown was hung and Mr. Garrison imprisoned. You cannot justly charge the north with disobedience to statutes or with failing to enforce them." Seddon wagged his head in disapproval, maintaining that the leading men of the North failed to return "fugitive slaves."

Lincoln wouldn't back down, saying that Seddon was "wrong," noting that even in the shadow of Faneuil Hall in the heart of Boston, enslaved people were returned, no matter how odious it felt to Northerners.

Seddon countered with more accusations, more invective, accusing the Northern press of being "incendiary," advocating "insurrection," and advising the enslaved people to cut their "masters' throats." Southern heads nodded in agreement. Once more, Lincoln hit back, defending the freedom of the press. "Are we peculiar in that respect? Is that not the same doctrine held in the South?"

Crittenden himself was listening carefully, and he felt that Lincoln's words about his constitutional duties "stilled" the crowd.

Then, perhaps as never before, Lincoln gave a window into his thinking surrounding the impending crisis: "In a choice of evils, war may not always be the worst. Still I would do all in my power to avert it, except to neglect a constitutional duty. As to slavery, it must be content with what it has. The voice of the civilized world is against it." Rives, whom Lincoln once quoted in a speech twenty-two years earlier, felt Lincoln was good-natured and well-intentioned, but "utterly unimpressed with the gravity of the crisis and the magnitude of his duties," adding, "He seems to think of nothing but jokes and stories."

But the jokes were Lincoln's rapier, the stories his métier. And one thing Lincoln did not do was make any direct comment on the work of the peace commissioners themselves.

The Peace Conference delegates reconvened the next day, Monday, February 25, at 10:00 a.m. Time was running out for them to reach a solution before the presidential inauguration on March 4. A number of amendments were introduced by the conferees yet again, and in contrast to the tepid evasions of the past, there was a concerted effort by some in the South to make it clear that the Constitution does recognize slavery, while still standing against resurrection of the international slave trade. William H. Stephens of Tennessee, feeling things were getting out of control, warned, "We have come here to arrange old difficulties, not to make new ones."

Yet old fears were difficult to dispense. Charles S. Morehead of Kentucky predicted that the commissioners were opening up the greatest scheme of emancipation "ever devised." There would be an underground railroad at every principal route of travel; there would be canoes furnished to ferry "Negroes" over the Potomac and Ohio; there would be long pikes stacked up in every little village for enslaved people to defend themselves.

There was talk of making secession unconstitutional. There was talk, too, of legitimizing "the right of revolution."

Now Salmon P. Chase stepped into the breach, proposing a national convention to ratify the work of the Peace Conference. He pleaded, "Let us not rush headlong into that unfathomable gulf. Let us not tempt this unutterable woe. We offer you a plain and honorable mode of adjusting all difficulties... Is it too much to ask you, gentlemen of the South, to meet us on this honorable and practicable ground? Will you not, at least, concede this to the country?"

It was voted down.

Kentucky's Charles S. Morehead recalled that he told Lincoln he held the destiny of more than thirty million people in his hands; that if he acted the part of a "statesman in avoiding a collision, he would occupy a place in the future of his country second only to Washington." In a momentous gesture, Lincoln replied that he would withdraw his troops from Fort Sumter if Virginia would stay in the Union. And the reply? Lincoln listened carefully, with his elbows on his knees and his hands on his face; he then told an Aesop fable regarding an elephant who agreed to be disarmed of his tusk only to be clubbed to death. Yes, Morehead said, but he warned of injury to the "cause of humanity" if Lincoln permitted a "fratricidal war." By this stage, all those around Lincoln spoke with great emotion. As for former president Tyler, he pledged, "I go to finish the work you have assigned me": presenting the Peace Conference's recommendations to the two houses of Congress.

With that, General Winfield Scott ordered a 100-gun salute in homage to the just concluded Peace Conference and its delegates. The roadways shook and the windows of the Willard rattled. And then, almost inexplicably, rather than stay in Washington to advocate the Peace Conference proposals, Tyler hopped in a carriage and hastily left for Richmond to take his seat at the Virginia Secession Convention.

For many of the conferees, it was downright depressing, if not madness.

As the days went on, the commissioners were buffeted by soaring oratory, implied threats, ongoing confrontations, and emotional pleas for conciliation. As secession conventions were meeting in far-off states like Arkansas, Missouri, and, above all, Virginia, the commissioners had much to debate and much to anguish over.

In a short time, however, the convention would be embracing the very policies embodied in the Crittenden plan.

So on the evening that Lincoln and Douglas met in Suite 6, Lincoln assured Douglas that he appreciated his sharing his views. Yet he still was unwilling to approve of the convention. This, of course, was what Douglas had on his mind when he dropped by to meet with the president-elect.

At stake, Douglas was convinced, was the integrity of the United States.

It was on Tuesday, February 26, that the Peace Conference began voting on the resolutions and amendments that they would advocate for the final package. Dejected, Tyler felt that too many had come with no olive branch in their hands—"nothing to give—nothing to yield...Not an 'I' dotted nor a 'T' crossed."

It wasn't just Douglas and the peace delegates who were pressuring Lincoln now; it was Virginia and the border states, too. One group came to Suite 6 from the Virginia Secession Convention, which was holding back from voting either to secede or adjourn, anxiously waiting to see how Lincoln would address the crisis. The Virginians exhorted Lincoln to convey "a message of peace" that they could take back to Virginia. There was that word again: peace. This was a momentous offer, as peace or war would likely be decided by which way Virginia went. But Lincoln would only go as far as saying that he would protect the Southerners' "legal rights."

Then another delegation representing the border state Unionists, including three Virginians, knocked on Lincoln's door; they were from the Peace Conference itself. They said that Lincoln must avoid coercion at all costs. That he should evacuate Fort Sumter, whose Union flag only whipped the Confederates up into a frenzy. And that he should offer "satisfactory guarantees" to the eight slave states still in the Union. Here, they had William H. Seward's promises in mind. Seward, in a remarkable act of diplomatic double-dealing, had been acting as a de facto member of the Washington Peace Conference. He had assured border Unionists that within sixty days of Lincoln's inauguration, the crisis would "melt away." But the delegation insisted that they hear this from Lincoln himself.

After weeks of hesitancy and fudging, Lincoln was now specific and blunt. Momentously, he promised that he would support the newly proposed (and passed) Thirteenth Amendment to the Constitution, "to the effect that the federal government, shall never interfere with the domestic institutions of the States." In short, this amendment, which was sponsored by no less than Charles Francis Adams Sr. in the House, would enshrine slavery as it stood in the Constitution for time immemorial. It was a momentous step for the slave-hating Lincoln. Lincoln now promised that "such a provision to now be implied constitutional law, I have no objection to its being made express, and irrevocable." What he could not do, however, was allow slavery in the territories to expand. Frankly, Lincoln was flabbergasted. He asked: How was it coercion to maintain the integrity of the government? How was it coercion to collect revenues in the Deep South and retake the forts that rebels had captured? He did, however, have a deal in mind, repeating what he had told the Peace Conference itself. If the three Virginians could persuade the Virginia Secession Convention to dismantle itself, he reiterated that he would give up Sumter.

Here was possibility.

26

Weighty Decisions

Never were peril and promise wrestling with each other more than in these high-pitched weeks. Lincoln's only respite from the commotion of inaugural week and what to do about Sumter and the Peace Conference was the comparable headache of assembling his cabinet—his first test. One shrewd unofficial appointment he made was in appointing Frank P. Blair Sr., a powerful Maryland Republican, as the "elder statesman" of the administration, whose political clout the president could use when needed. A former Democrat, Blair was one of the founders of the national Republican Party. He lived in an elegant country estate in Silver Spring, Maryland; he knew everyone in Washington and everyone in Washington knew him. Meantime, his son Montgomery Blair would be the postmaster general. On its face, this also looked like a shrewd political move, a way of appealing to the South since the Blairs had Kentucky ancestry. However, this ignored the fact that Blair had nothing but contempt for Seward's attempts to woo the seceded states back. "Violence is not to be met with peace," Blair snorted. This didn't sit well with Seward, who was rarely hesitant about insisting that he was the administration's towering figure, more so than even the president-elect. Seward thus hoped to control the cabinet, if not the administration itself. As for Lincoln's other appointments, Seward, of course, was secretary of state. Edward Bates was attorney general. Simon Cameron was the war secretary. Gideon Welles was head of the Navy.

When all was said and done, Lincoln hammered together a cabinet representative of the broad expanse of Republicans, encompassing all the discordant elements in the party—lapsed Democrats and former Whigs, extant liberals and old-fashioned conservatives, easterners, westerners, and border Southerners. After the Revolutionary War, one British officer had marveled, "The Americans are a curious people; they know how to govern themselves, but nobody else can govern them."

But when it came to the Republicans and the brewing crisis, they remained largely a blank slate.

———

In a sudden surprise, the Virginians weighed Lincoln's proposal for giving up Sumter and vetoed it. Unwilling to make promises on specifics, all they would guarantee was "devotion" to the Union. And having come with so much promise, the delegates from the Peace Conference ultimately left Lincoln, too, having solved nothing. "We have saved this Union so often," one delegate forlornly observed, "that I am afraid we shall save it to death." In late February, the convention did finally send Congress a plan. It was Crittenden redux. Among other things, it called for reviving the Missouri line and extending it westward, with slavery to be protected south of that line. At this stage, this was more than the exhausted Republicans could stomach; worn and fed up, they said no. But then again, so did Virginia's leaders, as well as other border Southerners.

So when the convention's recommendation, similar to Crittenden's, went before Congress, it was stifled by Republican obstinacy, hamstrung by resistance from Lincoln, and paralyzed by the babel of Southern voices and ineffective moderates.

Thus, the last-ditch effort for compromise was rejected by both sides, and ignominiously strangled in the Senate crib.

In the end, hope against hope, the Peace Conference proposals suffered an unceremonious defeat in the Congress. Suddenly, the revolutionary wheel was about to take its most frenetic turn to date.

———

All Lincoln could do was look forward. With Inauguration Day approaching, Lincoln now sat for hours in his study, scribbling the final draft of his speech, paragraph by paragraph, sentence by sentence. More than anything else, this would be his introduction to the nation as well as the world, and he wasn't taking anything for granted. So he reworked, rewrote, and revised his paragraphs with utmost diligence. In doing this, he was guided by four documents: the Constitution, Andrew Jackson's nullification proclamation, Daniel Webster's immortal "Liberty and Union Forever" speech, and Henry Clay's address to the Senate arguing for the Compromise of 1850. He knew his task was to somehow find a way to soften the anxieties of the Southern states, while at the same time stiffening the spine of the Union. Finally, on March 3, he was ready for Seward to critique the speech. After reading it, Seward wrote a long letter back to Lincoln. Predictably, Seward advised that Lincoln offer more concessions to the South and, moreover, that Lincoln remove his provocative promise to recapture all federal forts and arsenals the rebels had taken. While Lincoln thought it important, reality was settling in; he was now willing to accede to Seward's wishes, lest he alienate the all-critical Southern Unionists who Lincoln believed to be the crucial hinge for avoiding war.

Yet that was as far as Lincoln would go. As he saw it, the very future of self-government and freedom now depended on his being resolute. He was adamant that he would adhere to the Republican platform, as well as his promises to the people who had voted for him. At stake, for him, was the right of a free people everywhere to "choose their leaders." At stake, too, was a simple principle for him. If Southerners didn't like him, they could simply vote him out of office in 1864. Moreover, there was the tenuous precedent of secession, the notion that any unhappy state could leave the Union at any time. This he could not, and did not, accept. As he saw it, no president could. To his eyes, secession was merely "an ingenious sophism," having no legal defense, no real historical basis, and no grounding in logic. For Lincoln, it was as plain as the morning's day: The Union was "perpetual" (actually, this was debatable); "supreme" (also debatable); and "permanent" (debatable too), and should not be governed by the whims of a disaffected minority. Sounding a little like William Pitt or Catherine the Great, both of whom presided over great empires, he believed no government in history had ever been established that blithely allowed for its own dismemberment.

And then there was the matter of him somehow being illegitimate, or that he should "apologize" for his victory. This gnawed at him. Democrats never did that, so why should he? And the more he thought about it, the more he was adamant that he would not surrender the party creed on which he had presented himself to the people.

That night, Lincoln uneasily climbed into bed, with the heavy thought that twelve hours from now, the fate of the United States would rest in his hands, and a noose was around his neck.

27

Inauguration

March 4, 1861. In the predawn darkness, the people were already gathering in expectation. As dawn broke, temperatures were in the fifties, clouds appeared overhead, and the sky looked menacing. And despite the wee hours of the early morning, there was already the steady clip-clop of cavalry and the incessant rumble of artillery being set up. Meanwhile, in Suite 6 at the Willard Hotel, Lincoln, who had been awake pacing nervously since before sunrise, was alone with his thoughts. Then, joined by his family, he read the inaugural address to them, after which he once again asked to be alone. Staring out the window, he could see the troops marching and massing outside—hundreds of them—there to guard against any attempted assassination. At the same time, military patrols formed a watchful guard, and sharpshooters raced from building to building, positioning themselves on rooftops and in windows.

Belying his country roots, Lincoln was dressed for the occasion, wearing a new black suit, shiny black boots, and his trademark stovepipe hat, which framed his trimmed Quaker's beard. In a small irony given the caning of Boston's Charles Sumner—or was it a hint of defiance?—Lincoln carried a cane sporting a gold head. At long last, the clock struck noon. The clock also struck noon for President Buchanan, who arrived at the Willard to complete the traditional peaceful transfer of power—from one man to the other, from one party to the other—and to escort the president-elect to the ceremony. It was hard to imagine a greater contrast: a worn-out Buchanan was nearly seventy; a tireless Lincoln, already drained, was only fifty-two. Buchanan was short and mesomorphic; Lincoln was tall and muscular. Buchanan was experienced, one of America's great statesmen who spoke the King's English; while Lincoln was a novice, a backwoods country lawyer who spoke in homilies and little stories. As they climbed their way into the open carriage, the Marine band struck up "Hail to the Chief."

It was time.

Enveloped by horse-drawn floats, the carriage made its way up Pennsylvania Avenue while hundreds of dignitaries clapped and tens of thousands of people cheered. The Stars and Stripes hung from second- and third-story windows, gawkers hung out of their balconies, and clutches of handkerchiefs fluttered up and down the avenues. Reporters and photographers were there, too, ready to record the event for posterity. More flags waved, more people cheered, and the military bands continued to play.

When Lincoln appeared on the square platform of the east portico of the Capitol, slowly making his way to his seat, he was once again met with a roar of applause. In the front row along with Lincoln, surrounded by three hundred dignitaries as well as plainclothes detectives on the lookout for assassins, Buchanan sat next to a sickly Senator Douglas and Chief Justice Taney, architect of the *Dred Scott* decision. Ironically, here were three of the four men accused by Lincoln of conspiring to destroy the work of the framers in his "House Divided" speech.

As Lincoln rose and moved forward, the collective pulse quickened. The sky now cleared, and a stiff wind began to howl and blow. In the distance, on a nearby hill, a battery of howitzers stood ready to strafe the streets at the first hint of problems.

Lincoln could not find a place for his hat, and in a touching act of bipartisan symbolism, Senator Douglas reached out and held it during the ceremony. Lincoln then slipped on a pair of steel-rimmed spectacles and positioned his speech. Summoning his energies, his voice crackling but firm, he began to read. It was one of the great orations uttered in American history.

He started by telling Southerners that his policies were not about coercion, but accommodation and forbearance. He acknowledged that Southerners were afraid that he would endanger their property and their personal security, not to mention their peace. But he promised, as he had said all along, that he would not threaten the institution of slavery and, indeed, that he had "no lawful right to do so." Here he quoted from his own Republican Party platform, which acknowledged the right of states to control their own institutions.

Equally significantly, now before the eyes of the world, he publicly endorsed the Thirteenth Amendment just passed by Congress and signed by Buchanan. It was, after all, he pointed out, consistent with Republican ideology. As he spoke, the crowd pressed forward to catch every word.

Now he directed his remarks less to the crowd and more to the Southern Unionists, speaking about the supremacy of the national government. He insisted that the Union was perpetual and could not legitimately be destroyed; that secession was in fact constitutionally illegal; and that violent resistance to federal authority was "insurrectionary" and "revolutionary." He would be guided by the Constitution, he insisted, which meant enforcing federal laws in other states and defending the Union. But stretching out his hand, he promised that the government would shed "no blood" unless it was forced to do so. Therefore, he would "hold, occupy, and possess" those forts still held by the Union, which included Fort Pickens at Pensacola Bay and Fort Sumter in Charleston Harbor. Yet "there would be no invasion—no use of force," he maintained, even as he made no pledge ruling out the use of force to secure Pickens and Sumter.

Having laid down the marker in defense of federal authority, he then offered what he saw as a series of concessions. He would deliver mail in the South only if Southerners allowed him, would collect tariff duties only offshore, and would hold back on patronage appointments in the South until matters were resolved.

Now he marched to his conclusion: "In your hands, my dissatisfied fellow countrymen, and not in mine, is the momentous issue of civil war. The government will not assail you. You can have no conflict, without being yourselves the aggressors. You have no oath registered in heaven to destroy the government, while I shall have the most solemn one to preserve, protect and defend it."

He saved his most soaring and trenchant words for his sum-up, among the most eloquent words ever uttered by a president. "I am loath to close. We are not enemies, but friends. We must not be enemies. Though passion may have strained, it must not break our bonds of affection. The mystic chords of memory, stretching from every battlefield, and every patriot grave, to every living heart and hearthstone, all over this broad land, will yet swell the course of the Union, when again touched, as surely they will be, by the better angels of our nature."

Lincoln swiveled to face Chief Justice Taney, placed his hand on the Bible, and soberly took his oath as the sixteenth president of the United States. The people cheered, and on the east plaza an artillery salvo exploded in the wind. Lincoln now rode back to the White House past a deliriously cheering assembly, accompanied by a dejected Buchanan, who then shook Lincoln's hand and, with less a hint of sarcasm than a touch of humor, wished him luck.

Meanwhile, the aging general-in-chief Winfield Scott spoke for many when he roared, "Thank God, we now have a government."

Carried by telegraph, Lincoln's words quickly raced their way across the country and were printed in dozens of evening newspapers.

———————

Throughout the nation, reactions to the speech varied widely. Predictably, Republican newspapers praised the speech. The *Philadelphia Bulletin* called it "eminently conciliatory," while the *Commercial Advertiser* of New York maintained (wrongly) that the inaugural was solely "the work of Mr. Lincoln's own pen and hand." Democratic papers from the North were considerably more hostile. The *Hartford Times* bellowed that the speech was "wretchedly parched and unstatesmanlike," while the Albany *Atlas and Argus* sputtered, "It is he that defies the will of the majority. It is he that initiates Civil War." The tone of the Southern response was harsher still, damning the address as a declaration of hostilities. The *Richmond Enquirer* called the speech the "deliberate language of the fanatic," while the North Carolina *Herald* insisted that Americans "might as well open their eyes to the solemn fact that war is inevitable." For its part, the Montgomery *Weekly Advertiser* grandiloquently proclaimed that the address meant "War. War, and nothing less than War, will satisfy the abolition chief." The *Arkansas True Democrat* agreed, proclaiming, "If declaring the Union perpetual means coercion, then LINCOLN'S INAUGURAL MEANS WAR!" Predictably, the *Charleston Mercury* sought to have the last word: "A more lamentable display of feeble inability to grasp the circumstances of this momentous emergency, could scarcely have been exhibited."

That said, in the pivotal slave states of Virginia and North Carolina, there were pockets of greater receptivity to Lincoln's speech, seemingly vindicating Seward's contention that there were indeed Southern Unionists secretly praying for peace. Ironically, some of the most withering criticism came from radicals and abolitionists within the Republican Party itself, who were disgusted by the words of seeming appeasement. Frederick Douglass, who originally was heartened by Lincoln's victory as heralding an "anti-slavery reputation to the presidency," was now disgusted by Lincoln's declaration that he had "no lawful power to interfere with slavery in the States" and, moreover, no "inclination" to do so.

For Douglass, the speech was little more than Lincoln paying obeisance before the "foul and withering curse of slavery." And he spit out his final assessment: "Some thought we had in Mr. Lincoln the nerve and decision of an Oliver Cromwell. But the result shows that we merely have a continuation of the Pierces and Buchanans."

Douglass couldn't have been more wrong.

The next day, on March 5, Lincoln's first day in office, already there was a military crisis—"the very first thing placed in his hands." The War Department sent over a staggering report from Major Robert Anderson, Fort Sumter's commander. The news was stark. Rebel batteries had now surrounded the Union stronghold, and Anderson questioned whether he could even hold on to Sumter, let alone mount an offensive operation. Already his supplies were perilously close to running out, and he estimated he had only six weeks to hold on. Were the president to try to relieve the garrison and enable it to fend for itself, it would necessitate a much larger force of "70,000 good and well disciplined men."

What was Lincoln to do? The problem, and it was indeed a problem, was that he had virtually no military experience, and what he did have was almost pitiful: commanding a small company of ill-disciplined volunteers in the Black Hawk War who trained with wooden sticks as rifles. Lincoln understood that he didn't yet have the strategic acumen to adequately assess the threat facing Sumter. So he turned to his general-in-chief of the Army, Scott, a lofty military voice in Washington. With his unimpeachable credentials, Scott remained a legendary soldier. True, he was physically failing. Seventy-five years old, he suffered from vertigo and dropsy and was so obese that he was unable to climb the steps of the White House or mount a horse on his own without assistance. Nonetheless, he had seen it all; his prestige was immense, and Lincoln regarded him as a valued resource. The president asked him for his opinions.

That night, Scott promptly got back to him. It was a bleak picture.

Explaining that he couldn't send enough men for several months, he explained, "I now see no alternative but a surrender in some weeks. Evacuation seems almost inevitable"; and, in any case, he held up the possibility that Sumter could be "assaulted" as early as the present week. Further, Scott said Anderson could hold out for only twenty-six days and that it would require "6 to 8 months" to assemble the fleet of "war vessels and transports, 5,000 additional regular troops and 20,000 volunteers" necessary to reinforce the garrison. For an enervated Lincoln, this was a disaster. Repeatedly he had been saying, in public as well as in private, that he would hold on to Sumter. He knew that Anderson had become a national hero and his fort the most pronounced symbol of federal authority in the nation. What would the country say if he played the role of supplicant and abandoned the very place he'd promised only the day before in his inauguration speech to "hold, occupy, and possess"? How would the party react to this? How would the North react? And how even would his own cabinet react?

Consumed with "anxiety," and already distressed, in the days that followed Lincoln repeatedly gathered his advisers around a long and heavy oak table in his White House office, where they would discuss and deliberate, argue and assess. Rarely did Lincoln sit; most of the time he nervously paced up and down as he spoke. Significantly, a portrait of President Andrew Jackson, the president's guiding spirit, was draped over the fireplace mantel, while old maps hung on the walls. So here he met with high-ranking officers of the Navy and the Army, and his own sage cabinet secretaries, all consequential figures in their own right.

Here, surely, he would find the answers he needed.

By one side, he had the renowned William H. Seward, the senior member of his cabinet. A celebrated raconteur who loved to pun and banter, he was revered in DC. Cosmopolitan, he, unlike Lincoln, was schooled in the ways of Washington; indeed, he was so sure of himself that he laughed at his own jokes while perpetually munching on a Cuban cigar. On the other side sat Gideon Welles, the secretary of the Navy, in his long-haired wig and with his massive white beard hanging from his eternally misanthropic scowl. Here, too, was the ambitious and handsome Salmon P. Chase, fresh off the Peace Conference, speaking solemnly yet firmly with a lisp. Here also was the tendentious Simon Cameron, the secretary of war, his arms folded, "openly discourteous" (Lincoln's words) to the president himself. And here was Montgomery Blair, the postmaster general, who freely wielded a powerful political influence far beyond his young years and junior seniority, and who was at once hot-tempered and controversial and never backed down from a good fight. And here, of course, was the irrepressible Winfield Scott, a devotee of chess with his knowing looks and his trembling hands, whose imperial presence forged by decades of service imposed his will upon everyone caught up in his wake. Like his good friend Seward, his prestige was enormous.

Mentally fatigued and physically exhausted, Lincoln already looked beaten down by the presidency he'd so recently entered. "You will wear yourself out," Senator Henry Wilson of Massachusetts had solemnly warned him. One subtext of the meetings was his lack of experience.

Senator Charles Sumner put it bluntly: Lincoln "has no conception of the situation. He is ignorant and must have help." As Lincoln met with his advisers early on, he had bags under his eyes that betrayed the unremitting strain he was feeling, even as he carefully listened to the arguments.

On the question of Fort Pickens, the cabinet all agreed that it should be reinforced and held. Unlike Charleston Harbor, it was not inflammatory to the South; thus, reinforcing Pensacola Bay was unlikely to galvanize hostilities. So Lincoln ordered that a troop ship be sent to reinforce Pickens promptly.

That was the easy part. Then came the discussions about Fort Sumter.

Ultimately, did Lincoln have the stomach for a bloody pitched battle at Sumter? That remained to be seen. And no matter which way Lincoln turned with his cabinet, he found disagreement or despair, and the prospect of his freedom of action narrowing rapidly. When he raised the specter of reinforcements, the Army was convinced that would be a disaster (although the Navy thought problems would be minimal). Lincoln asked what if he instead sent in a flotilla to provision the fort? Gideon Welles vacillated, first supporting the idea, then changing his mind. By contrast, an unwavering Seward wanted to evacuate as quickly as possible. He announced in a clear, firm voice that he favored making Fort Pickens the symbol of federal authority, where there was minimal risk. Yet he felt strongly that Sumter "must be given up." He contended that any aggressive move there would almost certainly precipitate a civil war, wiping out South Carolinian Unionism and Virginia Unionism as well. Militarily, too, an attack would be challenging: Rebel batteries were positioned around the harbor with a preponderance of troops, while South Carolina politicians were daily whipping the people up into a frenzy. So Seward counseled playing the long game. Surrender Sumter and give ammunition to Unionists around the South to consolidate their strength and to "take over" the secessionist states, thus returning them to the Union. Seward was adamant; this was the only way to end the crisis, the only way to prevent civil war.

What Seward did not do, however, was tell the cabinet about his ongoing secret negotiations with Confederate emissaries. On his own, he had already assured the Southerners that Sumter would be "evacuated"—in fact, on March 14 he told Justice John Archibald Campbell that Sumter would be evacuated within three days. Under the assumption that Seward spoke for Lincoln as well, the Carolinians relayed the message to Jefferson Davis back in Montgomery. In truth, Lincoln had not authorized anything of the sort. But Seward, playing a perilous gambit, just assumed the president would follow his lead and let him run the administration concerning the South.

Seward continued to speak the language of a statesman: "I have believed firmly that everywhere, and even in South Carolina, devotion to the Union is a profound and permanent national sentiment, which, although it may be suppressed and silenced by terror for a time, could if encouraged, be ultimately relied upon to rally the people of the seceding states to reverse."

For his part, Montgomery Blair, the only cabinet member with military experience, pointedly disagreed with Seward's plans. As it happened, he thought Seward was a coward. Scott, too. Both Montgomery Blair and his father urged Lincoln to retain Sumter and deal with the consequences. Don't be like Buchanan, the Blairs exhorted; instead, be Andrew Jackson. Make a proclamation. Mass the Army around South Carolina and threaten to send them in. Deal with the traitors. He maintained that this would completely "demoralize the rebellion." But the Blairs constituted a lonely voice. Other than that, the cabinet, falling lockstep behind Seward, was grimly unanimous.

On March 13, at Blair's suggestion, the president had also met with his brother-in-law Gustavus Fox, a thirty-nine-year-old former naval officer with a rather shrewd proposal for relieving Sumter by water. The proposal was a relief for Lincoln; for once, this was information that gave him time to reflect and held the possibility of success. Fox believed supplies could be loaded onto a transport while three sturdy tugboats followed by a large steamer conveying troops could be used in case the tugs were opposed. Lincoln liked the plan and presented it to the cabinet. Once more, the cabinet was split.

With his cabinet so divided, with Seward on one side and Blair on another, on March 15 Lincoln called on his secretaries to submit written opinions on the Fox proposal and related matters. By this stage, the president seemed to be tilting toward provisioning Sumter "without reinforcements." Lincoln asked a difficult question to the cabinet: Was it, he wondered, even possible to supply the fort, as Fox believed? And in the same breath, Lincoln wanted to know, was it wise? (His exact words: "Assuming it to be possible to now provision Fort Sumter, under all the circumstances, is it wise to attempt it?") Only Chase and the younger Blair said yes. The other secretaries all sided with Seward and voted to evacuate. It was as though Lincoln could feel his power steadily slipping from his hands.

The president was desperately concerned, but it was indisputable that Seward and his allies had strong arguments. The attempt to supply Fort Sumter with armed forces would, Seward maintained again and again, inevitably provoke the remaining slave states to secede and launch a civil war—that "most disastrous and deplorable of national calamities." And it would undercut Unionist sentiment in Virginia, North Carolina, Arkansas, and the border states. Yet, if the North assumed a defensive position, "we should have the spirit of the country and the approval of mankind on our side." Edward Bates agreed, arguing that he was against any act that would have a semblance before the world of "beginning a Civil War." Cameron thought surrendering the fort was "inevitable," and "the sooner it be done, the better." Interior Secretary Caleb B. Smith thought while the plan might succeed in reinforcing the fort, it would not be "wise" under any circumstance. As Welles saw it, the world was already laboring under the impression that Sumter was to be evacuated; reversal in this course could result in "untold disaster."

Chase was the wild card, and unexpectedly gave Lincoln an equivocal reply. This was surprising given his hard-line inclinations. He favored allowing the seven seceded states to be an *"accomplished revolution,"* and endorsed letting the Confederacy "try its experiment." But he softened his analysis with the conclusion that he thought war "highly improbable."

It ultimately fell to Montgomery Blair. Tall, spare, the youngest cabinet officer and its lowest-ranking member, he was to be the only unequivocal yes, insisting that every new conquest made by the rebels would "strengthen their hands at home" and their claims for recognition as "an independent people abroad."

Save for Blair, Lincoln was once more virtually alone. It would be an understatement by now to say that he was desperately concerned. Moreover, the turn of events only emboldened Seward, who believed that the president would never go against the weight of such unified and prestigious military and political counsel.

That night, a subdued and downhearted Lincoln stayed up late and tried to push the crisis away from his thoughts. He sat in a big chair by the window in his library, wearing a faded dressing gown, where he would read and think. At morning he awakened early to walk around the spacious grounds of the White House—this was his exercise—followed by a simple meal, usually a single egg eaten with a cup of coffee. Beyond the second-floor sleeping quarters, there was an oval room filled with bookcases, which Mary had turned into the family's library. In the afternoon the president would sometimes wander in there to munch on an apple or wash down some bread with a glass of milk.

But there was no way of getting around the fact that he would soon be forced to make a dramatic decision, which would affect not only his political career and the fate of his party, but the very nature of the United States.

While Lincoln was deciding, the world was watching. Rumors flew that Sumter was to be surrendered, prompting the disgust of many Republicans and concern over Lincoln's indecisiveness. One newspaper headline screamed, "HAVE WE A GOVERNMENT?" Other Republican organs evidently thought not. "The bird of our country is a debilitated chicken, disguised in eagle feathers," commented a horrified George Templeton Strong. "We are a weak, divided, disgraced people, unable to maintain our national existence." Meanwhile, the *New York Times* editorialized, "WANTED, A POLICY." A letter summed up the feeling of many when it said simply, "Reinforce Fort Sumter at all hazards!" Another predicted doom for Lincoln and his party if Fort Sumter were evacuated—"the new administration is done forever." Even Democrats were swept up by war fever and called for reinforcements of Robert Anderson's "gallant band" who were defending their country's "honor and its flag in the midst of a hostile and traitorous fire." For its part, the *New York Times* worried that the Lincoln cabinet was timid and dangerously adrift: "The administration *must*," it demanded, "have a policy of action." Other papers echoed a similar refrain that almost anything was better than "additional suspense." Finally, the New York *Morning Express* noted that the people wanted something to be decided to serve "as a rallying point" for the abundant but "discouraged loyalty of the American heart."

At its core, the view was mounting that the administration had no policy adequate to meet the secession crisis or to deal with an "active, resolute, and determined enemy." For Lincoln, the pressures were unremitting, and he was quickly losing control of events. There were those who favored letting the South go in peace and good riddance. Yet there were those who insisted that Lincoln be firm with the Southerners and come to the rescue of federal property. Never had an inexperienced president been trapped in the jaws of such problems. Whereas Charles Sumner was the self-styled new Henry Clay guiding the nation through its crisis and bringing it back together into eventual reunion, Lincoln was a newcomer in Washington with almost no experience in national affairs. One day, a tired Lincoln revealed to Orville Hickman Browning that "all the troubles and anxieties of my life" could not equal those that attended "the Sumter nightmare." They were so great that he "did not think it possible to survive them."

Lincoln took solace in the fact that he still had roughly four weeks before the Sumter garrison ran out of provisions, which gave him time to make better sense of the events embroiling him. He decided he would send some trusted advisers down to South Carolina on fact-gathering missions so that he had more solid evidence on which to make up his mind.

Key to this was dispatching Stephen A. Hurlbut, an old Illinois friend who had been born and educated in South Carolina and still had family there. With his finger on the pulse, Hurlbut would measure the temper of the people, holding discussions with rebel leaders as well as old friends in Charleston. Then he would report his findings back to Lincoln. At the same time, Lincoln also sent Gustavus Fox, by now becoming a fixture in the administration—a sort of minister without portfolio. He was to speak directly with Major Anderson and determine, once and for all, exactly how long his supplies would last.

Pacing back and forth in the White House alone, for Lincoln the mental strain was unbearable. Yet, for now, all he could do was wait.

Part VI

THE LOST
PEACE OF 1861

28

Sumter

The president wasn't the only one waiting. Trapped at Fort Sumter, Major Robert Anderson had to depend on the papers for news, which everybody knew was tendentious or potentially inaccurate. He didn't know that his report on the number of men needed to reinforce him had provoked a cascade of cabinet meetings in Washington and piqued the president. He did not know that there were moments when Lincoln questioned his very loyalty. But he did know the facts staring him in the face: that Sumter had become a stifling prison of apathy, of endless waiting and unceasing discomfort, and that the troops would've welcomed bloody clashes if for no other reason than to combat the mind-numbing boredom. He did know that his irregular supply of fresh meat and vegetables had now been cut off, and his men were subsisting largely on salt pork. And he did know that under the leadership of the flamboyant general P. G. T. Beauregard, the Georges Danton of the South—"De l'audace, encore de l'audace, toujours l'audace!" (We have to dare, to dare again, always to dare!)—the Carolinians were arranging increasing numbers of twenty-four-pound guns along with cargoes of ammunition at the strategically placed Cummings Point.

The great question for Anderson was, what would the new administration do? What was Lincoln's frame of mind? What options was he weighing? To the beleaguered officers of Fort Sumter, awaiting the instructions from General Scott that would decide their fate, the continued silence from Washington seemed to be almost surreal.

In Charleston, the *Courier* echoed the problem of the hour: "Well, what is it, peace or war?"

This question was asked and answered by the *Courier* itself, which headlined, "THE EVACUATION OF FORT SUMTER DETER-MINED...ANDERSON TO GO TO FORT MONROE." Meanwhile, Charleston itself was awash with rumor. It was first whispered, then shouted, that Anderson's soldiers were openly in mutiny. It was also believed that Major Anderson was resigning his commission. Then, spies in Washington relayed the news that Anderson had mined the wharf at Sumter, and that he would "blow up the Fort rather than see it fall to the enemy." In truth, it was hard to tell by now what was fact and what was fiction.

Anderson did receive a number of visitors. South Carolina governor Francis Wilkinson Pickens went to Sumter one day on an official errand and lingered to talk with the officers. Ironically, everyone got along so well that Pickens sent cigars as well as claret to Anderson's men afterward. Then, Fox, the denizen of reinforcement, met with Anderson bearing the news that General Scott had *not* forgotten him. Here he received Anderson's estimate that with the current state of his provisions, he could not hold out beyond April 15, even if he put his men on short rations. That was their D-Day. After two hours, Fox had the information he needed, and he returned to Charleston. It was at this point that Ward Hill Lamon, one of Lincoln's closest friends, registered at the Charleston Hotel on March 24 after arriving with Hurlbut. Presenting himself as "a confidential agent" of the president's, he gave all indications to Governor Pickens that he was there to discuss details of the removal of the Sumter force.

By the time Lamon had left Charleston, there was little doubt in anyone's mind that Anderson and his men would clear out soon. Heartened by this news, General Beauregard wrote to Anderson that no "formal surrender or capitulation" would be necessary when he left.

Still unsure, and feeling his way in this Kabuki dance of potential death, Anderson cabled back to Washington: "I must, therefore, most respectfully and urgently ask for instructions what I am to do as soon as my provisions are exhausted."

———————

Yet cooler heads were indeed prevailing. Now that Fox had received permission to meet with Anderson, he, too, learned indisputably that Anderson could only last until April 15. At the same time, Hurlbut examined Seward's contention that Unionist feelings throughout the South would intensify and expand so long as the United States refrained from any provocative action or perceived aggression against the rebels. For two days Hurlbut queried politicians, lawyers, and citizens, and upon his return on March 27 provided a detailed report of what he found. Contrary to Seward's claims, Hurlbut was convinced by his "unquestionable" sources that South Carolinians had "no attachment to the Union," and many even relished a battle with the Union capital as a way of unifying the Confederacy. The only man in the city of Charleston who avowedly adhered to the Union was, it seemed, Judge James Louis Petigru. Moreover, Hurlbut was categorical in reporting to the president that Unionist sentiment in both the city and the state was dead, and indeed was so everywhere else in the South. As he put it, "That separate nationality is a fixed fact" and the seceded states were "irrevocably gone." What would quell the secessionist ardor of the rebels? Nothing, Hurlbut said, except for "unqualified recognition of absolute independence."

Charleston already envisaged a role for itself as a bustling commercial emporium in the South, much as New York was for the North. Here, then, was the quandary for Lincoln. He had been trying to decide whether to reinforce or merely reprovision Sumter, but was now being told by Hurlbut that the rebels would actually open fire on any ships Lincoln sent to Charleston Harbor, including even a peaceful flotilla strictly for provisioning the garrison.

Back came the question: Should Lincoln then evacuate? Once more, Hurlbut was certain. Withdrawal, he maintained, wouldn't do anything.

If Lincoln surrendered Sumter, the rebels would then demand that he give up Fort Pickens as well. "Nor do I believe," he said, "that any policy which may be adopted by the government will prevent the policy of armed collision."

This was a splash of cold water in Lincoln's face, a harsh awakening for a president who for countless months had maintained that Southern Unionism was alive and well, and that at bottom Southerners were attached to the Union with the same devotion that he was. His dilemma now seemed less a dilemma. It appeared that a bloody showdown with the rebels was unavoidable.

As far as he was concerned, even if he evacuated the fort as the South wanted, it would only postpone the inevitable: civil war.

―――――――

Throughout this period, activity in the South was frenetic. In Montgomery, the Confederate Congress was engrossed with such issues as rail transportation, postage, the Lighthouse Bureau, lightships, liquor control, registration of vessels, and Indian agents. The committee on the Confederate flag was busy endorsing the first flag, the Stars and Bars, which now floated over the state capitol in Montgomery, Alabama. And in Washington the Confederacy dispatched three commissioners to attempt to open relations with the new Lincoln administration—in vain as it happened: The president adamantly refused to recognize the rebels or meet with them face-to-face. He would instead only communicate with them through a series of intermediaries. In a flurry of activity and ambition, Jefferson Davis also named three commissioners to Britain to attempt to negotiate for recognition. And on the military front, General P. G. T. Beauregard assumed command of Confederate troops around Charleston Harbor, while Brigadier General Braxton Bragg assumed command of Confederate forces in Florida.

It was wartime in Carolina, and people felt it. Most felt it with anticipation, a few with grief. The apprehension came and it went, but mostly came. For President Davis, this was a challenging task. He had to organize everything virtually from scratch, and neither he nor many of the other Southern politicians had the capacity or training to do so effectively. To be sure, Lincoln was a loose administrator with scant experience, but at least he was a master at handling men. As it happened, Davis had little experience as an administrator as well. True, he had been secretary of war, but contrary to standard belief, this was misleading. He had directed only seven clerks and supervised a pitifully small army of between 10,000 and 15,000 men. As Confederate president, his task would be much more complicated, and the day would come when he would preside over 70,257 civilian employees, the largest number being in the War Department and the smallest number, 29, being in the State Department. Even as the head of his slave plantation, he was, like so many other planters, anything but a careful administrator. The Confederacy would one day be rightly compared to an underdeveloped country fighting against a well-organized and comparatively powerful modern nation.

While the South was regarded as an aristocratic society in the North, it is significant that in 1861 few of the leading Southern statesmen were of an aristocratic lineage. Postmaster General John H. Reagan's father was a tanner, and at one time he himself had been an overseer. Stephen R. Mallory, the secretary of the Navy, was the son of a Connecticut Yankee who had assisted his widowed mother in running a boardinghouse for sailors in Key West. Christopher G. Memminger of South Carolina was a German immigrant who had spent his early youth in a Charleston orphanage. The immensely talented Judah P. Benjamin was the son of a Jewish merchant. Even Davis himself was the son of a yeoman farmer and was born in a house not much more significant than the modest log cabin in which Abraham Lincoln was born. The same could be said of many of the South's Civil War governors.

Back at the White House, Lincoln's cabinet members were endlessly squabbling with one another, not over policy but influence, all united in their resentment of Seward's dominant position. Lincoln sought to quell matters by holding regular cabinet meetings on Tuesdays and Fridays at noon. Then, on March 28, Lincoln received more earth-shattering information in another memorandum from General Scott. This time around, Scott advised that Lincoln surrender *both* Sumter and Pickens so as to appease the eight remaining loyal slave states. President Lincoln was outraged. *Surrender both?* Unable to fathom this, he asked himself, Wasn't Pickens settled business? He regarded his general-in-chief as a towering military figure, but Scott's memorandum appeared to be based far less on military considerations than on political advice from a man whose roots clearly still lay in Virginia. Lincoln could scarcely contain his anger.

That night Lincoln attended a formal cabinet dinner, the first of his administration. William Howard Russell of the *Times* observed that there was "a babble of small talk," punctuated by a cascade of amusing anecdotes by Lincoln—Lincoln characterized the *Times* as "one of the greatest powers in the world"—belying the fact that beneath this bantering facade he was churning.

When dinner was over, he urgently summoned his secretaries into another room and, with much "excitement" and "emotion," told them what Scott had proposed. Lincoln was visibly angry. "A very oppressive silence" fell over the room, interrupted only by Montgomery Blair's disdainful reply that Scott was playing "politician and not general." With a pursed mouth, Lincoln angrily instructed them to turn in another opinion about Sumter for the next morning.

Yet, after they left, the president's inner struggle resolved itself; he decided the days of depending so exclusively on cabinet secretaries or generals had run their course. It was then that he had an epiphany. This matter would have to be decided by himself, not his retinue of advisers. So, tired and trembling, he trudged upstairs, returned to his office, and turned on his gas lamp.

He worked through the night.

Later, an anxious Lincoln confessed to Orville Browning that of all the trials he'd had since he came to Washington, "none begin to compare with those I had between the inauguration and the fall of Fort Sumter."

The next morning, before talking with his cabinet, he acted unilaterally, requesting that Fox send a list of the "ships, men, and supplies he would need for his expedition."

At noon he met again with his cabinet. One by one they filed into the White House and took their seats around the president.

It turns out that by dawn, March 29, Lincoln had made up his mind. He informed his cabinet that he would dispatch a supply fleet to Fort Sumter and leave the onerous decision to the rebels whether to start a civil war or not—just as he had said in his inaugural address. Later in the day, he set the process in motion, instructing the War and Navy Departments to start putting together a relief expedition for Charleston Harbor. Knowing the storm that was about to break, Lincoln also drastically restructured his daily schedule, limiting the amount of time office seekers could call on him. At Seward's urging, three days later he would also order an expedition to sail for Fort Pickens.

This time, hearing the vehemence in his voice, the cabinet reversed course. Everyone except for William H. Seward and Caleb B. Smith now supported Lincoln's muscular Sumter policy. Later in the day Welles, Blair, and Fox met with Lincoln at the White House, where it was finally determined, "with the president's approval," to reinforce Fort Sumter.

As for Seward? This was a nightmare, leaving him out in the cold and potentially leaving Lincoln's policy in tatters, with one hand not talking to the other hand. Seward, long believing he was the real power behind the throne, had promised the Confederate government that Sumter would be relinquished, and he'd said the same thing to the Virginia Unionists. But this was illusion. In effect, he was seduced by his own vanity, not to mention the honeyed words coming from Union Democrats and some Republicans as well in the South, calling Lincoln "a third rate man," while Seward was "the Atlas of not only his cabinet, but the giant intellect of the whole North."

Or as Charles Francis Adams Sr. put it about Lincoln: "The man is not equal to the hour." The only hope, he repeatedly wrote, lay in the secretary of state's influence with the president.

Seward, of course, agreed. All those delicate negotiations that Seward had privately undertaken to save the Union now were for naught, according to the secretary.

Because of Lincoln. Because of this narrow-minded, backwoods man. Because of this rank incompetent, this so-called president who had "no system," "no conception of the situation." Seward feared that unless he undertook radical action, government policy would lay in tatters, along with his reputation, and an unnecessary, bloody war would surely follow. He howled to his friend George R. Harrington, "We are not yet in a position to go to war."

Desperate to rehabilitate himself, the secretary of state spent the next couple of days composing a memorandum for Lincoln, which he handed in on April 1. Its title was simple, "Some thoughts for the President's consideration," but its substance was grandiloquent. The document announced, "We are at the end of a month's administration and yet without a policy either domestic or foreign." And absent a policy, the Union was sliding toward catastrophe. To forestall that, Seward now was offering a policy for Lincoln to adapt as his own. For starters, Seward, embracing a form of realpolitik, now maintained that the present urgency was due to the real issue, union or disunion, and not slavery. Indeed, slavery must be left out of it. The next step was that the United States should withdraw from Sumter, and instead hold the Florida garrison by establishing a blockade. Next, the government must arouse a vigorous "*spirit of independence* on this continent against European intervention." In effect, Seward was counseling that the United States should manufacture a war against Spain, France, and England, or, for that matter, Great Britain, Canada, and Russia, all of whom had designs on Mexico—or each other—for which the United States should demand an immediate "explanation," and if it were unsatisfactory, then America must declare war.

In any case, whatever policy Lincoln would pursue, it must be done so energetically either by the president or "devolve it on some member of his cabinet"; in other words, to Seward himself. Then all debate needed to halt. Everyone in the administration must agree with the policy and execute it loyally.

To Lincoln, this "effrontery" was disgraceful. His own secretary of state was not only dressing him down but offering to take over his administration; it was nothing short of a mutiny wrapped in a shiny diplomatic cloth. Lincoln sat down and composed a terse response to Seward, but then backed off and tucked his letter away in a drawer. Rather than potentially escalate matters, the president chose not to rebuke him in writing. John G. Nicolay and John M. Hay later noted that a less gracious president would have swiftly dismissed Seward. Aware of the difficulties that lay ahead, Lincoln instead wisely confronted Seward in private. He rejected his advice, sharply disagreeing that the administration had "no policy." On the question of who actually carries out policy, Lincoln was emphatic. "I must do it," he countered, because he was president. Finally, he eschewed any smothering of cabinet discussion. "I am entitled to have the advice," he said, "of all the cabinet." Backed into a corner, Seward suddenly appreciated Lincoln as a vigorous leader. As he learned, Lincoln could be pushed only so far. "Executive force and vigor are rare qualities," a shamed Seward wrote to his wife. "The president is the best of us." From then on, Seward became the president's most faithful cabinet secretary.

That service would be sorely needed in the days to come.

29

The Face of War

Curiously, there was one matter that the cabinet, amid its constant discussions, did not go over: the face and the cost of war.

In 1861, what did war look like to Lincoln and his cabinet as they weighed steps toward resupplying Sumter? This was as important a question as could be asked, yet there is little evidence that the cabinet even discussed it. However, the issue loomed large: What did war presage as Lincoln and his men knew it? What did it tell them about the fiery trial they were about to enter? Did they take it as inevitable that because of their greater numbers, there was no way they could lose a potential war against the Confederacy?

In truth, if they had spent some time addressing war throughout the ages, it would have been a sobering picture. They would have seen that armies countering numerical superiority, like the Confederacy, were not without options. They could employ secrecy, deception, and terror as their ultimate tools. They could move quickly, attack fast, and just as quickly scatter. They could rain terror—witness Missouri's carnage—when enemy troops were eating or when they had just concluded an exhausting march; they could assault military targets, or just as often hunt down random civilians. In short they could hit the enemy in his rear, or in his infrastructure, or just as devastating, in his psyche. The one constant for the smaller army was that it could move when least expected, and invariably in a way to maximize impact. Put differently, it could seek to erode the adversary's strength, and just as importantly, the enemy's morale as well.

Among the things that Lincoln could have been aware of was the fact that in Spain, no less a military force than the Romans required several long centuries before they could finally surmount the hit-and-run tactics of the Lusitanians and Celtiberians. Much later, in Wales, the English conquest succeeded only after some two hundred years of stubborn, acrimonious struggle and the widespread use of castellation—covering the country with strongholds. Equally familiar to Lincoln and nineteenth-century Americans were the Thirty Years' War and the French Wars of Religion; the experience of Frederick the Great in Bohemia, of the Duke of Wellington in Portugal, and the partisan war against Revolutionary France in the Royalist Vendée. And there was more, such as the stories of the Netherlands against the Spanish rule of Philip II; of Switzerland against the Habsburg Empire; of the Polish uprising in 1831; and of the nineteenth-century struggle of the Caucasian tribes against their Russian invaders. Remarkably, the Crimean War was witnessed by no less than the future general-in-chief of the Union, George B. McClellan, who was sent there by the then secretary of war, Jefferson Davis, to observe the hostilities and report back to Washington.

And then, of course, there was the most honorable example of them all, the American experience employing guerrilla methods against the British in the War of Independence. Using muddy roads and swollen streams to their advantage, as well as novel tactics on the open battlefield, including winning battles by losing them, American heroes successfully took on the British, who had been bred and trained on European battlefields. British general Lord Charles Cornwallis aptly spoke for England when he labeled as "truly savage" the American way of war, which another British general spoke of as "the sort of victory which ruins an army." For their part, after the success of the levée en masse for the French, what was needed was "un peu de fanatisme." General Baron de Jomini, the most widely studied theorist of war in the mid-nineteenth century, warned in his famous work,

Précis de l'art de la guerre (Summary of the art of war), that the growing nationalist passions sweeping the continent unchecked presaged the "bellum omnium contra omnes," or "the war of all against all."

If Lincoln and his cabinet had stopped to reflect upon the wider implications of war and its inherent unpredictability, not to mention its horrors and death toll, might he have chosen a different approach toward Sumter? Had the public known the calculus of war, or that the butcher's bill would one day consume four ghastly years and 620,000 lives, might it have insisted upon greater caution? Or had Lincoln read the masterwork on war by the great theorist Carl von Clausewitz, who brilliantly spoke of mustering the deadly passions of whole populaces on the battlefield, would he have seen the logic of Seward's dogged actions to strengthen efforts to preserve peace?

But now, as time dragged on, matters were hardening on both sides.

April 4, 1861. Peace was still very much on William H. Seward's mind. The secretary made arrangements for John B. Baldwin, a Virginia Unionist, to talk with Lincoln about the Virginia Secession Convention and Fort Sumter. This had long been of interest to Lincoln, who was desperate for the convention to adjourn and for Virginia to stay out of hostilities. In the interest of peace, would she do so? Now, to Seward's dismay, Baldwin was singing a different tune than he had been just weeks earlier. Suddenly, he insisted that Lincoln must pull out of Sumter first, warning that if he didn't and a shot were fired, then "as sure as there is a God in heaven the thing is gone" and Virginia would secede in forty-eight hours. Where Lincoln had flirted before with giving up Sumter if the Virginia Secession Convention disbanded, he now made no such offer. Of Baldwin's insistence, Lincoln emphatically scoffed: "Sir, that is impossible."

On the same day, Lincoln turned command of the Sumter expedition over to Gustavus Fox. As planned, it would consist of three warships, a gunboat, and a steamer containing two hundred soldiers and a year's worth of provisions. At the same time, the president sent a special messenger to inform Major Anderson: A relief fleet was on its way.

Still hoping that Lincoln would change his mind concerning Sumter, Seward tirelessly continued to work on plans for reinforcing Fort Pickens. He called on Captain Montgomery Meigs to meet with him at his home. Seward requested that a detailed estimate for "relieving and holding Fort Pickens" be brought to the president by late that day. Back at the White House, Lincoln was waiting. He welcomed the report, although he still planned on reinforcing both forts. The president said, "Tell [Scott] that I wish this thing done," and "not to let it fail."

Part of not letting it fail was engaging in subterfuge. Seward was worried that because a sizable number of men in the Navy had been openly disloyal to the Union, the Army's expedition to Pickens should be kept from naval authorities. Such was the undercurrent of sedition and confusion in the Union capital. So the plan was to employ the US Navy's most powerful warship, the *Powhatan*, with its hefty guns and three hundred sailors, for a secret mission to Pensacola under the command of Lieutenant David Porter. Incredibly, Lincoln emphasized that under no circumstances should these plans be disclosed to the Navy Department. Yet there was considerable mayhem as it turned out that the relief for Fort Sumter also depended on the *Powhatan*, which would play an essential role in backing up the tugboats carrying supplies to the garrison. But Navy secretary Gideon Welles and Captain Gustavus Fox were unaware of the Pensacola operation, just as the Pensacola operation knew little about the Sumter plans.

In truth, Lincoln was sloppy in perusing the orders, and inadvertently assigned the *Powhatan* both to Pickens and to Sumter. Already, in a grim sign of things to come, even before any fighting had begun, Lincoln was experiencing what Clausewitz himself had called "the fog of war." However unreliable the clerks in the War and Navy Departments were, Lincoln in these feverish hours could have at least pulled aside secretaries Cameron and Welles and told them what was afoot. He did not.

Totally unaware of the confusion, Welles wrote to the commander of the *Powhatan* on April 5 instructing him to "leave New York with the Powhatan in time to be at Charleston Bay" by the morning of April 11. Lincoln's plan was straightforward. If the supply boats were permitted to land at Fort Sumter, the *Powhatan* would return to New York at once. But if Porter's entry was opposed, then the *Powhatan* and its support ships should be used "to open the way." And should the peaceable supply mission fail, a reinforcement of the garrison should be attempted by "disposing of your force," as needed. Welles's order to the commander of the *Powhatan* was read to the president the same day and authorized. However, the mix-up would prove to be deeply fatal to the mission.

Then, on April 6, Lincoln sent the most important letter of his presidency thus far, and indeed one of the most important messages in the life of the United States: a communiqué for Cameron to dispatch a special message to the governor of South Carolina. The Union ships would not open fire, Lincoln said, unless South Carolina resisted them or bombarded the fort. "I am directed by the president of the United States to notify you to expect an attempt will be made, to supply Fort Sumter with provisions only; and that, if such attempt be not resisted, no effort to throw men, arms, or ammunition, will be made without further notice." On paper, this was the genius of Lincoln's plan. By informing the governor of South Carolina that America was sending provisions to Sumter, he left the rebel governor with a hard choice of allowing food to enter peacefully or starting a war.

The actual message itself was not relayed over telegraph by a member of Lincoln's cabinet but hand-delivered by Robert Chu, a mid-level State Department clerk. Chu boarded a train in DC bound for South Carolina on April 6, four days before Captain Fox sailed from New York.

———————

In the meantime, before Chu arrived, confusion reigned in the South about Lincoln's actual plans. Were they still to believe Seward's promises of abandoning Sumter? Having no reliable information, they were driven by a cacophony of whispers and rumor. Increasingly, the three unrecognized Confederate commissioners tasked with keeping South Carolina updated on events felt doubt creep into their convictions.

Daily they sent wild telegraphs to the Confederate secretary of state, Robert Toombs. It was a miasma of confusion.

On April 4 they telegraphed: "Strengthen the defenses at the mouth of the Mississippi."

On April 5: "The statement that the armament is intended for Santa Domingo may be a mere ruse."

April 6: "The rumors that they are destined against Pickens, and perhaps Sumter, are getting every day stronger."

April 7: "It may be Sumter and the Mississippi; it is almost certain that it is Pickens and the Texas frontier."

And while Seward had continued to peddle the idea that Sumter would not be reinforced, Unionist Justice Campbell was full of forebodings and alarm at the warlike preparations taking place.

Meanwhile, the men of Sumter were now living in a sort of twilight zone. They had long since finished packing their belongings in preparation for departure and were wondering why the government was taking so long to give the order. They knew that it wasn't unusual for the White House to be slow, but now its pace felt glacial. Like a man stranded on a desert island, almost daily Major Robert Anderson warned Washington of his diminishing supplies and asked desperately for orders. None were forthcoming. All Anderson knew was what he was reading in the newspapers. Unhappy and anxious, he reported back to Washington: "The truth is that the sooner we are out of this harbor the better. Our flag runs an hourly risk of being insulted and my hands are tied." Former senator Louis T. Wigfall, a rebel and a fire-eater always ready to secede, left Baltimore, where he had been recruiting Confederates in secret, and registered at the Mills House in Charleston on April 3. He strode out to the balcony and gave an inflammatory speech.

"Whether Major Anderson shall be shelled out or starved out," he boomed, "is a question merely of expediency."

Yet the uncertainty was getting on everyone's nerves. The famed South Carolinian diarist, Mary Chesnut, tried in vain to enjoy her pâté de foie gras salad. "How can one settle down to anything?" she asked. "One's heart is in one's mouth all the time." Intuiting what was to come, a pair of prominent Northern journalists arrived in Charleston, settling into well-appointed hotel rooms: George Salter of the *New York Times* and F. G. de Fontaine of the *Herald*, both war correspondents. General P. G. T. Beauregard gave them something to think about; unwilling to take Seward's promises of withdrawal at their face value now—he was right—he began work on the harbor fortifications, which had lagged during the peace talks.

Chesnut astutely remarked, "The plot thickens, the air is red-hot with rumors."

That same evening of April 8, Lincoln's emissary, Robert Chu, arrived at Northeastern Station in a city giddy with expectation. He rushed to the Charleston Hotel, and soon was meeting with General Beauregard and Governor Pickens. Cradling a sheet of paper by candlelight, he read the fateful message from Lincoln that put an end to all the rumors.

The ambiguity was gone. Governor Pickens now knew the score.

Chu then handed Pickens a copy of the message for him to keep. It was unaddressed and unsigned, not at all according to formal protocols between a president and the governor of a state. This was Lincoln's not-so-subtle way of sending a message to Pickens—he did not accept the South Carolinians as a legitimate country.

———

On April 4, Simon Cameron, Lincoln's secretary of war, had sent a letter to Major Robert Anderson. He informed Anderson that his report to the president occasioned "some anxiety" to Lincoln; that Lincoln had assumed Anderson could hold out until the fifteenth without any great inconvenience; and that an expedition was on the way to relieve Anderson before that. He added that if in Anderson's judgment he needed "to save" himself and capitulation becomes "a necessity," he was authorized to make it.

Anderson was "deeply affected" by the letter; indeed, he was crushed. He had endured long hardship and great strain and above all humiliation, and now Lincoln was sounding the alarums. As it happened, Anderson wrote back, informing Lincoln and Cameron that he didn't even have enough oil to light the way in lanterns for his own boats. Nonetheless, Anderson was stoic; he said he would strive to do his duty although his heart was "not in the war," and that he hoped God would still "avert it." No doubt Lincoln would've found this report of great consequence, but it never reached him. It fell into the hands of the enemy: General Beauregard.

Major Anderson promptly began to put the fort on a war footing. Men were detailed to carry ammunition to the guns. Flagstones were piled in tiers to offer more protection to the gunners. The ship bringing them supplies, if it got by enemy batteries, would anchor the fort's left flank, which was not prepared for the entry of men and supplies. They frantically began to address that. Anderson had no illusions that the enemy would allow provisions to enter unopposed. Thus he made ready for an expedition bringing him not only provisions, but also reinforcements.

Around this time General Beauregard informed Anderson that no further mail would be allowed into or from Sumter. The blackout was complete.

Meanwhile, on Sunday morning, April 8, the men of Sumter got a rude awakening. The Confederates blew up the house on Sullivan's Island west of Fort Moultrie, unmasking a previously hidden battery of heavy guns. So what else did the Confederates have waiting for them? Anderson was certain they would be in a position to unleash a hail of enfilading fire on the flank where the relief ship would anchor. However, this would be a disaster of the highest consequences.

Meanwhile, five thousand more Confederate soldiers were now pouring into Charleston in streams. Charleston's streets were clogged with marching soldiers, rumbling wagons filled with powder, and excited citizens milling in the roadways. Soon, some six thousand men all told would be surrounding Major Anderson and his minuscule command. Still, among the Confederates there were hesitations. Toombs, in a prophetic moment, told Davis, "The firing upon that fort will inaugurate a Civil War greater than any the world has yet seen."

Yet patience was running out, and the Confederate war secretary, LeRoy Pope Walker, telegraphed Beauregard to at once demand Sumter's "evacuation." And "if this is refused, proceed, in such manner as you may determine, to reduce it."

Beauregard received that order on April 10. For his part, he was sending out orders as fast as he could write them, and he continued preparations.

He promptly set up two new guns: a heavy Dahlgren, and a rifle/ Blakely gun, which was capable of a twelve-pound shot with the accuracy of a dueling pistol. The Charleston *Courier* boldly editorialized, "Let the strife begin—we have no fear of the issue." At the same time, the Virginian ex-congressman Roger Pryor gave a fiery balcony speech to help prod a cautious Virginia to move.

At the top of his lungs, he enthused, "Strike a blow!"

———————

For Lincoln, things went quickly awry. The flagship of the Fort Sumter expedition, the *Powhatan*, was transferred to the Pickens fleet and instead of reinforcing Sumter, sailed off for Florida. Upon realizing this, Lincoln tried to retrieve the missing ship, but to no avail. It was already gone. On April 9, without its protective flagship, Fox's little fleet set out on its fateful mission to Charleston Harbor, sailing bravely into the jaws of hell.

In the White House, Lincoln stood at his office windows staring out at a darkening sky. It had rained incessantly over the last couple of days, drumming on rooftops and running in streams. The president at least took satisfaction in knowing that he was defending the United States flag snapping in the wind over Sumter, that he had refused to give in to the browbeating of Southern insurrectionaries, and that he was abiding by his oath of office and doing what most Union men wanted him to do.

If the rebels opened fire, the momentous issue of civil war was indeed in their hands.

April 11 dawned bright and clear. In Sumter, Anderson received yet another sobering surprise. At the west end of Sullivan's Island, he saw 24-pounders and 23-pounders added to the heavy guns already aimed at Sumter's left flank; that was where the relief boat would anchor, if it was even lucky enough to reach the fort. Anderson realized what President Lincoln did not: There was no help now.

The brave little Sumter garrison was cut off from the world.

Anderson's men nibbled their remaining bits of bread. All that was left to eat was some salt pork and a few broken crackers. Anderson then ordered everybody to move their bedding from the vulnerable barracks and officers' quarters to the protection of the casemates. Here they would live as well as fight, and if necessary, die. Head bowed, face grim, Anderson paced alone, back and forth and back and forth, seeing nothing but tragedy for the nation.

He once again put up a stoic front in his daily report. "I shall continue," he said sternly, "as long as I can."

As if in a dreamlike state, on April 11, some of Anderson's men stared endlessly out at the sea. "We're looking for the relief promised to us," wrote one soldier, "and men can be seen at all hours on the parapet." They saw no warships, but at 3:30 p.m. that afternoon they spied a small boat bearing a white flag approaching from the city. It was a Confederate lieutenant, ironically named Jefferson Davis, bearing a dispatch from Beauregard for Anderson. In it the general said the Confederacy could wait no longer: "I am ordered by the government of the Confederate States to demand the evacuation of Fort Sumter."

Anderson had a fateful decision to make: to capitulate or to fight back, however long the odds. He convened his closest advisers and polled them. He asked each of his officers the fateful question: Should we give up?

Doubleday: "No."

Foster: "No."

Seymour: "No."

Snyder: "No."

Davis: "No."

Hall: "No."

Crawford: "No."

Anderson wrote back to Beauregard, replying that his sense of honor and obligations prevented his "compliance." He then remarked to Colonel James Chesnut, "I shall await the first shot, and if you do not batter us to pieces, we shall be starved out in a few days."

For dinner that night, they downed the remaining salt pork and rice. Meanwhile, the men kept glancing out to sea.

No warships were visible.

———————

Mary Chesnut recorded, "We had an unspoken foreboding that it was to be our last pleasant evening." Deeply anxious, she sighed, "I do not pretend to go to sleep."

Anderson's men sized up the enemy batteries bearing down on Sumter. And sized up what they had in return to defend themselves. It was not enough, and Anderson and his men knew it. It was just a matter of time before Armageddon.

Then at 12:45 a.m. on April 12, the sentinels of Sumter spotted a boat in the distance approaching under a white flag once more; it was the three Confederate aides, accompanied by a fourth man. Colonel James Chesnut was one of them. Intrigued by Anderson's comment about the men being starved by April 15, Beauregard wanted to know *exactly* when Anderson would have to evacuate the fort. Perhaps this way war could be avoided.

For one last time, Anderson asked his men how long they could last as a fighting force. Now Dr. Crawford rendered his professional opinion; he estimated the enervated garrison could last for three days entirely without food. But there was enough doubt that in one room Anderson and his men had a fervent debate, while in another, Chesnut and his Confederate companions waited and grew impatient. Finally, the Sumter officers agreed that they could hold out until noon on April 15, but no longer. Instructed to ask for Beauregard, Chesnut shook his head upon hearing this; there were too many conditions, too many "ifs."

Now at the crack of dawn, Chesnut informed Anderson that hostilities would commence in one hour. It was nearing 3:30 a.m. when one of the Confederates, Captain Lee, gave a sigh and poignantly called out to Anderson, "If we never meet in this world again, God grant that we may meet in the next." Underneath a canopy of stars and a tray of wispy clouds, the four Confederates got back into their little boat and glided across a calm sea to Charleston.

They wouldn't make it. Shortly thereafter they saw a flash of flame rise high in the sky, followed by a whistle and an ear-busting roar. The shell soared in an arc, then curved downward in a violent burst almost directly over Fort Sumter. There was enough of a pause for everyone to absorb the drama of what had just happened.

It was the first shot of the Civil War.

Then the darkness was split by thunder as a dozen batteries let loose from various points in the harbor. In her suite at the Mills House, Mary Chesnut was now tossing and turning, unable to sleep. "At 4:30 the heavy bombing of a cannon," she wrote. "I sprang out of bed, and on my knees prostrate I prayed as I never prayed before."

———————

On April 13, telegraph messages about Sumter came pouring into Washington. It was everything Lincoln expected, and nothing that he expected. Lincoln's commander for Sumter, Gustavus Fox, asked, where was the *Powhatan*? No answer was forthcoming.

The first epic battle was about to be waged and lost.

In Charleston, citizens shimmied onto rooftops and sat on chimneys to watch the show. In Sumter itself, the men could hear the boom of the first single shot. Then another, then another, as the firing became one jumbled roar. Remarkably, Anderson's men kept up a veneer of normality—or was it a state of denial? They had breakfast, a quick affair—a glass of warm water and a bit of fat pork. As it happened, the dark-skinned waiter serving them was almost white with fear, wincing with each explosion.

In the meantime, Major Anderson fired off a series of instructions to his tiny group of seventy men. He allowed Captain Abner Doubleday, his second-in-command, to fire the first gun back—an honor that Doubleday accepted with relish. For most of these men, in fact, war seemed an exciting spectacle, not the province of moaning victims and endless casualty lists. They would be soon enlightened. The air was quickly thick with choking smoke and deafening sound. Soon the operation at each gun became mechanical: "Sponge barrel, load cartridge, RAM it, load ball, RAM it, fire!" The brick-and-frame barracks and officers' quarters, built three stories high, began to take a dreadful beating. But Anderson's men couldn't seem to make a dent in the well-protected Confederate batteries. Even when they scored direct hits, to their horror the balls merely bounced off harmlessly, not having enough weight or power. If the Sumter men were unable to make much of an impression on the Confederates, they at least had the satisfaction of knowing that their own walls, twelve feet thick, were turning away shots with equal disdain.

But then in midmorning, the upper story of the barracks caught fire; the rebels were firing red-hot balls. Despite efforts to extinguish the flames, the barracks continued to burn. Where, Anderson's men asked, was the relief expedition Secretary Cameron said would arrive on the eleventh or the twelfth?

That wasn't the only question. Anderson realized that it was entirely possible that the enemy would attempt a storming assault during the night, and then, how to tell friend from foe? As Sergeant Chester observed,

"Both would come in boats, both would answer in English. It would be horrible to fire upon friends; it would be fatal not to fire upon enemies."

By midnight, no relief boats had come. But then almost miraculously, beyond the bar in the distance, there were two ships steaming closer, still distant but visible through the haze and smoke, flying the Stars and Stripes. Shortly they were joined by a third ship. To Anderson and his men, this was as good as the *Powhatan*. They thought that this was what they most needed: a chance to give the South Carolinians a sturdy taste of the Yankee blade between the ribs.

———

For Lincoln's handpicked emissary, Captain Gustavus Fox, his relief expedition was increasingly shaping up to be a nightmare. Everything went wrong. The voyage south was made in a howling gale that cost precious time and caused many sailors to be seasick. At 3:00 a.m. on April 12, Fox was ten miles out from Charleston Harbor, desperately waiting for the *Powhatan*, the *Pocahontas*, and the *Pawnee*, as well as the three tugs, the *Yankee*, *Uncle Ben*, and *Freeborn*. Of all these, the *Powhatan* was the most important, and Fox still did not know that the frigate had been rerouted by Seward and Lincoln. Nor did he know that the tug *Uncle Ben* was caught up in a storm in Wilmington, North Carolina, or that the *Yankee* missed Charleston altogether and ended up in Savannah. More inexplicably still, the *Freeborn*, the third of the tugs, never even left New York.

So Fox had no choice but to wait in the capsizing heavy seas hoping for six additional ships—miles out. But it refused to "stand in for the bar" because its orders were to await the arrival of the *Powhatan* for further instructions. This was yet more poisonous fruit from the bureaucratic confusion in Lincoln's White House.

When darkness came, Fox began signaling with lights for the *Powhatan*, still not realizing that something had gone tragically wrong.

———

Between seven and eight o'clock that evening, a heavy rain began to fall. Around eight o'clock the skies cleared, and sunshine turned the harbor waters a vivid blue. Now the barracks caught fire, and the Sumter men were unable to douse it. Some took axes to the flaming woodwork, but this was useless. Despite all their efforts, the flames continued to spread. To the rebels off in the distance, Sumter was an inferno, flames shooting high in the sky. Surely now, the Confederates thought, Anderson would have to surrender. It was all the more problematic for the Union men given that cartridges were so short in supply that Anderson restricted its firing one gun to every ten minutes. And any hope that the fire might burn itself out proved to be a vain one as well. With each passing minute it only got worse. Then came the explosions; the heat caused the stockpiles of shells and grenades to explode. By this stage, the heat from the fire was so oppressive that soldiers had to rip off their outer clothing, which was smoking.

The men of Sumter were hot, unnerved, sweating, and scared. With numbed blank looks, they felt like they were suffocating, smothered by the heat and fumes. The sound of masonry falling in every direction only added to the growing chaos. Inside the fort, it was pandemonium. Discipline broke down as both officers and men abandoned everything else in search of air. In successive thrusts, the flames spread, hissing and sparking and crackling. And the men's cartridges were almost gone. So the gunners resorted to an ingenious but ultimately ineffective substitute for cartridge bags—socks. Then came perhaps the greatest indignity. Shortly before one o'clock, the flagpole bearing the Stars and Stripes was decapitated, and the flag itself floated slowly to the ground.

Things were moving very quickly now. Former senator Louis T. Wigfall, over at Cummings Point, could see that the Union was in distress once the Sumter flag went down. In these stirring, emotion-packed hours, there were also tender moments that transcended the gritty realities of war. Taking matters into his own hands, he got into a boat with two oarsmen and headed for Sumter with a white flag draped on his sword—he was going to suggest "surrender." There was so much flame and smoke that Anderson and his men didn't even see Wigfall coming until he pulled into Sumter. Once there, the Texan shouted excitedly, "You are on fire and you are not firing your guns! General Beauregard desires to stop this."

He was taken to see Major Anderson.

"You have defended your flag nobly, sir," he told the commander. "It's madness to persevere in useless resistance." Anderson nodded in agreement and said he would surrender now, instead of noon on the fifteenth. They set terms: Anderson said he would quit his command, take all company property, and salute his country with a touching 50-round salute to the shredded American flag. In a moment of supreme poignancy, Beauregard said it was honorable testimony to the gallantry and fortitude with which Major Anderson had defended his post. There were no battle deaths. As Horace Greeley, the great New York journalist, said later of the supreme irony, "It was a comparatively bloodless beginning for the bloodiest war America ever knew."

Thirty-four hours after the fighting began, Anderson's men, some sitting on the ground, were exhausted. Some began gathering their things in silence, as if they were dim, purgatorial souls. Others just lay down, stared blankly into the distance, and slept. Covered in grime and soot, Anderson himself looked haggard. The fort looked haggard, too. Its gates were gone, its parapet a ruin, and the barracks had collapsed and were still blazing out of control. Ironically, all this could've been avoided. In a few days at most, the garrison would've been facing starvation, and the command could've evacuated the fort peacefully. The war was already chaos.

In Charleston, people were gripped by a fever of excitement. Without a thought of what was to come next, business was at a standstill; the whole town was taking "a holiday." They were giddy and elated and thronging to the harbor front to view the heroic spectacle. The excitement, declared one dispatch, was "indescribable." Few of the townspeople stopped to reflect on the fact that the battle was little more than 7,000 men who defeated a paltry seventy hungry soldiers, musicians, and workmen. The South Carolinian Unionist judge James Louis Petigru may have been the wisest of the lot when he said: "It is an odd feeling to be in the midst of joy that one does not feel. The universal applause that waits on secessionists and secession has not the slightest tendency to shake my conviction that we are on the road to ruin."

Meanwhile, still out at sea, Gustavus Fox was sick with chagrin. The *Powhatan* and the three tugs had never come, and the *Pocahontas* finally arrived just as Sumter was surrendering.

30

It Begins

On April 14, with Sumter surrendering, Lincoln went to church and then had a lengthy meeting with his cabinet. As the minutes ticked by, the meeting was consumed with frustration and fear. Lincoln declared in a voice trembling with emotion that the rebels had fired the first shot, thereby hamstringing him with a fateful decision of "immediate dissolution, or blood." To stamp out the rebellion, he announced, he would call up seventy-five thousand militia to suppress it, along with convening Congress in a special session on Independence Day. (Lincoln, however, did go to great pains to underscore that he was not going to wait for Congress to shape "a war policy.") And he repeated that this was not a war between the states, but a "domestic insurrection" against the national government. Lincoln wouldn't even acknowledge that the Deep South states had left the Union; rather, their actions were akin to a large coup: Rebellious citizens had taken over and created a "pretended" Confederate government that Washington could not and would not recognize. Lincoln's objective, then, was not so much to win a war but to reestablish the rightful authority of the government in the territories seized by a radical South.

That afternoon after the cabinet meeting, Lincoln's former rival Stephen A. Douglas sauntered into the president's office. Douglas's voice was parched. Actually, he was unwell, and in two months, he would be dead. But for several hours that day, they talked strategy and politics. Without reference to the past, Douglas offered his wholehearted support, declaring himself ready "to sustain the President in the exercise of his constitutional functions to preserve the Union." Crucially, Douglas agreed with Lincoln's plans; he, too, would mobilize Union troops to suppress the rebels, except that he favored bumping up the figure to two hundred thousand men. He and the president treated the dispute as if it were an unruly riot rather than a devastating war between opposing nations. The two former opponents then walked over to Lincoln's wall and studied a large map, dissecting the strategic choke points that had to be reinforced. One thing they did not discuss was the possibility that this would be a cataclysmic conflict stretching over not months but years, and washed not with the stamping out of pockets of rioters but with an ocean of dead.

Later in the day, Douglas issued a press release promising his unwavering support for the president "in this hour of trial." After that, Douglas rushed back to Illinois to stir up fellow Democrats to the Union cause, urging every man to lay aside his party bias and go "heart and hand, to put down treason and traitors."

On April 15, Lincoln crossed the Rubicon. His proclamation for seventy-five thousand militia men now swept across the states; whether they were in the North or the South, everyone now had to choose their sides. Once more in the South, the ghastly specter of federal troops invading and massacring Southerners and liberating enslaved people was more than even Southern Unionists could countenance. In the final blow to Lincoln's once Unionist dream, the Virginia convention on April 17 launched a thunderbolt, adopting a secession ordinance. With this one stroke, Virginia, the crown jewel of the South, the "mother of presidents," joined the Confederacy, and the federal capital was moved from Montgomery to Richmond. Hailing the call, other Southern states followed suit over the next two months: Arkansas, North Carolina, and Tennessee also became Confederate states.

Meanwhile, to Lincoln's existential fears, the crucial border states of Maryland, Missouri, and Kentucky seemed poised to leave the Union as well.

Staring out his windows, chin tucked to his chest, an embittered Lincoln looked out at the church spires and chimneys dotting the landscape in Alexandria; all around him, he felt, were images of treachery and sedition. There was one ray of hope, however. In the distance, a depressed Lincoln could see the Lee family mansion perched high above on Arlington Heights, the border separating North from South. Amid the day's slow-growing chaos, he expected that Lee, the hero of the Mexican-American War who put down the rebellion of John Brown, the beloved son of West Point, and the great Union soldier driven by an antique sense of honor, would surely respond to Lincoln's entreaties to lead the Union forces to crush the insurrection. Also, Colonel Lee was married to Mary Custis, the daughter of George Washington's adopted son. But questions lingered. How, Lincoln wondered, could Virginia's Union men join a traitorous secessionist movement with such incredible rapidity? How, he wondered, did men who repeatedly insisted upon their "lasting devotion" to the national flag so suddenly raise their hands in defense of disunion? How, he asked himself, did these "professed Union men" overnight become insurrectionists themselves? For that matter, how did they allow this "giant insurrection" to plant its roots so close to the White House?

And how did they succumb to the irony of following in John Brown's footsteps and seizing the federal arsenal at Harpers Ferry, as well as importing large bodies of troops "from the so-called Confederate states"?

Part VII

TURNING POINT

31

The End of an Era

On Sunday morning, April 14, 1861, Charleston awoke early. Sunlight sparkled on the waves, and shafts of brilliant light filtered into the piazzaed houses of the city; at the same time the towers of St. Michael's were as perfectly visible as a gorgeous French Impressionist painting; so was the harbor, thronging with sailing vessels, rowboats, skiffs, dories, and launches. The guns were silent and the Stars and Stripes were seen nowhere, while the palmetto and Confederate flags were everywhere, side by side.

The old order—the United States of America—was truly dead, or certainly not the same.

In Washington and New York, too, it was truly the end of an era. As Lincoln met with his cabinet members, the men of Sumter boarded the *Baltic* and were soon on their way north, catching up on sleep, while Major Robert Anderson, the lion of the nation, had been indelibly transformed into a rallying cry for the Union. Here was the North's answer to Charleston. With the tattered Sumter flag flying proudly, it was warmly saluted by the din of whistles and the cry of bells from every steamer and tug in sight in New York Harbor. Anderson was cheered, paraded, and given medals. Walt Whitman would never forget this moment. Emerging from an opera on Fourteenth Street, he strolled down Broadway late Saturday night. He was stunned to see the great lamps still brightly blazing at the Metropolitan Hotel and to hear the shouts of newsboys announcing the reports of war. Whitman likened the Northern response to a "volcanic upheaval." Yet, as pride mingled with determination, few appreciated that this was the beginning of an unimagined ordeal.

Both sides clung to their ideals. Both sides were seduced by their own illusions. Both sides dismissed Major Anderson's feeling that every gun fired from Sumter, every return salvo from the South, signaled another chip in the edifice of comity. Both sides believed this would be an easy war to win. The Confederate secretary of war, LeRoy Pope Walker, had already predicted that his handkerchief "would absorb all the blood spilled in the war." Now, with a sneer, he ventured a new prediction. "No man can tell where the war this day commenced will end," he insisted, adding, "I will prophecy that the flag which now flaunts the breeze here will float over the dome of the old capitol at Washington before May one."

Meanwhile, Northerners had little regard for the strength or determination of the South: Seward brazenly predicted that the war would be over in sixty days, while Lincoln's close adviser John M. Hay said that the Southern army was nothing more than "a vast mob, insubordinate and hungry." The New York *Tribune* had a more vivid prediction, one shared widely in the North.

"Jeff Davis & Co. will," it predicted, "be swinging from the battlements at Washington...by the Fourth of July."

Epilogue

The same day that Robert E. Lee learned of Virginia's withdrawal from the Union, US general-in-chief Winfield Scott and, separately, Francis P. Blair Sr. summoned Lee for an urgent meeting in Washington. It was here, first with Blair, that a stunning offer was made, bearing Abraham Lincoln's seal of approval: command of the new Union army. This was no surprise. Scott had termed Lee a "military genius" and "the best soldier I ever saw in the field." Scott even boasted that should hostilities break out, the US government should insure Lee's life for $5 million a year. Today, Lincoln made his desires plain. The Union wanted Lee.

All his life, this was one position that Lee had coveted. It offered him a chance to walk in the footsteps of not only his own father but also the father of the country, with a chance for military glory rivaling even Washington's. In the three hours that Scott and Lee spoke—of which no record exists—echoing his discussion with Blair, Lee not only declined, surely the most painful decision of his life, but also resigned his commission from the Army. However much the son of an ardent Federalist longed for compromise to save the Union ("Mr. Blair," he said candidly, "I look upon secession as anarchy"), however much he had a distaste for slavery (deeming it "a moral and political evil"), in the end, the permanency of birth and blood won out. "I cannot raise my hand against my birthplace, my home, my children," he said to a friend. And he explained that save in defense of his native state, "I never desire again to draw my sword."

But draw his sword he would. Despite Lincoln's offer, five days later Lee accepted an appointment as commander in chief of Virginia's military forces; three weeks after that he was made a brigadier general in the Confederate army. He did it for "honor" but with no illusions and the heaviest of hearts: "I foresee that the country will have to pass through a terrible ordeal," he warned soberly.

Would Lee be equal to the task? He was one of the best-known and most watched men of his era, and surely if someone could best the daunting odds arrayed against him and lead the Confederacy to victory, he would be the one.

Thus, the peace was lost and a great war would begin. Lincoln's decision at Sumter to maneuver the South into firing the first shot would become the most profound decision in this nation's history.

Over the next four years, a series of battles in once little-known places would take on immortality. First, Sumter. Then Manassas, Second Manassas, Antietam, Fredericksburg, Chancellorsville, Shiloh, Chickamauga, Vicksburg, Gettysburg, the Cold Harbor in the Wilderness Campaign, the carnage of the burning of Atlanta and the march to the sea, the siege around Petersburg and Richmond, the haunting specter of guerrilla war, and, of course, Appomattox. All told, it is estimated there were ten thousand confrontations in the war to come. And, too, a series of generals and political figures would equally take on immortality, whether revered or reviled. Ulysses S. Grant and Robert E. Lee, William Tecumseh Sherman and Stonewall Jackson, Philip H. Sheridan, Jefferson Davis, James Longstreet, and Patrick R. Cleburne, George G. Meade and General George B. McClellan and Joseph Hooker, Pierre G. T. Beauregard, Nathan Bedford Forrest, William Clarke Quantrill, and "Bloody" Bill Anderson.

What was begun by Lincoln in a nation of 31.5 million as an effort to quell a seeming insurrection would consume more than 600,000 lives, perhaps as many as 850,000, totaling more casualties than America would accumulate in all its other wars, from the Revolution in the 1700s to Iraq and Afghanistan in the twenty-first century. The butcher's bill was staggering; it was as if five million were killed: an almost unthinkable number. Also staggering was the legacy of the leftover soldiers who barely survived, this mass of filthy, bleeding and bruised, permanently maimed and tired men.

Across the Confederacy itself the legacy of the lost peace was everywhere. There were few poignant reminders of the prewar days in a landscape that was hopelessly battered and indelibly scarred. Where proud antebellum homes and mansions once stood, there was now little more than rotting wood, cracked paint, and weed-choked grass—and ubiquitous chimney stacks, charred and lonely reminders of once thriving cities and bustling plantations. A whole generation of men in the South were dead, dismembered, or gone.

And above all, the lost peace gave us the genius of Abraham Lincoln, who saved the United States and who fought tirelessly for the long-overdue Thirteenth Amendment banning slavery, who before he gave us his life as the victim of John Wilkes Booth's assassin's bullet, bequeathed to the nation the three most memorable series of orations in American history: the Gettysburg Address, the First Inaugural, and the Second Inaugural.

The lost peace of 1861 also bequeathed to America and the world the most enduring democracy, not to mention a reunited Union, or, in today's parlance, the United States.

And for Black Americans and lovers of liberty everywhere, the lost peace was the necessary war, and would provide for them their own struggle for true freedom, a principal legacy of the war that would still haunt the country for over a century to come. There would be the exhilaration of emancipation but also its unfilled promise, marred by terrible brutality, horrific violence, and often unspeakable racial repression on which, paradoxically, the strands of national reconciliation frequently rested. To be sure, the lost peace and the historic Thirteenth Amendment did not eradicate overnight the old and deep know-nothing streak of nativism that would not wither away easily in America: a virulent mix of Black haters, Catholic haters, Jew haters, immigrant haters, Northern haters, and just plain haters. Matching Lincoln's eloquence, Frederick Douglass amply articulated the complicated chapter in the United States that was just beginning after the lost peace.

"Verily," he said, "the work does not end with the abolition of slavery, it only begins."

But upon the end of the war, in the former slave quarters and plantation houses, in the hot fields and steaming kitchens, there arose excited talk of a changing world: the ability to choose where one lived and worked; how to educate one's children or oneself; where and whom one married—and when; and instead of being property, owning property. By all accounts, however flawed, the lost peace, the ultimate legacy of the necessary war, was at once a moment fervent with hope and paralyzing possibilities, as people of color caught sight of the edges of the new reality that now existed, a life with freedom.

Here, then, was the final benefit of the lost peace and the necessary war of 1861.

As Houston Holloway, whose own painful journey mirrored Silas Jackson's, and who had been sold three times before the age of twenty, put it: "I felt like a bird out of the cage. Amen, Amen! AMEN!"

Acknowledgments

To Evan and Oscie Thomas, my master historians and dear friends whose regular lunches with me did so much to enrich *1861*.

To Michael Humphries, a gifted historian in his own right who poured energy and research into this book.

To Nancy Jacobson and Mark Penn, longtime friends who have always done so much to enhance my projects.

To Wayne and Cathy Reynolds, who have provided indispensable support to my writing.

To Paul Kalb, who provided vital readings of *1861* and made extensive and useful comments. And to his wife, Susan Ascher, a good friend and always encouraging voice.

To Gordon Wood, a great friend who showed the way of history.

To Bruce Vinokour, for his keen understandings of the meaning of *1861*.

To Maureen Scalia, my cherished friend and confidant.

To Scooter Libby, for his enduring friendship and support.

To my longtime agent, Michael Carlisle, for his steadfast support during this entire project.

To Victoria Turner, who was there when I needed her with support and good counsel.

To Larry Camp, whose friendship always injected good cheer.

To John Dillon, friend extraordinaire, who in countless ways has always been there above and beyond the call of duty.

To Mark Werksman, my lifelong best friend.

To Amar Deol, whose flair and vision made this all possible.

A Note on Sources

In *1861*, a book that provides a very different understanding of the start of the Civil War, I have extensively woven primary with secondary sources, including contemporary newspaper accounts, letters, articles, books, and pamphlets. In countless ways, the strength of *1861* lies in its interpretations of these various sources. Case in point, a subject as vast as Abraham Lincoln ultimately has few new facts available. Yet there can be so much to say. So, in *1861*, I labored intensively to find novel and hidden insights about a subject otherwise obscured in the sea of historical information.

The reality remains, as I was reminded in writing *1861*, that sometimes, little details can yield the largest insights, and make for the most powerful understandings. For instance, I'm forever haunted by the little-known story of how, on the day that four influential confederates resigned from the United States Senate, that night Varina Davis wandered into her living room only to find her otherwise stoic husband, Jefferson Davis, weeping over the emerging death of the United States. But this detail is but one drop in a continued quest for historical treasures that ineluctably illuminate the gravity of the year of 1861.

Index